We Kept
Our Towns
Going

We Kept Our Towns Going

THE GOSSARD GIRLS OF MICHIGAN'S UPPER PENINSULA

Phyllis Michael Wong

MICHIGAN STATE UNIVERSITY PRESS

East Lansing

Michigan State University Press
East Lansing, Michigan 48823-5245

Support for this publication provided by the Leslie and Phyllis Wong Family Trust

Library of Congress Cataloging-in-Publication Data

Names: Wong, Phyllis Michael, author.
Title: We kept our towns going : the Gossard girls of Michigan's Upper Peninsula /
Phyllis Michael Wong.
Description: East Lansing : Michigan State University Press, [2021] | Includes bibliographical
references and index.
Identifiers: LCCN 2021017434 | ISBN 9781611864205 (paperback ; alk. paper) | ISBN
9781609176860 (PDF) | ISBN 9781628954524 (epub) | ISBN 9781628964462 (Kindle)
Subjects: LCSH: H.W. Gossard Company--Employees--History--20th century. | Foundation
garment industry--Employees--Michigan--History--20th century. | Women lingerie industry
workers--Michigan--History--20th century.
Classification: LCC HD9969.F653 U596 2021 | DDC 331.4/88722092277496--dc23 LC record
available at https://lccn.loc.gov/2021017434

Book design by Shaun Allshouse, www.shaunallshouse.com
Cover design by Erin Kirk
Cover art: Corset, 1890s, The Metropolitan Museum of Art, Gift of C.J. Vincente Minetti, 1972.

Visit Michigan State University Press at *www.msupress.org*

To all of the courageous Gossard Girls and Gossard men who shared their impressive stories—family history, factory work, culture, and challenges—through their own voices so that others may learn of their strength, accomplishments, and contributions to the American story. This story is yours and I am grateful.

To workers' relatives, friends of Gossard workers, and community members whose voices enhanced the largely untold story of Upper Peninsula women taking charge, your help is deeply appreciated.

In memory of the 1,500 Gossard workers who worked in the H. W. Gossard plants in Ishpeming and Gwinn, Michigan, from 1920 to 1976, your life is a key part of the history in this book.

In memory of the late Elaine Peterson, Gossard Girl and friend, who spent hours explaining to me the multifaceted world of undergarment factory work, words cannot convey the depth of my appreciation.

Contents

Foreword

Lisa Fine

I am writing this during what everyone hopes will be the final months of the COVID-19 global pandemic, a singular historical event, along with many other momentous events during this extraordinary year that will reverberate for many decades to come. There will be much raw material for historians to process, but one enduring issue the pandemic has illuminated is the unique, vital, and varied labors of women. Women's labor was revealed as "essential" to the smooth running of life inside and outside the home, just as many came to see in stark relief how many women work multiple "shifts" and are often poorly paid (or not paid at all) for these services. The pandemic also shined a bright light on embedded inequalities in the female labor force itself—inequalities based on race, skill, class background, region, and many others. None of these issues was created by the pandemic; the crisis of the pandemic revealed these long-standing circumstances. Despite the myths about female labor force participation common in popular culture, women have always worked. They have not yet achieved parity by most measures, and they are still doing more than their equal share of all of the labors of homelife.

Phyllis Michael Wong's *We Kept Our Towns Going* tells the story of women factory workers who were also wives, mothers, daughters, vital members of their communities, activists, trailblazers, and citizens. This book reminds us of all of the work women have done and still do and how important it truly is. Wong begins her story of the Gossard Girls, the women who worked in the H. W. Gossard undergarment factories of Ishpeming and Gwinn, in the Upper Peninsula of Michigan, in the 1920s with the arrival of the factories producing undergarments by women in these small, primarily mining communities. Even though both plants closed by 1976, the memories of working in the plant remained with the women that formed the basis of the over ninety oral histories that shaped this book. Working in these plants formed a core feature of the identities of generations of women, rooted in their work, their place, and their solidarity as Gossard Girls.

The Gossard Girls, whether they knew it or not, were part of a very enduring practice of women working in some aspect of the production of textiles and clothing. This was a traditional skill of women in the home, which before industrialization scholars refer to as the domestic economy. Women textile workers were among the first factory workers in the United States. Starting primarily in the New England and mid-Atlantic states, the most famous were the Lowell Mill Girls, recruited from their farms in New England to work in textile factories in Lowell, Massachusetts, starting in the 1820s.[1] It was considered acceptable to communities where clothing production was primarily done by women in homes to relocate this labor into central workshops for more rational, coordinated, and increased production. These workshops became factories with the addition of machinery and a larger scale of production.

H. W. Gossard sited its undergarment factory in a northern Michigan community dominated by the overwhelmingly masculine enterprise of mining, populated by immigrant families from England, Finland, Ireland, Italy, Norway, Canada (French Canadian), and Sweden, to take advantage of this work. The Ishpeming Industrial Association saw multiple benefits: utilizing a defunct department store, employing "boys and girls seeking employment," and luring a quality company to town. Few could have anticipated that within a few years this company would employ hundreds, keep them employed through the Great Depression, and expand further until the 1970s, to employ generations of women.

In the early years, work was long and hard, but the income and the independence this local employer provided was crucial to a variety of survival strategies of the working girls and women in the community. Everyone in the plant, including managers, office staff, and factory workers, lived and shared in the same community. Since the employment brought women downtown, local businesses benefited from the traffic and patronage. As early as the 1920s, the company sponsored events such as dances, holiday parties, summer picnics, and a baseball team called the "Gossard Girlies." Around the time of World War II, the Gossard began providing the workers with free hot lunches as well. Factory workers on piecework recalled how they were able to maximize their earnings, while others used the factory as a first step for limited upward mobility. Some women learned how to be independent at the same time they learned about other cultures and backgrounds. Laila Poutanen even described how working at Gossard provided her with sex education: "When the young girls were about to get married, the older women gave us sex education and things like that." The work was available to women at various times in their life cycles—right out of high school, as a single parent, when their children went to school, or even later for self-support.

Nevertheless, changed conditions in the industry and within the labor force brought new developments to the North. In 1941, the International

Ladies Garment Workers Union (ILGWU) began a lengthy and difficult campaign to organize the Gossard Girls that escalated in the mid-1940s, but many workers wanted to remain "independent," free of the union. Increasingly though, as a result of unfair piecework rates and speedups, hostile work environments, remote ownership, and skilled organizing, the workers came around. They staged a sixteen-week strike in the summer of 1949 and won representation by the ILGWU. Not all of the workers were in favor of the union or involved in its founding, but those that participated through organizing and picketing learned important skills and lessons to last a lifetime.

Some workers blamed the arrival of the union as the beginning of the end of the Gossard plants, but the real reasons were more complicated: a changing business climate in the United States, Michigan in general and northern Michigan in particular; a global oil crisis; changing fashions (the design of bras certainly changed between 1920 and 1970); and corporate consolidations. The region of northern Michigan where the two main industries were mining and underwear would change forever. Rita Roberts Corradina stated, "'It was just like the company took the heart out of Ishpeming,' when it shut the factory's doors in December 1976."

I have been a women's/gender labor and working-class historian for thirty-five years, and throughout my career I have been dedicated to teaching and writing about women and work in twentieth-century America. Many of the foundational texts that formed the basis of this field did precisely what Wong has done in this volume—preserving, documenting, contextualizing, and sharing the voices of working women of the past. There are many important and satisfying aspects of this book, but the vivid voices bursting off of the pages will undoubtedly be the most valuable and enduring contribution. This feature, and the work this book showcases through the oral histories of working-class women, places it with two of the most formative and important volumes on working-class women (and some men, too). Tamara Hareven and Randolph Langenbach's *Amoskeag: Life and Work in an American Factory City*, features the oral histories of female (and some male) textile workers from several of the now-defunct Manchester, New Hampshire, textile factories. These precious interviews were done in the 1970s with many of the last workers in these shops that shuttered their doors during the 1930s. The women, from a variety of ethnic backgrounds, recounted how this textile work figured into their own personal and family life-cycles. The work was sometimes grinding and hard. Nevertheless, the authors/editors assert, "contrary to the prevailing popular idea that large factories and the urban environment cause individual anomie and social fragmentation, most of these people had a highly developed sense of place and formed tightly knit societies around their kin and ethnic associations. Despite the hardships and conflicts they experienced, they shared the feeling they so frequently expressed about their lives in the mills: 'We were all like a family.'"[2]

Jacqueline Dowd Hall et al.'s *Like a Family: The Making of a Southern Cotton Mill World* is also based, in part, on over two hundred oral histories. It recounts the poignant and vivid stories of southern textile mill workers around the turn of the twentieth century, culminating in their great strike for union representation in the 1930s. This story of textile workers occurred in a very different place but also demonstrates that women's work, both inside and outside of the factory, was essential to individual, family, and community survival. The authors recounted that when workers used the family metaphor to describe mill village life, "they were explaining their relationships to one another. Family, as an image and an institution, winds its way through [their] book, multilayered and deeply felt."[3] The authors end their book with the words of Icy Norman who worked in one of the mills for forty-seven years. She claimed she got pleasure out of her job: "When I come out of that mill, I know that I had done the very best I could. Somewhere along the way I felt a peaceable mind. We had good years, we had bad years. I reckon that goes through life. Like I said, everybody up there felt like just one family."[4]

Phyllis Michael Wong's *We Kept Our Towns Going* reveals the multiple strategies and relationships women employed negotiating their roles. Like textile workers before them, they too forged close meaningful bonds with others in the factory. This family imagery was common. Cecilia Marra Rovedo Kangas started at fourteen years old in the Gossard in 1925. Despite the hard labor of her life inside and outside of her family, she remembered, "The Gossard was like a happy family." Thirty years later, Gloria Koski LaFave started packing bra boxes right out of high school in the Gwinn plant and eventually moved up to office work. With her mother and sister in the company, she described, "We were actually a close family, . . . workers taking care of each other." All of these books, based on the experiences of women workers, first and foremost reveal valuable historical lessons about the importance of work for the women workers. They documented the importance of family life and community. They all reported on the importance of the work in the regional, national, and global economies. They all documented the vagaries of their industry and the impact this had on the women, families, and communities. Finally, all three books reflect on how these stories contribute to the centuries-long relationship between women workers and textile/clothing production.

Wong's book is a worthy addition to these volumes as she engages all of these important themes and issues into the twentieth century, with lingerie workers, and in a new location—northern Michigan.

When the Gossard factories shuttered their door in the mid-1970s, the story was not over. The importance of this experience endured in the hearts and minds of those who worked there and their families. This book chronicles those efforts in poignant ways. And now, new groups of workers, primarily women, are engaging in this type of labor. According to a 2016 article in the *Economist*, most of the world's bras now come from China where conditions are both similar to and different from what our Gossard Girls experienced. Hundreds of thousands of rural people, many women, flood into towns like Gurao, one of many single-industry towns in China. "Gurao is one of several underwear hubs that have made China the world's largest lingerie producer. The country made 2.9 billion bras in 2014, 60% of the world's total."[5] We can only imagine the type of impact that will have on the women working these factories, their communities, and the global market. Hopefully someone is documenting their stories.

Notes

1. See Thomas Dublin, *Women at Work: The Transformation of Work and Community in Lowell, Massachusetts, 1826–1860* (New York: Columbia University Press, 1979); Anthony Wallace, *Rockdale: The Growth of an American Village in the Early Industrial Revolution* (New York: Knopf 1978); Christine Stansell, *City of Women: Sex and Class in New York, 1789–1860* (New York: Knopf, 1986).
2. Tamara K. Hareven and Randolph Langenbach, *Amoskeag: Life and Work in an American Factory-City* (New York: Pantheon, 1978), 12.
3. Jacquelyn Dowd Hall et al., *Like a Family: The Making of a Southern Cotton Mill World* (Chapel Hill: University of North Carolina Press, 1987), xvii. I also found this family metaphor was ubiquitous in my own work on the REO Motor Car Company of Lansing. See Lisa M. Fine, *The Story of REO Joe: Work, Kin, and Community in Autotown, USA* (Philadelphia: Temple University Press, 2004).
4. Hall et al., *Like a Family*, 362–63.
5. "Bleak Times in Bra Town; Industrial Clusters," *The Economist* 419, no. 8985 (April 16, 2016), 36.

Preface

YOU WILL NEVER KNOW what someone is thinking unless you give them a voice.

The seeds of this idea germinated in March 2010, when I made a presentation on women's labor in Michigan's Upper Peninsula (U.P.) during Women's History Month at Northern Michigan University (NMU). Six women who had worked in Ishpeming's undergarment factory also spoke about their experiences.

I had been speaking on this untapped piece of local history since 2007 when Century Club members (of which I was one) researched "women who made a difference" locally, regionally, or nationally. Fellow club member Carolyn McDonald and I partnered to research a local woman: Geraldine Gordon Defant (I have also seen it spelled DeFant) who organized and led a strike by and for almost seven hundred rural women in the U.P. in 1949. We interviewed seven women about their work at the H. W. Gossard undergarment factory in Ishpeming and their knowledge of Geraldine's role in the four-month strike. Two of the seven women had knowledge of Geraldine's unionizing work. The remaining five interviewees created a compelling snapshot of rural women workers empowered by workforce challenges and contributions between 1920 and 1976.

What began as a research project focused on *one* woman who made a difference quickly shifted to a project about the collective voices of rural women factory workers. I intended to continue interviewing former workers now in their seventies, eighties, and nineties, to enlarge the snapshot of "Gossard Girls"—those who worked at one of the H. W. Gossard Company factories in Michigan's Upper Peninsula, where high-quality ladies' undergarments were made—for future historians. I sought advice and direction from Ishpeming native Lily Korpi (affectionately referred to as the woman "with a velvet hammer"), Kaye Hiebel, then the director of Marquette County Historical Center, and Russ Magnaghi, a history professor at NMU. Through word of mouth, social settings, and community events, I sought individuals with knowledge of the factory, including Paul Arsenault, the owner of the Gossard building. These informal and formal conversations often led to names of more former workers.

In 2008, I was asked to participate in NMU's Sonderegger Symposium VIII, an annual conference on the culture, history, and nature of the U.P. The Gossard snapshot had grown to forty individuals whose oral histories suggested rural women's wages in two undergarment factories (Ishpeming and Gwinn) sustained and enriched their communities economically, socially, and politically. From that university event came more references for future interviews, as well as requests to speak in other venues.

In the ensuing year, I participated in a variety of social and business gatherings in Marquette County (including Ishpeming Carnegie Library) and learned, among other things, that a number of citizens were only vaguely aware of the 1949 strike or the presence of what was the largest women-dominated business in the U.P. Nonetheless, I was encouraged to do more interviews, to preserve this largely untold piece of history for future experts. Gossard artifacts such as photos, quilts, or newspaper articles that had been given to me during the interviews or presentations would be donated on behalf of those generous individuals.

In March 2010, my intentions for preserving Gossard oral histories would shift. Not because I no longer wanted to conduct oral interviews but because of two unexpected incidents during my talk for Women's History Month at NMU.

First, each of six Gossard women, whose work histories spanned the 1920s to 1976, told her story, and the audience then queried former workers. At one point, a brief exchange ensued between two Gossard women with differing perspectives. Their exchange did not go unnoticed by some in the audience; rather it became a golden opportunity for me to underscore the importance of collective voices, which by now was well over sixty oral histories that I had collected. There wasn't one lens of workers' experiences.

Once the program was over, a handful of the audience lingered to speak with the special guests or to me. Among this group was a stranger holding a cardboard box of Gossard fabric remnants, some of which had been fashioned by hand into quilt squares. I accepted her box, assuring her that the antique material would be preserved at the local history center. This box would travel with me to more Gossard presentations, and I began to formulate an idea for a memorial quilt. Over the next twelve months, the now complete Gossard memorial quilt was displayed in an annual quilt show and in Marquette's Peter White Public Library, resulting in more interviews and Gossard talks.

In 2011, the expanding list of Gossard-related events included a presentation at the Historical Society of Michigan's sixty-second Annual Upper

Peninsula History Conference. Former workers, relatives of workers, and community members would add their voices to the growing list of those sharing the Gossard Girls' story, now approaching ninety individuals.

I moved to the West Coast in 2012, and the oral histories followed me. The idea of a history on the U.P.'s Gossard factories from workers' perspective began to take shape in my mind. Regular trips to Michigan's Upper Peninsula in the ensuing years yielded more stories, research, and endless writing. On each of these trips I would run into people I knew when my husband and I worked at NMU. When they asked me about my return, I'd end up telling the stories of the Gossard Girls and the role they played in the economic welfare of the central U.P. from just before the Great Depression through two world wars, a civil rights movement, and the start of the technology revolution. So often the response to my narrative was surprise, then pride at the Gossard Girls' contributions. Many would say their grandmothers or great-aunts were Gossard Girls, but I never knew the whole story. Even more would respond, "There should be a book about that." One day I thought, there really should be, and started writing the impressive story of the women of the U.P.'s Gossard factories.

Introduction

SUCCESSFUL LABOR STRIKES LED BY and for women during the 1940s were a rare moment in U.S. labor history, let alone one occurring in Michigan's Upper Peninsula within the garment industry. This book highlights the oral history of the women who worked at the H. W. Gossard factories and were known as Gossard Girls, unsung heroines who went on strike for four months in 1949 in an effort to unionize their workplace. These were ordinary women who made news and a difference in their communities. Hidden by location, this unheralded strike remains a significant piece of labor history unknown to most.

The moniker "Gossard Girl" has its roots as early as the 1940s, according to Laila Poutanen, who worked in both Upper Peninsula Gossard factories. Gossard Girl was a term often used by workers (women and men) in conversations among themselves and in conversations within and outside of their communities. The source of the nickname may be unknown, but its influence remains.

In a very real sense, Gossard Girl conveyed an identity to and connection between hundreds of diverse rural women. To this day, many Gossard Girls still speak of the way their employment elevated workers' status within towns and communities, an important recognition given differences in their age, ethnicity, and economic standings.

What may have accounted for this unofficial status? One possibility is to consider that as late as the 1960s, cultural expectations for women were vastly different than today. Generally speaking, sixty years ago a husband, not a wife, was supposed to provide for the family. Marriage, housekeeping, and rearing children were women's primary avocation.

Yet for over a half century, a pair of undergarment factories, whose workforce comprised 85–90 percent female workers, would introduce a new idea: women working outside of the home. The Gossard factories tested the norms of the time. Some women, such as Cecilia Kangas, Dorothy Waters, and Rose Collick, worked at the factory because they had to help support their families. Some, like Alice Haapala, Arlene Felt, and Verna Holmgren, did it to have their own pocket money or to enable their families to purchase nonessential items. Others, like Clara Joseph, would work briefly between high school graduation and marriage.

Raised during the Depression, Gossard Girl Clara Joseph described herself as "a shy person" who didn't go out much. When she graduated from Ishpeming High School in 1943, she worked at Woolworth's for two years. She would follow two older sisters to the Gossard factory in Ishpeming, where her piecework wages in wide binding exceeded hourly wages from the "five and dime store." ("Piecework" is work paid by the number of items made, not the time required to make them or hours on the job.) Clara's sisters worked longer in the undergarment factory, while she worked less than a year: long enough to help her siblings buy a bedroom set for their parents and until Clara got married. Two months after Clara was married in a double-ring ceremony with her older sister, and after her husband "put [her] in a house in West Ishpeming," she left the undergarment factory. Clara's husband, who was raised in an orphanage, preferred that his bride stop working at the Gossard. She did not have a car, and living in West Ishpeming was too far from the factory. Clara worked full-time as a homemaker raising eight children. "We didn't have everything, but we had a good life."

The Gossard factory was considered the best place for all types of women, including single women like Nancy Valenzio and Marie Patron who had to work. "Those were different times compared to today," said Nancy, who grew up during the Great Depression. The young teenager left Republic High School after ninth grade and moved to Ishpeming to live with one of her older sisters. Nancy began at the Gossard in 1947 because "it was the place to work for women. It was the thing in those days."

With few options for single rural women, Nancy was pleased she had a job. "I was lucky the Gossard factory was here." She would work in at least eight different areas during her twenty-five years: bar-tacking straps, attaching bows, attaching bar-tack tiny bows, burning lace with a hot wire for decoration, packaging bows, folding and boxing bras for shipping, elastic binding, and elastic tabs. As such, Nancy exemplified important workplace abilities—flexibility, resilience, and diligence. When Nancy took a leave of absence to recover from a car accident and later to give birth to her daughter, Gossard management rehired her.

Nancy worked until December 1976 when the Gossard factory closed, an uncertain time for all workers, but especially for single, older women. Nancy received unemployment for a year, "one lump sum" from Trade Readjustment Assistance, and a modest pension. In 1981, Nancy completed an important life goal, earning her high school diploma.

Similarly, Marie Patron and her son Barry would benefit from the presence of the women-dominated factory. Marie lived with her mother in Ishpeming during Barry's childhood, an arrangement that enabled Marie to fulfill her ardent wish to send her son to college.

The Gossard factories in Ishpeming and Gwinn, Michigan, were highly desirable places for untrained workers. Not only did they employ a high number of women, but wages were generally higher than grocery and clothing stores or the phone company, businesses with decidedly fewer employees. In turn, Gossard Girls spent their wages in town, which made the communities of Ishpeming and Gwinn significantly more vibrant. Newspaper articles often extolled the economic health of downtown Ishpeming and Gwinn, a consequence of hundreds of Gossard workers whose incomes kept their communities and families going strong for over a half century.

Drawing on scores of interviews with Gossard Girls and their families, as well as research in the newspapers and other publications of the time, this book tells their story. In addition to outlining their shared history at the plant, I include profiles of many individuals whose lives reveal the diverse experiences and perspectives of these ordinary, extraordinary women.

CHAPTER 1

The Beginnings of the
H. W. Gossard Company

CORSETS WERE WORN BY "virtually all free-born women in the United States" during the nineteenth century, Jill Fields wrote in *An Intimate Affair: Women, Lingerie, and Sexuality*. However, beginning in the mid-nineteenth century and continuing in the early twentieth century, physicians, ministers, couturiers, feminist dress reformers, health and hygiene activists, and "advocates of tight lacing" were debating the value for tight-fitting corsets and Victorian clothing styles. Concurrently, the roots of America's commercial production of women's undergarments can be traced to the Second Industrial Revolution (1870–1914). This was a period in which low startup costs, advancements in technology, and cheap labor employing women (many were immigrants) drove the swift rise in undergarment factories. In 1874, for example, Warner Brother's Corset Company of Bridgeport, Connecticut, was started, and by 1900, new companies entered this growing industry in states such as Illinois, New York, and Massachusetts. In 1913 New York City had "13,517 workers in the trade of whom 11,762 were women ... in 375 shops" according to Fields. The Royal Worcester Corset Company in Worcester, Massachusetts, employed 1,500 workers, mostly women, in 1917, reported *The Corset and Underwear Review*. The undergarment industry grew rapidly, and so did the number of women wage earners across America, many of whom would buy rather than make clothing, thereby increasing the number of consumers. These and other factors would, as Fields suggests, be viewed as "an attractive entry point" for aspiring entrepreneurs in the early twentieth century.

One such entrepreneur was Henry Williamson Gossard who, in 1900, founded the H. W. Gossard Company, a women's undergarment manufacturer. Born in 1871 and raised near Frankfort, Indiana, Gossard, started working as a salesman for G. H. Foster and Co., Chicago, a wholesale dressmaking company, when he was 18 years old, and he worked there from 1889 until 1895. During this period "the business of the French, Gossard and Company was established" and then was "succeeded by Gossard and Pinkerton." In 1900 Gossard and Pinkerton was "incorporated under the present style of the H. W. Gossard Company," according to editor John W. Leonard of *The Book of Chicagoans: A Biographical Dictionary of Leading Living Men of the City of Chicago.* The company would become known for its high standards, as was demonstrated in articles from its employee magazine, *The Gossardian,* which stressed high employee standards as a mechanism to producing high-quality merchandise that could demand a higher price than many other undergarments of the time.

During one of his buying trips to Paris for laces and trims, Gossard learned about a new style in women's corsets, a corset that laced in the front. Gossard was impressed when he attended a performance where French actress Sarah Bernhardt's figure had been transformed by a front-lacing corset. Gossard was unaware of any other American manufacturer exploring the revolutionary front-lacing corset, an undergarment that could provide a woman with more control over her body by enabling her to tighten the corset herself and not require assistance from someone else as the traditional corset of the day did.

Intent on testing the American market with this radically new undergarment, Gossard purchased 150 front-lacing corsets from a dressmaking manufacturer in Paris, for which he paid five dollars apiece. To recoup his costs and make a profit, the American businessman set the price of a corset at $25 each. Despite this 500 percent markup, the entrepreneur sold his entire inventory. Gossard then renovated the back section of his building in Chicago and hired twenty-five seamstresses. Within a few years, the demand for front-lacing corsets quickly outpaced production by those operators. In January 1904 the H. W. Gossard Company opened its first factory in Belvidere, Illinois, a town seventy miles northwest of Chicago. Demand for Gossard corsets and other women's undergarments rose steadily. Over the next sixteen years, the Chicago-based company opened a number of factories in Canada and the Midwest, including Michigan.

Gossard's strategic decision to extend his company's reach into an isolated area of northern Michigan, known as the Upper Peninsula, would reap significant dividends for the president and his company, and it would embolden hundreds of rural women in unexpected ways.

Ishpeming, an Ethnically Diverse, Self-Sufficient Mining Town

In 1920, the H. W. Gossard Company set its sights for expansion on Ishpeming, a mining town in Michigan's Upper Peninsula (U.P.). The vibrant, self-sufficient community of 10,500 was situated in a sparsely populated area of Marquette County, located in the north central portion of the U.P. Ishpeming, then and now, was reflective of the U.P. for its distinctive four seasons: long and white winters, with average snowfalls nearing two hundred inches per year; muddy and short springs leading to spectacular summers where sunlight bounced off the green of the ever-abundant trees and the twinkling blue of rivers and lakes, including Lake Superior, referenced by the locals as "the Big Lake"; and autumns on fire with dazzling miles of forests in reds, oranges, and yellows.

Gossard Girl Barbara Nuorala remembered her childhood on Vine Street, saying children played outside in all seasons. "We were always out of doors. We were out in snowstorms." Neighborhood children played "together in a big gang." Sometimes they played kick the can, and when the longest season of white—winter—arrived, the neighborhood gang played king of the castle on snowbanks. The Ishpeming native smiles when reflecting on this rough-and-tumble game where "everybody would get up and try to knock you down." Winter play was especially fun when the unsupervised gang "roasted potatoes over a bonfire on the bluff." Decades later, the Gossard pieceworker said, "It was great fun. The kids today don't know what they're missing."

Not only the winters but the economic challenges of the rural area required hearty residents. Gossard Girl Madeline Kaupilla said her mother, Theresa, was forced to take in boarders to support her three daughters after her husband died six months following a mining workplace accident. Conditions remained modest when Theresa remarried and moved the family to nearby Negaunee. "We had a kitchen stove. We would open the oven and have our breakfast in there because there was frost on the inside wall."

Marquette County was home to a handful of mining companies. These mining companies, according to U.P. historian Robert Archibald, had a "stake in seeing to the town's welfare," and the mining companies "could be seen as benevolent in some ways but with a self-interested benevolence." Some housing was owned and controlled by mining companies.

In the late 1920s and 1930s mining families could rent a company house, remembered Gossard Girl Verna Holmgren, who recalled when her father, a land agent for Oliver Mine Company, decided to upgrade the family's living conditions, renting "a nice company house for $12 a month." The upgraded rental, Verna recalled, was equipped with a furnace, wood floors, and a fully equipped bathroom (tub, sink, and toilet). However, families with less income paid $4–5 a month for a house with "no furnace and only a toilet in the basement," she said. The Gossard Girl recalled her family being "prudent with money," which she said helped lessen the impact of the Great Depression of the 1930s on Verna and her sister. Verna's mother, a homemaker and an excellent seamstress, never used cotton fabric to sew her daughters' winter clothing, only wool. Verna recalled "a beautiful grey tweed coat with red lining, cape-like shoulders, and ornate tiny red ornamental buttons." Not all were so fortunate. A young Verna had a friend whose family received "surplus food, such as grapefruit on certain days." The plethora of Ishpeming's shoe repairmen, who "did big business" resoling shoes, also showed the effects of the Depression, an older Verna would later observe.

In Ishpeming, the mining companies were, according to Archibald, "a conduit" into which money flowed into the community. For example, Ishpeming's hospital, visiting nurses, YMCA, and Ishpeming High School benefited from the presence of the Cleveland-Cliffs Iron Company (CCI) and its workforce. When the H. W. Gossard Company opened a factory in 1920, the company did so "in a milieu of a corporate community," where CCI was the largest employer. These mining companies provided a corporate paternalistic safety net in health and welfare for residents and other area businesses.

Mining companies "dominated the industrial potential of the region," said Russ Magnaghi, former director of Northern Michigan University's Center for Upper Peninsula Studies. Industries necessary to mining—railroads, boiler makers, machine ships, and lumber mills—could be found in and near these communities. Additionally, Magnaghi observed, there were "cottage industries: such as weavers (1–2 in town), breweries, shoemakers, custom clothing (tailors), cigar makers, tin smiths, butchers and related businesses providing for the local communities." Absent from these communities were large nonmining industries, especially industries targeting a female workforce. In "Gender and Factory Work in the Upper Peninsula through 1976," author Magnaghi cited a 1920 report by Michigan's Department of Labor, which listed seventy-seven women working "in a variety of occupations . . . in clothing stores, chain stores, and hotels. None were factory workers." The H. W. Gossard Company would enter this distant rural area where the combined populations of Ishpeming and neighboring Negaunee and their surrounding townships hovered around twenty thousand.

The undergarment company joined a community of relatively recent (first- and second-generation) immigrants from places such as England,

Finland, Ireland, Italy, Norway, and Sweden. The ethnic diversity during this period enriched the area, even though the diversity also contributed "to some level of ethnic conflict," said Archibald. Churches, social clubs, and lodges helped reinforce the sense of ethnicity from the old country, but they also provided a way for immigrants to become fully integrated into American society, he said. As Elizabeth Coron, the granddaughter of French Canadian immigrants, remembered it, "Back then people kind of tended to lean toward their ethnic background. That's the way it was."

Looking back at her childhood, Gossard Girl Ann Marie Stieve, one of thirteen siblings in an Italian family, felt growing up in Ishpeming during the 1930s was safe and comforting. "Our family was very close. We always took care of each other." A Christmas present for the family's youngest would have been a bag of nuts, an orange, and a bottle of pop. Siblings shared beds and chores, including helping with the family's vegetable garden. During cold winter periods, floor rugs provided another layer of heat. Reflecting on her childhood, Ann Marie mused, "It was just a nice way of family living."

Like many small towns, Ishpeming was a self-sufficient walking community, even after the advent of the automobile. Everything—grocery, clothing, hardware, department stores, as well as health care—was contained within a few blocks' walking distance in downtown Ishpeming. Stores were social places, and everyone, corporate management as well as the working class, "rubbed shoulders. By contrast, today's cities and towns are often segregated by income. There was less stratification by income in Ishpeming," according to Archibald.

Elizabeth, who was born in 1920, reflected fondly on her hometown. "It was a heyday in Ishpeming" with a downtown where "stores were just anchored in one next to the other," she said. The youngest of four children, she often walked downtown with her mother and grandmother from their house on Division Street. "I remember going down our streets when I was four. We had wooden sidewalks weather-beaten grayish with the lines in." Three generations would have had "loads of grocery stores" to frequent such as A. W. Meyer, Leflors, Arkesh, and Koski's. Elizabeth's parents did not own a car for a number of years. When the three generations wanted to travel to neighboring towns and areas during the 1920s, they rode the efficient streetcar line to Negaunee or Ishpeming Township.

Arleen Felt, who grew up in Negaunee in the 1930s and 1940s, said the modes of transportation for her and her childhood friends were roller skates, bicycles, and trains. "It was nothing to ride a bicycle from Negaunee to Ishpeming and back to Negaunee, just to see what was going on in the towns." If the circus was coming to town, she'd watch as carnival animals were unloaded from the trains. During high school, the Negaunee native and her peers would have taken trains to Marquette, the "big city" about twenty miles away, for school activities. "We never had to fear," she said.

One of the largest stores in Ishpeming's downtown was the F. Braastad and Company Store, built in 1904 by Frederick Braastad—immigrant, entrepreneur, businessman, and state and local political figure. On September 7, 1903, the *Mining Journal* described the structure as "one of the most imposing pieces of architecture in the city . . . with solid frontage of 150 feet, three stories in height, the corner adorned with a massive clock tower, extending twenty-five feet above the rest of the structure, and visible from all parts of the city." The much-anticipated opening of Braastad Block on the corner of Cleveland Avenue and Second Street drew thousands for the grand opening in early May 1904 to the "best and most complete store north of Milwaukee." Newspaper accounts of the day claimed ten thousand people visited the store, which sold just about anything and everything from "flour and straw to toys and needles." However, within ten years, Braastad threatened to close Braastad Block, citing overtaxation and referring to himself as "Ishpeming's heaviest individual tax payer." He died in 1917 before acting on this threat. Braastad's son, Arvid, managed the department store until 1919 when the company was dissolved. Over the course of the year, the grocery, dry goods, and furniture businesses closed, leaving an imposing three-story, 57,600 square foot building (excluding the basement) empty.

At the time the Braastad Company dissolved in 1919, the Chicago-based H. W. Gossard Company was rapidly expanding. "To meet a growing demand for Gossard corsets and other women's undergarments, the Gossard Company opened three new factories in 1919 and planned to open at least one more in 1920," according to *The Corset and Underwear Review*, volume 15. The new factories were in Logansport, Indiana (225 workers), Allentown, Pennsylvania (160 workers), and Drummondville, Quebec (225 workers). Ishpeming would be the fourth. What might have seemed like a giant eyesore to Ishpeming's business leaders in December 1919 would, in less than three months, be hailed as one of the best investments in the area.

Making the Deal

According to 1920 newspaper articles from Marquette's *Daily Mining Journal* and Ishpeming's *Iron Ore*, Randall P. Bronson and William Leininger, representatives of the Ishpeming Industrial Association, traveled to Chicago early in 1920 in search of new business opportunities for their town, including for the empty Braastad Block. During one of their visits, a bank representative "suggested the 'Gossard' sometimes built factories, that they were all right, and he might be able to interest them," reported the *Iron Ore*. Bank officials recommended Ishpeming Industrial Association representatives get in touch with the H. W. Gossard Company's sales representatives, Mr. Erickson and Mr. Pascoe.

It was perhaps fortuitous that Bronson and Leininger would speak with Erickson, who had roots in Marquette County; his father had worked as a miner in the Humboldt Mine. Erickson visited Ishpeming, the Braastad Block, and members of the Ishpeming Industrial Association. He was impressed with the spacious three-story building and the enthusiastic reception by Ishpeming's businessmen.

Meanwhile, local newspapers reported on a financial agreement between the H. W. Gossard Company and Ishpeming business community. Members of the Ishpeming Industrial Association "would do their part towards financing the property purchase [Braastad Block]" and solicit financial pledges from the business community. When the H. W. Gossard Company had paid out wages "twenty times the building costs" the company would "own the building," Ishpeming's newspaper reported. Furthermore, the undergarment company would pay for "all improvements . . . , taxes, insurance, etc.," according to the *Daily Mining Journal*.

In addition to the financial arrangement, there were a number of benefits, reported the Marquette newspaper on March 9, 1920.

- *Projected high employment*: The company planned to employ up to "250 hands" by July 1, 1920 (women and men), "300 hands by the end of 1920," and peak employment was expected to reach at least one thousand.
- *A reputable company*: With its "high financial rating and standing" and worldwide reputation in the undergarment industry, H. W. Gossard was considered one of the largest corset manufacturing companies in the country with factories dotting the Midwest and Canada. Its products were sold all over the world.
- *Quality product*: The company held a patent on the front-lacing corset, a revolutionary and healthier product, which might be prescribed by one's doctor.
- *Favorable working conditions*: "The making of corsets in a place where it is very hot has its disadvantages. The labor cannot work to the best advantage in such heat and then the goods easily soil. Labor troubles are not looked for in Ishpeming. The pay will be good and conditions ideal for those employed."

- *Economic advantage for families*: "It's worth considerable to every family in town that has boys and girls seeking employment. To get [a] place in outside towns means spending more money in travelling and hotel bills before the job is landed. . . . Better to live at home with family and with friends and relatives with whom you have been raised. More money will be saved in Ishpeming than in Detroit. . . . It's what you save that counts."
- *Distinctions*: Lastly, the Gossard Company intended to make Ishpeming "their chief factory." A spacious Braastad building coupled with a large labor supply in Marquette County may have influenced Gossard officials to project employment of "about one thousand hands" in less than two years.

And so, the Ishpeming Industrial Association had its way. Preparations were underway. By March 13, 1920, the *Iron Ore* reported members of the Ishpeming Industrial Association had raised $34,000 to finance the proposition. Many women from Negaunee, a small neighboring city to Ishpeming, had "registered for work," said the *Daily Mining Journal*. In turn, officials at Michigan Gas & Electric Company planned to increase the "street car schedule . . . to properly handle the increased morning and evening traffic, especially between Negaunee and Ishpeming," according to *Daily Mining Journal* accounts.

Meanwhile, on Monday, March 22, 1920, the mayor of Ishpeming, members of the Ishpeming Industrial Association, and "other prominent men" entertained Gossard Company officials at a celebratory dinner, the culmination of four to five weeks of negotiations. Mrs. John Gray, the only woman in attendance, had prepared "a substantial dinner, appropriate for 110 hungry men," said the *Iron Ore*. It was a happy occasion, and much speechifying took place. The mayor reflected on the importance of the gathering. "This was one of the days that would be referred to in history, a red-letter day." Gossard was impressed with "the open-hearted attributes and the keen business principles displayed by business men and the citizen[s] in general." Furthermore, as the *Daily Mining Journal* reported, Gossard heaped high praise for the *Iron Ore*, insisting it was only newspaper in the country that "handled the matter [Gossard factory] so masterly." No doubt the mood at dinner was high that evening. The importance of the day would, indeed, be remembered in years to come.

Much work was needed in preparation of the factory's opening in April 1920. E. S. Axline from Gossard's Chicago office, who would become the Ishpeming factory's first superintendent and first manager, oversaw the remodel of the building from a department store to a typical Gossard factory. Equipment, supplies, and a trained workforce were needed. A shortage of steel slowed work on the third floor, and strikes in Chicago delayed the factory's opening by a month. However, there was no shortage of a female labor supply, according to Ishpeming's newspaper. With more than five hundred employment applications already filled out, the newspaper urged the business community to forego plans for a cigar factory. "Women would prefer corset making to the making of cigars," and "the cigar makers will have to seek some other place for starting up a business," reported the *Iron Ore* in May.

Ishpeming Plant Begins Manufacturing

By April 24, production commenced for "seventy-five women and girls," but only on brassieres, according to the town's newspaper. Agnes Harnett was the first female employee at Ishpeming's plant, while "railroad transportation troubles," a switchmen's strike in Chicago, delayed delivery of industrial machinery and supplies, reported the *Iron Ore*. It would take almost four weeks for the delivery, installation, and fine-tuning of 188 machines, but by May 17, the factory had more than one hundred workers involved in the production of undergarments.

Over the next six months, more workers were hired, and more industrial machines were installed. By October, the local newspaper stated Ishpeming's plant "is already one of our leading business enterprises, with semi-monthly pay roll which amounts to thousands of dollars. It is giving employment to many men and women, and it is going to have a healthy growth."

Gossard management believed in supplying every convenience for its employees, so in July the company added a rest room, a lunchroom, and a phonograph on the third floor. Initially, the company provided free coffee in its lunchroom, said the *Iron Ore* in a July article, but future plans called for free hot meals "every noon at the close of the summer months" for employees living in Negaunee and other outlying districts.

When Ishpeming's factory opened in 1920, company president Gossard and his management team intended to make the factory one of its largest. A year later (October 1, 1921), the *Iron Ore* reported the factory "is now employing more hands than some of the best mines, and paying good wages. Many a family the head of which is out of employment is being maintained by the girls working in this factory, and it is saving the town much in many ways."

In 1928, the H. W. Gossard Company was operating ten factories, and Ishpeming's factory, which then employed 470 workers, was rated the best factory in the United States. That year the factory was "the second largest industry in Ishpeming," according to the local paper. The factory was poised to grow its work force even more, reported the *Iron Ore* on June 9, 1928. "The Gossard company recently closed its factory at Janesville, Wisconsin, and most of the machinery that was in use there has been shipped here and installed." These changes, said the article, augured a bright future for the Ishpeming factory.

Prosperous Times despite the Great Depression

The economic future for Ishpeming's factory and workers seemed bright into the next decade despite the effects of the Great Depression across the United States and despite the fact that the H. W. Gossard Company, an American corporation, became a British company in the 1930s. In September 1928, "stockholders of the H. W. Gossard company . . . voted to change the name to Associated Apparel Industries, Inc., and to increase the authorized capital from 200,000 to 500,000 no-par shares and eliminate the present 5,730 preferred shares. The additional common stock will be held in the treasury for purposes of future expansion," according to the *Iron Ore*. Though ownership of the Gossard had changed, the brand name continued.

In 1930, when Peter Koskela died in a mining accident, leaving his wife Anna-Lisa to raise twelve children, their sixteen-year-old daughter Olga became a Gossard machine operator. "I thought the day would never end. My neck hurt so much," Olga Honkala would tell her daughter Maxine decades later. Initially, Olga earned sixteen cents an hour during the nine-hour day (presumably the piecework rate for newly hired seaming operators in 1930). Using public transportation and later carpooling, she was "never afraid of work" whether in ladder stitching or as a cutting room worker. Olga worked thirty years in two separate periods (1930–42, 1958–76), enjoying the camaraderie of Gossard friends, yet according to daughter Maxine, mindful "about always wanting to make her rate" in a system where wages were based on the minimum number of completed units.

In December 1931, Ishpeming's undergarment factory was six months into operating on a six-day work schedule. "All departments are busy daily" for a record 475 employees, resulting in the largest payroll ever in the plant's history, said the *Iron Ore*. Claude Tripp, the plant's manager, announced the workforce would be increased to six hundred, and the third-floor dining room "would be abandoned" to accommodate new equipment, the newspaper reported.

But the economic effects of the Depression soon began to affect the undergarment industry. Five months later (May 1932), the *Iron Ore* wrote that some machine operators worked nine hours daily on samples of new models, which were expected to increase the plant's workload capacity even more. Many, however, worked a modified schedule, because the Gossard Company "maintained a policy all during the Depression of keeping people working on a part-time basis" to benefit all workers, Ishpeming's local paper reported on May 21, 1932. At the national level, Congress passed the National Industrial Recovery Act in 1933, which was intended to stimulate the nation's economic recovery by granting authority to President Franklin Roosevelt to regulate a number of industries' wages and prices, as well as the hours worked. As a result, workers' wages and hours at Ishpeming's Gossard factory increased to thirty-five cents per hour for a forty-hour work week (Monday–Friday), an increase, according to Marquette's *Mining Journal* on June 20, 1939, that allowed "scores of the more experienced and adept girls to earn more than four and five dollars a day."

The wage increase would have helped wife and mother Pierina Forchini who traveled thirty miles, one way, to Ishpeming's factory. Decades later, her daughter and Gossard Girl Virginia Ayotte said, "war and Mussolini" drove her parents from Italy to New Swanzy, Michigan, where Louis worked in the lumber industry until "he was unable to continue his heavy lumber work." Travel in "these times" was different from today, said Virginia. Her mother took the Negrinelli bus, along with miners, daily from Gwinn to Ishpeming. "There were times rather than her take this bus back to Gwinn, a lady friend and her husband would take her in. She'd spend the night up there rather than drive all the way home. . . . There were no daycare centers or after school programs like they have now," said Pierina's daughter.

Ishpeming High School graduate Mary Jacobson, however, had a much shorter commute; she walked a few blocks. In 1937, "I needed the job, and it was the only option," said the oldest sibling whose wages helped the large Valela family (four sisters and two brothers). Once married, her husband, Robert, supported her decision to leave. "I didn't like sewing, so I was happy when I quit."

By 1939 employment at the factory reached five hundred. Not quite the six hundred Manager Tripp had predicted, but still an impressive number. Moreover, 90 percent of the workers were women, whose economic power benefited the economic health of Ishpeming and surrounding communities. While many workers hailed from the twin cities of Ishpeming and Negaunee, there were also workers from the neighboring townships—Forsyth and Negaunee—and farther points like Marquette. Workers' pay at the undergarment plant was considered one of the highest for women, and no other industries in Marquette County or the U.P. employed large numbers of women.

In 1939, the Gossard factory was acknowledged by Marquette's *Mining Journal* as "one of the great stabilizing factors in the economic welfare of the local community." What began in 1920 "with a staff of 50 girls, none of them experienced in the needle trade" employed five hundred workers (450 women, 50 men) who operated "between 600–700 machines of various types." In 1920, the factory produced "less than 2,000 dozen garments." In 1939, reported the newspaper, the factory's "annual output was between 150,000–200,000 dozen garments." Moreover, Ishpeming's factory was now in its nineteenth year of continuous operation—except for inventory—during two major depressions (1922–25 and 1930–35). Without a doubt, the factory had become an important contributor in Ishpeming's economic success. Much of the credit for the upbeat news, said the paper, was Manager Tripp's "wise administration" over fifteen years.

Two additional Upper Peninsula newspapers mentioned Ishpeming's positive economic news. The *Bessemer Herald* noted that undergarments made in Ishpeming's factory were sold "in many sections of the country and to foreign lands. A great boom to Ishpeming in this local plant."

A second newspaper, the *Wakefield News*, reprinted an editorial from the *Iron Ore* that among other things, viewed the expansion of Ishpeming's women-dominated factory favorably when viewed within the area's receding iron market. "What Ishpeming has done, Wakefield can do. A shunting to one side of petty jealousy, a little less criticism of the city, and a substitution of the hammer for some of the community spirit which we hear much about and see but little, would make this community the best little town," wrote Wakefield's editorial staff.

CECILIA KANGAS, GOSSARD GIRL

Cecilia Marra was born March 24, 1911, in Houghton, Michigan, the third oldest of nine children (five boys and four girls). Parents Joseph and Rose Marra emigrated from southern Italy to Houghton when a promise of employment in the copper mines attracted Joseph to what would become known as the Copper Country.

Cecilia was still a toddler in 1913, when mining labor issues resulted in a nine-month strike affecting all mines in the Copper Country. The uncertainty in mining persisted, so in 1919, her parents left the area when again "mines were having troubles" and settled about one hundred miles south. Within five years, Cecilia would become a fourteen-year-old employee in Ishpeming's Gossard factory.

Cecilia's childhood memories reflect a time when families, bonded by culture, language, and tradition, lived near each other. Her memories reflected the challenges and pleasures of a "very poor" but close-knit family. As was the custom in an Italian family like Cecilia's, her father and mother raised and preserved many vegetables and fruits. The homegrown food helped the family of eleven, especially during the Upper Peninsula's long harsh winters, but the father's income from the mines did not always meet the family's needs. When a young Cecilia needed a pair of shoes, she independently sought help from "a government official" in Ishpeming, who sent her away empty-handed and with a stern rebuke: "Your parents, yes, go ask them."

Cecilia described her childhood as one governed more by work than play. "It was work. It was a lot of work." Cecilia was not the oldest; she had two older brothers. Nevertheless, she was the oldest daughter of Italian immigrants. She was expected to be "momma's helper with all the babies and everything else," including repurposing "one-hundred-pound flour sacks into bloomers and pillowcases." During those rare moments when Cecilia was not momma's helper, she played on the street with neighborhood children and her cousins where they often communicated in their native languages whether Italian, English, or Finnish. "We had relatives living on the same street. My dad's brother, they lived a few houses down from us. They had a big family. And we got together outside there. That was our playground on the street there. So that is how we got together with the family and the neighbors. They were all like a big family at one time, not like today. You don't know who's living next door to you."

Although helping her mother governed much of Cecilia's childhood, she did attend a convent school in Ishpeming. One of her fondest grade-school memories involved music. Cecilia wanted to take piano lessons, but her parents did not own a piano. A determined Cecilia was resourceful. In eighth grade, she took piano lessons at the convent school, practicing daily on the school's piano while a nun sat in a rocking chair. But when Cecilia made the difficult decision not to attend high school, she had to quit piano lessons. Her decision was, in large part, based on cultural and societal expectations of boys and girls in the 1920s. Cecilia said, "Now you take these older people. When they raised a family, the boys were supposed to get educated, not the girls." Cecilia respected her mother, Rose, an intelligent woman, and yet she never attended school in Italy.

Cecilia reasoned, "My mother never went to school," so "I told my mother you can't send me to college. Why should I go to high school? So, I might as well try to get a job somewhere." She became a Gossard Girl. Cecilia would be the only sibling in her family of five brothers and three sisters who did not earn a high school diploma.

Cecilia started work at the H. W. Gossard in 1925 when she was fourteen. Underage girls could and did work at the Gossard. For example, Wilma Sparks, also born in 1911, started when she was fifteen. "All you had to do was say you were 16. You didn't have to worry about child labor laws," said Wilma in a 1989 *Mining Journal* article.

The Marra family lived on East Pearl in a neighborhood behind the Gossard factory. This was convenient for fourteen-year-old Cecilia and her family. Too young to drive and too young to live independently, she'd walk three minutes to the factory and walk home for lunch. An older Cecilia said her minimum piece-rate wages on seaming in 1925 were modest by today's standard, an amount equivalent to seventeen cents per hour. Even so, her wages were valuable for the Marra family. Cecilia would work as a Gossard Girl for forty-two years. "It was hard work," she said, "I had to work. In them days you didn't make much. I had to keep working."

Cecilia remembered her first day vividly. "They showed you how to thread the machine, and they gave you some [material] scraps to sew on the machine. I was doing that for a while when I said to the girl next to me, 'When is that noise going to stop?' She said, 'What noise?'" Years later, Cecilia blamed her hearing loss on four decades of work with industrial machines.

Despite the din in a fast-paced work environment, Cecilia held good memories from her years as a Gossard Girl. "The Gossard was like a happy family," a family that regularly laughed and joked together, she said. Machine operators, grouped by department (i.e., seamers, a wide binder, or a two-needle binder), worked five days a week (except for periodic overtime) in an environment and system that generally rewarded the fast worker. The more pieces one finished over the basic rate, the more money one made. That was the incentive, according to Cecilia.

The Gossard family stepped up during times of crisis; according to Cecilia, "When someone died in the family, they'd collect." In 1951, Cecilia's first husband, Amelino Rovedo, died unexpectedly in a drowning accident. His sudden death at thirty-eight was a bitter pill for Cecilia. It was difficult not only because of the loss in family income (he was a shift boss in the mines), but his sudden death threatened to derail the husband and wife's dream of sending their only child to college. Gina's parents were each denied the opportunity of a college education. Cecilia knew an education was beyond her reach, so it had become her and her husband's dream to send their daughter, "a book worm," to college. Not just any college; they would send her to the University of Michigan to study medicine. When Amelino died unexpectedly a month before Gina began her college experience, the parents' dream seemed lost. However, that's when the Gossard family stepped up to help. Still moved by the act of generosity, Cecilia said, the Gossard Girls "gave towards a check." Not just those who worked in seaming, but also those from other departments. Cecilia has kept the typewritten list of almost 150 generous Gossard Girls, which she opens carefully so as not to damage the list bearing a poignant handwritten sentence by her: "The Gossard Girls gave me a gift."

Nineteen years later, an independent-minded Cecilia married Gossard cutter Ray Kangas, who held a union leadership position in Ishpeming's factory. At first, "he would talk to me, asking how my day was and the work and all that. So, we got acquainted, and then he called me up to take me out." Cecilia declined his offer, but Ray persisted. Cecilia and Ray went out for coffee on their first date. Thus began a special friendship between Ray and a reluctant Cecilia. "It was a hard thing for me to go out with him because I had been a widow for nineteen years, and I said, 'I don't want to get married anymore.'" Ray continued to show up unexpectedly at her house to take her for drives in his car. "I couldn't get rid of him," said Cecilia, her eyes smiling while she shared a photo of her deceased husband.

When asked to reflect on a legacy of Ishpeming's Gossard factory, Cecilia answered quickly, "The Gossard was the bread and butter for lots of people." Over her years, Cecilia had worked with countless Gossard Girls like her who had to work. Some were single. Some married. Some divorced. Some widowed. Regardless of their marital status, their economic situations were serious. Like Cecilia, they knew the best-paying jobs could only be found at the Gossard factory. And the best position was pieceworker. Those who were fast and whose work regularly met the company's high standards made well above the company's basic rate.

It was perhaps early in Cecilia's employment (1925–30), when she learned firsthand the downside of speed. One day, Cecilia worked quickly completing many bundles, not knowing that she had sewn the pieces incorrectly until the inspector said her work did not pass inspection. Every Gossard product—brassieres and corsets—was required to meet specific company standards. She would not be paid for her mistakes, only for work that passed inspection. Cecilia said, "I made only twenty-two cents that day." At other times, it was work on "sale samples" that cut into Cecilia's ability to earn above her daily average. It was a time-consuming project not just because everything had to be perfect, but also because the project involved feedback from Gossard workers who wore the sample bra for two weeks. Cecilia's daughter Gina recalled, "She did not like her supervisor singling her out."

Looking back, Cecilia was thankful for the Gossard factory because she helped her parents and then her own family. Even so, it was a highly competitive work environment. "It was a hard-working place. The girl that's doing the same work as you, well, you were trying to beat her. You're trying to see if you can make more money than her. You were always thinking, 'She's going to finish that before I am.'" Cecilia said her coworkers impressed *and* pushed each other to work harder. It's what Ishpeming's Gossard factory became known for—motivated, hard-working women who took tremendous pride in creating well-made lingerie for women throughout the country and beyond.

CHAPTER 2

The Factory

Each day hundreds of female workers from rural towns made their way to 308 Cleveland Avenue in Ishpeming, the Gossard factory. Some drove, some carpooled, and some rode a bus. But most just walked whether it was one block, twelve blocks, or several miles. In the fall, morning temperatures would start hovering in the 30s and continue to fall throughout the winter months. As female workers, many in work dresses and bundled under wool coats and scarves, clogged Ishpeming's sidewalks and streets, the Gossard clock chimed four times an hour, informing walkers to increase or slow down their pace.

The workday began at 7:00 a.m., but some machine operators would arrive early to "beat the clock." Harold Johnson, a mechanic, "opened the plant in the morning no earlier than a few minutes before seven a.m.," according to his son Peter.

Gossard Girl Elaine Peterson also knew "there would be girls lined up alongside the building anxious to be let in to work when the power to the machines would have been turned off." In the absence of power, these workers "turned their machines' wheels manually," said Elaine.

When the doors were unlocked, the factory's interior came alive as hundreds of women, talking and laughing, poured through one of three Gossard entrances and headed to the first-floor numbered coat racks packed with four hundred to five hundred hangers. Workers, some in galoshes (rubber boots that zipped in the front), some in leather heels, and some in sturdy flats, filed up wood stairs with a daily staccato rhythm of clicking heels.

Office workers, most of whom were women, began their daily routines on the first floor while machine operators headed to their workstations on the second and third floors. Lighting in the 14 ft., 2 in. high ceilings provided critical illumination in the large airy rooms. Large wood-frame windows helped ventilate a workspace where heat was generated from hundreds of workers and hundreds of whirring sewing machines. A metal tube called a shaft powered clusters of ten to twelve industrial machines mounted on endlessly long rows of rectangular wood tables.

"They just had rows and rows of machines," said Gossard Girl Remigia Davey. "Rows of machines on one side and more machines on the other side. Just girls facing each other and sewing." Added Gossard Girl Marjorie Ketola, "Everybody was facing each other. We each had a little wooden box. You would get your own thread and needles. Everyone brought their own pad to sit on as the chairs were not comfortable." Furthermore, said machine operator Phyllis Miller, "We sat in the same seat, and we had to get permission from our boss to use the bathroom. There were so many big, long shafts. They examined our work very carefully." Like Cecilia Kangas many Gossard Girls would also remember the deafening level of noise from hundreds of sewing machines.

Before power to the machines was turned on by a mechanic, machine operators pumped oil from a common metal drum on the second and third floors into their Singer oil cans, oiled their machines, and inventoried supplies or "findings" (i.e., bobbins, thread, zippers) in their personal wooden work boxes. Meanwhile, department heads (also called supervisors) distributed bundles to operators under their direction.

Preparing for Production

Monday mornings signaled another routine. Three days a week—Mondays, Wednesdays, and Fridays—a Gossard Company truck delivered "raw materials and findings" (i.e., bows, lace, bias tape, hooks and eyes, and elastic) to Ishpeming's factory. Men from the shipping department unloaded the freight from the landing bay and transported it by elevator to the appropriate floor where three workers processed the orders. The first worker determined the amount of material needed for the orders delivered that day, the second worker processed the findings, and the third female worker figured out what general labels and inventory tags were needed. The information was then given to male cutters. Once the material was inventoried, it was stored in large wood bins built by male workers.

Don Merrill, who worked in multiple departments, said production of undergarments commenced when the head male stockroom worker brought "a big roll of raw material" to a male cloth inspector responsible for identifying and removing fabric defects (i.e., tears, knots, holes, uneven dyeing, dropped stitches, or snags). The inspector first threaded the heavy roll of cloth through the bottom of a fabric inspection machine. As the material was fed over a special light, he looked for flaws, counted the flaws, and reported them to the foreman, who then recalibrated the amount of usable cloth and adjusted the value of the fabric. Meanwhile, the inspector removed defects and set aside a small portion of the raw material for use in repairing finished undergarments damaged by oil or other stains.

Next, a cloth layer used a fabric measuring device to cut the amount of needed material, and then, walking back and forth, he laid out twenty-four to forty-eight layers of fabric on a four-by-six-foot cutter's wood block table, which was "seasoned" with special oil once a week. The material was now ready to be cut. After securing the fabric edges with metal clamps, he positioned metal undergarment pattern pieces on the top layer, according to Don. The cutter then used overhead metal clamps to secure the pattern pieces onto the material. Next, he inserted "a sharp blade through a wood handle and tightened the metal blade." With "a steady but strong hand," he drove the knife though the layers of material. At least once a week, a cutter seasoned and sharpened his cutting tool. Years later, in the late 1960s, the clicker, a hydraulic cutting machine, would be used to cut up to ninety-two layers of material.

The cut pieces were sorted into one, two, or three dozen bunches and tied together with leftover fabric selvages. A woman bundler placed cut pattern pieces in a large cloth bag called a bundle. Next, she attached a units tag to the bundle and placed it in a large wood box mounted on wheels known as a truck. A bundler made sure the reference card affixed to the truck matched the bundle's units tag. The trucks were then delivered to one of two production floors, the second or third floor, where female department heads distributed bundles to the pieceworkers she supervised.

Undergarment Assembly

The assembly of undergarments was done by female machine operators known as piece-rate workers or pieceworkers, who accounted for at least 85–90 percent of the workforce. Broadly speaking, Gossard workers were divided into two categories: hourly workers and piece-rate workers. Hourly workers, regardless of their production pace, earned the same hourly rate. However, the pay structure for piece-rate workers, who received their work in bundles of twelve, twenty-four, and thirty-six, was different. Unlike hourly workers, the rate of pay by the late 1930s was calculated by two factors: a minimum or basic rate and an "above-the-minimum rate." The minimum rate signaled the company's minimum expectation for the number of items to be finished by workers within each department such as seaming, wide binding, zigzag, and other piece-related tasks. If, for example, an operator in seaming made $2.40 worth of pieces one day, and the basic rate was $4.80, she was paid $4.80. "Sometimes, workers who [continually] did not make their basic rate would receive a notice from the office," said Elaine Peterson. However, when a worker exceeded the minimum or basic rate, she earned "above the minimum rate for each additional piece." For example, if a seaming operator completed twenty-four pieces above the basic number established by the company, she would earn the daily basic rate ($4.80) plus the "above the minimum rate" per piece ($.05 x 24 pieces = $1.20) for a daily total of $6.00. The Gossard, like other companies, sometimes changed how the system worked as well as the rates per piece that workers received.

Third-floor assembly-line machine operators assembled garter belts, girdles, combinations, and small orders of specialty bras. Also on this floor was a separate space where an instructor trained new operators for up to six weeks on industrial sewing machines and Gossard sewing standards (i.e., number of stitches per inch, even stitching).

When management asked seventeen-year-old pieceworker Catherine Barbiere to train new operators, she respectfully declined. "I am not that capable of doing it; I have only been here a year." Management persisted noting she had the skills and "personality" to be successful. "I was uncomfortable supervising women thirty-five to forty years old. I hated to tell them what to do." Nevertheless, Catherine worked as an instructor for six years until she married.

Gossard Girl Jennie Melka spent twelve of her twenty-seven years training unskilled workers on the third floor. "They were beginners who came off of the street." Jennie's curriculum was straightforward for groups of up to thirty-five women at a time. "I sat at one of the industrial machines demonstrating the operation of and care for industrial sewing machines, as well as the basics of sewing: tension, stitch length, etc. Next, I would stand behind them and teach them. They always had six weeks to learn. They had to make graphs to put above their machine. The supervisor, the big shot, would come around, and if he didn't like the way the graph showed, that person would have to go. Some of the beginners would come out pretty good, and some quit before being fired because they didn't like the job."

The second floor was used only for large-scale bra assembly. Also among the second- and third-floor occupants were male sewing machine mechanics; their wood work tables served as their offices.

The assembly of an undergarment involved many different pieceworkers operating one-, two-, four-, six-, and twelve-needle machines. Depending on the undergarment and model number, the assembly might include a seamer, a binder (narrow, medium, or wide), a zigzagger, a zigzag ends person, a zipper person, a lace edger, an eyelet maker, a hooks and eyes person, a circular stitch operator, a Reece machine operator, or a boner operator.

Whether a pieceworker was on the second or third floor, the assembly process was similar. Beginning in the morning, each pieceworker received a bundle (cloth bag) filled with cut material bound in one, two, or three dozen bunches (also called units). She removed her work from the bundled units, untied the cut pattern pieces, and sewed only her part of each garment as quickly as possible. Once her portion was done, she retied the pattern pieces, placed them in the bundle, and removed a coupon from the bundle's tag for work she completed. Time meant money, so the faster an operator completed her task, the more she'd make.

Sometimes, pieceworkers worked on color-coded bundles, where a colored tag tied to the bundle dictated the order of production. Red-tag bundles were assembled immediately, green-tag bundles were assembled right away, and yellow-tag bundles were sewn as soon as possible.

Next, the department head or a floor lady delivered the bundle to the next operator who would complete her step. Meanwhile a roving female inspector, armed with a round metal gauge, periodically checked to see if operators' work adhered to company standards, such as the number of stitches per inch and proper seam allowances. This process continued until the end of the workday or until machine problems, workplace injuries, timings (a system using stop watches to establish costs in each step of undergarment assembly work), or other issues occurred.

Work Breaks

Workers had several breaks: midmorning, lunch, and midafternoon. Whether for fifteen minutes or one hour for lunch, the breaks were a welcome physical and mental pause from a fast-paced assembly-line environment that rewarded the fastest and most skilled workers.

At 10:00 a.m., the constant buzzing and whirring from the industrial machines paused when a mechanic turned off power to all machines. It was a break for operators to rest from the physical and mental demands of assembly-line work, a time for a Coke or snack in the factory's break room, which also supplied free coffee. The breaks were also a time to give the six hundred to seven hundred industrial machines a much-needed rest, to oil them, and to remove three hours of accumulated dust and lint.

After the fifteen-minute break, a mechanic switched the power on, and operators resumed their work pausing only for the usual interruptions, such as company timings, replacing broken needles, changing thread, replacing a bobbin, or readjusting the machine's tension setting.

Again, shortly before noon, a mechanic switched off power to all machines. Controlled chaos ensued as workers descended the wide stairs. Some snatched coats and raced home for a home-cooked meal, while others walked to their favorite lunch counter or restaurant. Those who brought their own food, such as a sandwich or leftovers, ambled to the factory's lunchroom. Others window-shopped or did family or personal errands and shopping during the noon hour.

Afternoons at the Gossard

Replenished and refreshed from a lunch break and stretching one's legs, pieceworkers returned, and the rhythms of the assembly line resumed. The mechanic turned on power to industrial machines; pieceworkers inventoried findings in their work boxes; department heads passed out bundles; machine operators resumed work; a highly skilled machine operator sewed a sale sample bra for Gossard traveling salespeople; inspectors, armed with special tools, scrutinized finished undergarments; repair cutters matched flawed materials; repair workers fixed damaged undergarments and returned them to their bundles via the hand elevator (bucket on a rope); floor ladies checked machine operators' work and notified operators about problems identified by department heads; the ironer prepared finished garments for shipping.

Some pieceworkers kept a notebook of their completed work (model type and number, completed units, and amount earned). They affixed their coupons—receipts for completed work—on a sticky, a card used daily to document workers' arrival and departure times. Three chimes from the Gossard clock signaled the end of a pieceworkers' day, though some worked longer to finish a bundle, to speak with a department head, or to meet with an office worker. Regardless, all pieceworkers punched out on their floor's time clock. As they left, they inserted their stickies through a designated slot in locked wooden boxes on the second and third floors. The staccato of heels and lively female chatter followed as hundreds of Gossard Girls, shoulder to shoulder, trundled down the worn wood stairs. Some workers stopped at the office while most grabbed their coats and joined Ishpeming's rush-hour foot and car traffic.

Postproduction

Throughout the eight-hour workday (an hour change implemented around 1933), the journey of finished undergarments was repeated. Assembled bras and corsets were returned to the original canvas bag (bundle), and a wood truck transported them to the inspection department on the first floor. Again, inspectors checked for defects such as poor stitching, poor workmanship, or soiled garments. Undergarments that did not pass inspection were set aside, returned to the operator whose work did not meet the company's inspection, or sent to a cutter and repair operator.

From inspection, the finished garments were moved to the boxing department, also on the first floor. Quality control mattered in every step of production, including boxing; inspectors routinely monitored the work of boxers. In the meantime, a box lid printer received print orders from the cutting room office. Using a special machine, she stamped critical inventory information, such as model number, sizes, color, and number of garments on cardboard box lids.

The cardboard lids were then delivered to boxers who were also piece-workers. Boxers worked at custom-built wood tables (one boxer per table) where packing materials (cardboard boxes and tissue paper) were stored in custom-built wood shelving. Precise packing instructions were dictated by the size of a cardboard box, the type and size of packing material, and the size, color, and type of undergarment. When boxing was complete, male shippers placed the boxed merchandise on a cart and moved it to the shipping room. Meanwhile, the production manager compiled lists of finished garments, which she delivered to the shipping department. Shippers then tied these boxes together and packed them in larger cardboard boxes. Next, male workers sealed boxes with a special machine that moistened and applied shipping tape. Three days a week shippers loaded merchandise onto trucks for delivery to company warehouses throughout the Midwest where the Gossard brand would be readied for delivery to national and international distribution centers.

Rose Collick, Gossard Girl

In 1921, Bruno and Concetta Nardi welcomed their first child, Rose, less than a year after the H. W. Gossard Company opened its plant in Ishpeming. That same year, Ishpeming's newspaper, the *Iron Ore*, heralded the year-old Gossard factory as a valuable community asset. "The Gossard factory in Ishpeming is now employing more hands than are some of our best mines and paying good wages. Many a family the head of which is out of employment is being maintained by the girls working in this factory." Rose's parents could not have predicted that their eldest daughter would become a proud Gossard Girl.

At that time, her immigrant parents, both from Calabria, Italy, were busy adjusting to life in a new country. Bruno worked long hours in the mines, but the birth of his first child made him quite proud. Father and daughter would be seen walking hand in hand everywhere, including to meetings for the St. Rocco-St. Anthony Society, an aid society benefiting Italian Americans in Ishpeming, Rose said with a smile.

The Nardi family was of modest means. During the Depression, Rose, as the eldest of eleven children, would be called upon to help. Sometimes, she stood in food lines for flour and sugar. Other times, her grandmother accompanied her. "They gave us a slip of paper [food voucher]," said an older Rose, who used it at a local grocery store. The Depression touched many lives in Ishpeming. It was hard times, Rose said, but at least her family's vegetable gardens helped feed the Nardi's eleven children.

The hard times caused Rose to stop her formal education. She attended St. John's Catholic School through eighth grade, and then an independent Rose made a difficult choice. "It was my decision. I wanted to help them." So she did. At fourteen, Rose was hired to do housework for Mr. Chase, his wife, and their three children. "I did everything except cooking." She earned $3 per week and gave her wages to her mother. Rose's job did not exempt her from responsibilities in the Nardi household. As the oldest, Rose had many duties, including weekly bathing of her siblings. Two years later as the Nardi family's needs grew, Rose, still a teenager, sought better employment.

In 1937, good-paying jobs were limited in Ishpeming for a sixteen-year-old girl. Child labor laws were changing at the federal and state levels, but according to Rose, she was still too young to work at Ishpeming's undergarment plant, now in its seventeenth year. Her family's needs persisted, so an uncle with special connections to the plant manager interceded. Like Manager Claude Tripp, Rose's uncle (and her father) had served in World War II. More importantly, Rose's uncle regularly played cards with Claude at the American Legion.

Rose went directly to Claude's house to ask for a job. Whether the manager knew Rose was not seventeen—the minimum age for work in a factory—is unknown. The sixteen-year-old would list her age as seventeen. "They [Gossard management] never found out. They never checked it [her age] out. I had to do things in those days because I knew my parents needed the money," said Rose.

Looking back, Rose spoke with great pride about her contribution. "In the first five years, I gave everything to my mother. I kept $3 every payday, so I could have silk stockings [50 cents] and lipstick [Tangee]. I never kept a whole check for myself." When Rose's younger sisters came of age, some followed Rose to the Gossard. Her sisters did give their parents some of their earnings, but they only worked a short time at the factory. Rose felt Gossard work requirements—the ability to work fast and produce high-quality undergarments—did not match up with the abilities of her sisters. On the other hand, Rose's speed, attention to detail, and exceptional work ethic were a good fit in the factory.

Following a brief orientation for new hires in 1937, Rose was placed in medium binding. What a change for someone raised on a treadle machine with one needle. "I started on a two-needle machine, and one day I ran both needles in my thumb," she said with a laugh. Typically, workplace injuries were resolved onsite. Rose's injury was more serious; two broken needles remained in her thumb. An older Rose reflected, "I kept pumping it. I was going faster than I should have been." Her loud "squealing" caught the attention of "the bundles' girls" who raced to her shaft and took the teenager to the emergency room. Decades later, Rose could be more circumspect about her injury, "That was nothing. I went back to work." And she learned to keep her fingers away from the machine's needles.

Rose was proud of her twenty years at the factory. "I always showed up for work. I liked going to work, getting my machine ready, getting my bundles ready, opening them up, getting my slip ready to put my price tags on it, making sure I had enough work in front of me." By her own admission, Rose had to work whether it was as the oldest daughter helping support her family or years later as the single mother supporting her own family. "I enjoyed it because I needed to work. I never thought, 'Oh, I hate going, I hate going.' I liked the work, and I stuck with it."

Rose returned to the unionized Gossard plant after divorcing her husband in 1961. She refused her father's offer to move home, choosing instead to raise her youngest child on her own. She began as a pieceworker, and over the next fifteen years, Rose took on leadership positions within the plant. She became a working department head and a department steward. In both positions, Rose was responsible for, among other things, a safe and fair working environment as set forth in the union contract even if it sometimes meant being "the squeaky wheel" intent on getting the needed oil to solve the problem of the day.

The packaging of undergarments, according to Rose, was as important as the assembly of undergarments. Throughout the boxing process, quality control mattered, and inspectors routinely monitored the work of boxers.

In 1975, Gossard officials visited Ishpeming's plant. Such visits were not unusual, and workers like Rose would not necessarily have known the purpose of the visits. During the course of the 1975 visit, Rose was asked to teach workers from a plant in Wisconsin how to fold and box a new bra model. Typically, multiple bras were placed in one cardboard box, but the new model would be boxed in a new container, a bubble. The bubble—a plastic holder—held only one bra. Rose said, "We had to fold them [bras] a certain way, so they would fit in a bubble, because that was how each bra was displayed."

During the visit, a photographer (presumably a Gossard official from the Wisconsin plant) asked Rose if he could photograph her while she demonstrated the process to Wisconsin employees. She agreed and later received an eight-by-ten-inch copy of her demonstration, and she also learned Gossard officials "took the model away from us," said Rose, to have it manufactured elsewhere. One year later (1976), Ishpeming's factory closed.

Decades later, the photo was a point of pride and an opportunity to discuss the boxer's work environment on the factory's first floor. A nearly century-old Rose pointed to the plastic bubble atop a wooden box. Thanks to Gossard male workers, she noted, every girl in the department had a handcrafted wood box on which she boxed the new bra model. Near the wooden box were two additional items: a clipboard and a small cup of water. "When you got a bundle, there was a tag on the end of it and you took your coupon off. Then you glued it to the paper, which was attached to the clipboard." Each day, she tallied her coupons, wrote her name and number, noted her pay, and submitted her paper to the office.

Rose was deeply proud of her tenure at the Ishpeming plant. "You could not find anything better than the Gossard," Rose stated while lovingly displaying a special Gossard negligee—Miss Elaine—which she donated along with her boxing photo to the Marquette Regional History Center (previously called Marquette County Historical Center). The orange and lace-edged negligee had defied its age of forty years. The delicate Gossard treasure embodied Rose's pride in being a Gossard Girl and her perseverance as a single parent to provide for her children.

CLAUDE TRIPP, GOSSARD MANAGER

In the fall of 1943, the city of Ishpeming lost one of its most prominent citizens, Claude H. Tripp: native of Belvidere, Illinois; World War I veteran; a two-term mayor in Ishpeming; a member of Rotary, the American Legion, the Ishpeming Town Club, the Masonic Blue Lodge, and the Presbyterian church; president, vice president, and director of Wawonowin Golf Club; director of the Ishpeming Hotel company; director of the YMCA; and director of the Community Chest. The forty-nine-year-old manager of the H. W. Gossard Plant had given twenty-two years (1921–43) of dedicated community service.

According to the *Mining Journal*'s (*MJ*) obituary, Claude exemplified the highest values for good citizenship: just, sincere, loyal, and conscientious. These values are what "give a community character," Mayor John Johnson was quoted in the newspaper. Civic leader Spencer Helden characterized Claude as a person willing to serve "whether you wanted a chairman or someone to park cars at a public event." No task was too large or too small.

Four years earlier, an article in the *MJ* had documented the importance of the Gossard to the city of Ishpeming, while also recognizing the leadership of its manager. By 1939, Claude had worked for seventeen of his nineteen Gossard years, with fifteen of those as plant manager. Under his leadership, Ishpeming's plant had grown into one of the largest and most productive undergarment plants within the Gossard Company portfolio, a company "considered the world's largest manufacturer of foundation garments" by 1939. Under Claude, the plant had "a record of continuous operation through two major depression periods (1922–1925 and 1930–1935), [which] was a testimonial to its general value, its wise administration, and its economic importance in Ishpeming's scheme of life," said the newspaper. The payroll for its work force of five hundred employees (450 women, 50 men) made it one of the largest in Marquette County. In 1939, the plant was "considered one of the great stabilizing factors in the economic welfare of the community," reported the *MJ*.

Under Gossard manager Claude's leadership, the city of Ishpeming continued to flourish. Within two years employment approached six hundred. Production increases, payroll increases, and employee benefits signaled a positive harbinger for local businesses' Christmas season. "One need only stand in front of the Gossard factory at 4 pm any work day to realize, as the workers come streaming out, its value to the community and why it brings cheer to Ishpeming's Christmas season," reported the *MJ* on December 24, 1940. Over the next several years, Claude oversaw a series of plant improvements, including the basement renovation for the factory's kitchen and cafeteria. Wishful businessmen hoped Claude's tenure would extend many years.

It did not. Claude died unexpectedly in September 1943 at a Chicago hospital while recuperating from a routine medical procedure, devastating his family: Claude's daughter Marjorie, a teenager; son Donald, a soldier stationed in Europe at the time; and wife Grace, a homemaker who had immigrated from England.

Marjorie never forgot her father's funeral because something "very unusual" happened. "When he died, the stores in downtown Ishpeming closed for the funeral," she wrote in a letter dated July 2009. Marjorie could understand if her father had been an important national or state figure, but this was her father. Her brother would not witness this rare tribute, nor would he witness the image of people lining Ishpeming's downtown streets in tribute to his father. Claude's daughter also recalled "some on the curb were crying."

What was it about Claude that compelled many citizens to pay tribute to Marjorie's father in an unusual way? For W. S. Pierce, president of Rotary and president of the Community Chest, Claude was "so thoroughly human, so utterly natural with all men regardless of their rank, that everyone found themselves attracted to him," reported the *MJ*.

Claude grew up in Belvidere, Illinois, 370 miles south of Ishpeming and 75 miles northwest of Chicago. Following completion of a two-year business program in nearby Rockford, he was hired by the H. W. Gossard Company in his hometown. Claude worked in the office of the Belvidere plant until 1917.

Within a short period, he was transferred to Canada. "Claude Tripp departed this morning for Toronto to take a position with the H. W. Gossard company [and assisted] with the organization of a [Gossard] plant in Drummondville, Quebec," reported his hometown newspaper, *Belvidere Daily Republican*, on October 13, 1915. Soon tensions across the Atlantic Ocean (World War I) lured him from factory work to military work, a pilot, something he wanted to do "more than anything," his daughter said.

Claude would serve overseas for eighteen months. When World War I ended, he returned to the Gossard plant in Drummondville, Quebec, but he could not erase memories of a very special woman he'd met on a beach in England during his furlough. Claude "sent for" Grace Stupple, "and the [young couple] were married on the boat before she stepped ashore [on] August 23, 1920," reported the *MJ*. He requested a transfer "back to the American division of the company," not because the young couple disliked Canada, but because they wanted their first child to be born in the United States, according to Claude's daughter. His request was timely. The H. W. Gossard Company had recently (May 1920) opened its first undergarment plant in Michigan's Upper Peninsula. Claude and his pregnant wife moved to Ishpeming in 1921 where he worked as assistant manager. When Manager M. E. Slater left several years later, Claude became the manager.

Gossard Girl Elizabeth Coron found the Gossard plant "a pleasant place to work," in part due to the factory's "wonderful boss." A "nice person, very revered," the former pieceworker stated emphatically. "He listened to you. He was so understanding. He'd never put anyone down. He always had time for you." The Gossard manager also encouraged workers to tell him if they "were unhappy about something or something wasn't just right." By his actions, workers like Elizabeth felt their boss, "was just there for you." When he died unexpectedly in 1943, it was a big loss for Gossard workers.

At Tripp's passing, Rev. C. G. Ziegler, veteran secretary of Ishpeming's Town Club would say in the *MJ*, "Claude Tripp was a fine example of the business man giving practical application in his daily life to the principles of Christian living. There was no hypocrisy about him. He hewed straight to the line of rugged honesty. His capacity to serve, his helpful counsel, his sincere encouragements will be missed by all who delighted in his companionship."

Grace Tripp became a Gossard Girl after Claude's untimely death because "she needed to pay for the house mortgage," said Marjorie. Her mother became the plant's personnel director, a position she held until 1954.

CHAPTER 3

A Decade of Expansion

A FTER CLAUDE TRIPP DIED UNEXPECTEDLY in the fall of 1943, assistant manager Harold Peterson became the factory's fourth manager and the man who would lead the Gossard through a great period of growth and, simultaneously, a great period of union contention.

America's undergarment industry continued to grow in the 1940s. According to the authors of *Uplift: The Bra in America*, "Most regions in the United States had at least one major producer by 1946." The growth in this industry was fed by women working in jobs vacated by America's men fighting in World War II. By 1945, women, who made up 36 percent of the work force, labored in a variety of areas such as "the Signal Corps, machine tool operators, censors in the post office, and a myriad of posts," including ship and airplane assembly.

The success of these undergarment companies was, among other things, dependent on their ability to adapt to women's diverse work environments. According to the authors of *Uplift*, the more successful companies exploited "serious marketing research" that guided their "product development and presentation." For example, an advertisement from *Women's Home Companion* and cited in *Uplift* depicted a factory worker in comfortable support undergarments. The more strategic-minded undergarment companies "recognized that export of brassieres and girdles outside of the United States held the key to solid and expanding post-war prosperity," said the *Uplift* authors.

Meanwhile, the British-owned Gossard Company continued its undergarment output while also assisting Britain's war effort. "Gossard produced everything from brassieres for the Women's Royal Naval Service to sails, parachutes and even single-seater fighter dinghies," according to the Gossard "Our Heritage" webpage. During the 1940s, the UK-owned company also introduced "a lightweight, pre-shrunk girdle featuring an innovative wonder fiber, called Silkskin."

Elizabeth Coron's five-year tenure as a Gossard Girl coincided with World War II. Uncertain of the exact year, she recalled a period when Gossard workers also did "sewing for the service." It was a time when the factory had a second eight-hour shift ending at 11 pm. Pieceworkers "made bras in the army color . . . a light shade of brown . . . not a darker green for the marines." With two brothers in the service, Elizabeth also proudly supported the war effort by purchasing war bonds through weekly payroll deductions.

Meanwhile, challenges and milestones marked the 1940s for Ishpeming's Gossard plant. In 1941, the International Ladies Garment Workers Union (ILGWU) targeted three women's garment factories in Michigan's Upper Peninsula (U.P.)—Escanaba, Marquette, and Ishpeming—in its efforts to improve workplace conditions and increase union membership.

However, the Gossard company had the reputation of providing good conditions for its workers. On March 20, 1944, Ishpeming's outside winter temperatures hovered in the 30s. Quite a contrast to the warm, cheerful atmosphere in the newly remodeled basement of the Ishpeming Gossard plant reported the *Mining Journal* (*MJ*) on March 25. What was once a modest-sized break and lunchroom in the basement had been enlarged and transformed into a spacious cafeteria serving free, well-balanced meals for 550 workers. The hot nutritious meals would be prepared by a newly hired staff of seven and tailored to the needs of factory employees.

The idea for company-sponsored meals was conceived by R. C. Stirton, president of the Gossard Company, developed by Manager Tripp before his death, and brought to fruition by Harold Peterson, the new manager of Ishpeming's plant.

Company officials "had been giving thought to means by which they could show further consideration for the welfare of the employees," notably women workers who comprised about 90 percent of the workforce, reported the newspaper. Most were married with families and some, with husbands serving abroad, "did the major part of their household work in the evenings. Each morning, they packed a lunch for themselves, many times taking what was left after giving the best, as mothers will, to other members of the family. Those who ate downtown had to hurry to get seats," said Peterson, who was quoted in the *MJ*.

Whether one brought leftovers or rushed downtown for lunch, there was, according to company officials, an economic concern. Rising prices affected restaurant owners who were faced with "serving less for the same money or charging more for the same food." Rising prices also affected those employees "from outlying sections who roomed in town," reported the *MJ*, and these workers "often followed the natural inclination to save as much as possible." Free meals helped all employees stretch their wages, reduced stress from quick lunches at a restaurant, and lessened women's household work. A menu of hot nutritious meals also helped further "good industrial practice," reported company officials, because there would be "less midafternoon fatigue and more efficiency." Moreover, nutritious meals could, according to President Stirton and Manager Peterson, increase workplace efficiency, which then increased workers' wages.

However, not all workers trusted management's rationale at the time. Gossard pieceworker Ruth Craine questioned the timing of the company benefit. She and other prounion workers were in the midst of organizing a campaign in 1944. From their perspective, free daily meals would dissuade workers from joining the ILGWU.

Remodeling the plant's basement wasn't easy. The partitioned basement in the three-story building housed a large furnace, a shipping department, and a break room for the two hundred to three hundred workers who brought lunches. Even so, a *Mining Journal* reporter stated, the plant manager "fell in line with the idea and took charge of the arrangements" with help from male Gossard workers. Renovation plans included reorganizing the shipping department, removing lunchroom dividers, decorating a cafeteria, and building "hundreds of storage bins" along the basement walls "to gain space needed to feed 550 persons."

Manager Peterson reported that equipping the cafeteria was harder than remodeling the basement, presumably due to wartime shortages of metal, rubber, and paper. "Trays alone were a problem. So far, it has been impossible to get 550. Plates, cups, knives, forks, spoons cannot be ordered from the nearest wholesale house," the manager informed the *MJ*. Similar challenges surfaced for equipping the kitchen. Peterson had "to scour the country" for kitchen and cafeteria service equipment. "Refrigerators, a sizeable stove, steam table, cafeteria service equipment, all had to be located, or built in the plant and much of it was done by the company's own carpenters," reported the newspaper.

Outfitting the cafeteria was a challenge, but seating 550 workers at one time was impossible. The basement could accommodate no more than fifty tables, and workers were allotted only one hour for lunch. Plan A—feed all the workers at the same time—was not sustainable. So Gossard management employed Plan B—use the factory's workforce structure. Workers were already divided into separate departments such as seaming, boxing, wide binding, mechanics, etc. "With approximately 80 [workers] to a unit, and each following the other in seven or eight-minute intervals, a steady line of employees comes to the cafeteria starting at 11:30. On the second day, the last department to report was being served at 12:10," said the *MJ*. Plan B, taking lunch by departments, was practical and sustainable.

Marquette's newspaper reported that on the first day, Gossard workers feasted on "baked sugar cured ham with champagne sauce, candied yams, choice of beets or minced carrots, chef's special salad, rolls and bread, ice cream, choice of coffee, tea or milk." A fine, nutritious meal prepared by Gossard chef Paul Maloney and served by six permanent kitchen staff. Once finished with their three-course meal (average time was twenty minutes), workers took their trays to a "garbage disposal table," where the kitchen staff quickly washed trays "to accommodate 550 employees with less than 200 trays."

Gossard Girl Ann Marie Stieve, a fast talker with a keen sense of humor, reflected on the company-sponsored meals. In a family of fifteen, she was used to her mother's Italian food, not Chef Maloney's varied menu, but the first time she ate sauerkraut, she thought, "How could something that smells so bad taste so good." Eating sauerkraut, even decades later, would make Ann Marie "think of work at the Gossard."

"If you worked here, you were lucky," said Margaret Sippola who became a seamer (employee #359) in 1944. She appreciated "complete meals prepared by the kitchen crew," especially on days when the menu included "baked turkey and Boston cream pie made from scratch." These three-course meals helped stretch her wages while also providing energy during "hot summer days," when heat generated from industrial machines and the high humidity made it difficult to work. On these warm days, Margaret put talcum powder on her arms, presumably to protect the undergarment material while also absorbing sweat or smells.

Gossard Girl Alvera Brisson whose parents immigrated from Solta Colino, Italy, to Negaunee in the 1920s grew up enjoying "a lot of polenta, chicken, and spaget." For the most part, she enjoyed free lunches at the factory. But "sometimes we would know ahead of time what we would have. If I didn't like what we had, I would go to the Brown Derby for lunch."

Most workers used the rest of their lunch break (forty minutes) "for a leisurely walk." Some window-shopped. Others frequented Ishpeming's many businesses, while those living near the factory walked home to relax or do housework. And some pieceworkers, intent on maximizing their wages even more, hurried back to work "to beat the clock." Regardless, Ishpeming's business center was congested at noon, and for some businessmen, like Carlo Maki, it was best to avoid Ishpeming's downtown during the lunch hour.

Frank Andriacchi, owner of Ishpeming's Venice Supper Club situated less than two hundred yards from the factory, said the free lunches were "a great deal and part of workers' benefits." While some local businesses may have feared this competition, Frank had a different perspective. Local restaurants were hurt, the Ishpeming native said, "but not that bad because so many people don't want to eat where they worked. That's just human nature. They want to go somewhere else and get out of the building."

Teenage Gossard Girl Donna Bergman was thankful for company-sponsored lunches not just because of "the great chef and real homemade meals," but also because the savings from free meals, free car rides, and living at home boosted her weekly wages from zigzag ends on brassieres and corsets.

The company continued offering free midday meals even after the plant became a union shop in 1949 but discontinued this benefit in the early 1950s. Providing nutritious, three-course meals five days a week was a significant investment by the H. W. Gossard Company for workers in a number of its plants, including those in Ishpeming and Gwinn. Surely, many workers were disappointed when the company stopped this employee benefit, especially those who had come to depend on free lunches.

Meanwhile, Ishpeming's plant continued to expand over the next two years, employing 580 workers and paying over $800,000 in wages and salaries in 1946, according to the *MJ*. "During the day the whir of machinery is heard as experienced employes [*sic*] finish 550 dozen garments every working day. Through power sewing machines comes a steady flow of garments, using up in a single day approximately 3,900 yards of materials," reported the newspaper. The factory, long considered one of the company's largest, was part of the extensive Gossard network of factories. Warehouses stacked with the Gossard brand "to serve women of all countries and races" were spread across the globe in Chicago, New York, Atlanta, Dallas, San Francisco, Toronto, Buenos Aires, Argentina, and Sydney, Australia. The global reach of the Gossard brand was viewed favorably in 1946, a sign the company enjoyed "greater stability than at any time in its history," reported the newspaper.

Gossard mechanic Bob Sihtala lived two blocks from the factory. As "a little boy" he walked "past the mysterious, towering stone building [where he] heard the same sounds: whrrr . . . whrrr . . . whrrr. All the windows would be open because it was always warm in here. Even in the wintertime it was warm. Lots of friction." Puzzling sounds to a young, curious boy in the 1940s who wondered "what [was] going on."

Bob also recalled a pastime of many of his peers: sneaking inside the pyramid-roof Gossard clock tower, mounted on the northwest corner of the plant. Presumably Bob and his male friends accessed the brick time-piece by way of the building's fire escapes. If they scaled the fire escapes at night, a light inside of the clock may have helped them navigate the clock's interior. Maybe the clock's interior light helped one evening when "one of the boys carved his initials on the inside of the clock backwards." Strategic on the part of the boy, Bob mused. His initials "could be read on the outside of the clock." Two decades later, the clock would be removed for safety reasons and stored in the plant's basement where mechanic Bob tripped over the relic from his childhood.

Many Gossard Girls used their economic power during the 1940s to benefit their communities, on both a local and national scale. "Gossard employes [*sic*] have developed a keen sense of competition in community affairs and take pride in the records they establish. The result has been a series of achievements in over-subscribing quotas for war bonds, Red Cross drives and all other relief programs in the community," said the *MJ* on September 6, 1946.

After twenty-six years of continuous operations, Ishpeming's second largest business showed no signs of slowing down. Rather, company officials anticipated its workforce "will cross the six hundred mark for an all-time record" during September 1946, wrote the *MJ*. Good news for women in search of work, good news for Ishpeming's business community, and good news for the Gossard Company.

Decades later, Bill Cohodas of Ishpeming, who oversaw Cohodas Brothers Produce, the largest wholesale fruit and produce dealer in the U.P., reflected on Ishpeming during the 1940s. "The Gossard corset factory was one of the shining lights for the people of Ishpeming. Women could go in and work, and come out of there with their weekly paycheck, a godsend for a family, [because] it was a period when the mines were not doing too well."

However, the ever-growing workforce in the three-story (excluding the basement) factory was "cramped for space even after efficiency experts and their own trained personnel have made several rearrangements of storage spaces after several years," said the *MJ*.

A Second Factory

In 1946, efficiency experts had determined the renovation of Ishpeming's Gossard factory would not adequately meet the needs of the U.P.'s growing Gossard workforce. This was a challenging issue for Ishpeming, and an exciting opportunity for Gwinn, "a pleasant tree-shaded village of 1,000 built on iron ore" in Forsyth Township, reported the *MJ* in September 1947. Twenty-six miles from Ishpeming, the mining village of Gwinn, also known as Model Town, was designed by Boston architect Warren Manning for William Gwinn Mather, president of the local mining company, Cleveland-Cliffs Iron Company (CCI), in 1907. Gwinn, named for the CCI president, was intended to be a self-contained town. "Besides the houses, scattered on a site along the east branch of the Escanaba River," said the *MJ*, "the company built a hospital, clubhouse, and other civic structures." However, when local mines closed, workers were forced to find employment elsewhere. Some found work in the pulpwood cutting industry, others commuted to Negaunee and Ishpeming businesses, and more would work in nearby service industries, such as gas stations and utilities. Without support from CCI mines, the two-story company hospital closed, remaining empty for a number of years.

In 1946, when Gossard officials began exploring locations in Marquette County, Gwinn's business leaders proposed using the vacant two-story hospital. Just as the Gossard Company had breathed new life into Ishpeming's vacant Braastad Block in the 1920s, so too would the company adopt a similar strategy in 1947 when it selected the former hospital in Gwinn as the site of its new factory. Whereas the Braastad structure had been vacant less than twelve months, Gwinn's hospital had been vacant for a number of years. As such, the facility required extensive remodeling, not the least of which was a new roof. Other improvements included "steel reinforcements, a new heating plant with blower device, and fluorescent lighting," reported the *MJ*.

When the two-story renovation was complete, small hospital rooms were converted into "two big, airy, well-lighted workrooms" and equipped with "10 shafts to power 120 sewing machines," reported the newspaper. Cutting of material was done in Ishpeming, trucked to Gwinn for assembly, inspected, boxed, and trucked back to Ishpeming for distribution.

In early 1947, Gossard officials visited Gwinn High School. During her job interview, seventeen-year-old Ruth Webb learned she was too young. Later that summer the high school graduate received a letter asking if she "would like to apply." Still too young to work on industrial machines, Ruth began in boxing. "It took me a long time to learn how do the boxes without breaking them. Later I moved to packing bras in the boxes." Working at the plant meant she could take care of herself. "My family was poor. They had all they could do to take care of themselves." Whether she worked in boxing or later as a seamer, Ruth knew the plant "was a pick-me-up for women in town. They could work, be close to their families, and contribute. It made them independent."

The former hospital's basement was outfitted with a cafeteria where workers, like those in Ishpeming's plant, were served free nutritious three-course meals five days a week. An older Ruth smiled as she recalled heading to lunch on her first day of work. "I supposed everyone else would have factory bread. I had this big ugly sandwich made with homemade bread. That was the day we all went down and ate a free midday meal." Thereafter, Ruth looked forward to trying different foods like baked salmon. "They had beautiful food and nice desserts."

Perhaps Gossard Girl Nathalie "Neggie" Hutchens was also inspired by the variety of foods served in Gwinn's cafeteria, including salmon. Decades later, her three children, a niece, and Rick Wills heaped praise for Neggie's legendary cooking skills, whether she made beef roast, ravioli, pasties, chop suey, bread, creamed salmon, or gnocchi. "She did everything to the best of her abilities, a trait that served her well at the Gossard," said daughter Kathryn. It was his mother's "attention to detail" that made Neggie's pasties famous, according to her son, Mike. "She put a pad of butter into each steam escape slit in the top of the pasty when they came out of the oven." Mike's childhood neighbor and friend Rick loved "delicious pasties made by Mike's mother, a woman in "a little body, a big heart, and a wonderful sense of humor."

"They weren't fancy meals, but they were something to eat," according to Madeleine DelBello. Her favorite dish consisted of a roll stuffed with meat. "They used to roll out the dough, and they put some kind of meat inside. You roll it and slice it and cook it. Everybody seemed to like that."

Gossard Girl Edna Roberts, who worked two years "just to earn money and wait until she married," leveled high praise at Gwinn's cooks. "They were good cooks. Oh we had the *best* meals there, and I got a lot of ideas for my own cooking. I don't remember all the things they cooked, but we went down in shifts. Whoever came back would let everyone else know what they were having. We were always anxious to see what Mrs. Sarasin and another woman from Little Lake had cooked for the day." Gossard Girl Judy Green said, "I never liked liver and onions, but when Mrs. Sarasin cooked this dish, I just loved it."

When operations reached full capacity, the branch factory would inject nearly $250,000 in wages annually to Gwinn's economic bloodstream, reported the *MJ*. The infusion of a quarter million dollars was viewed as a "barometer of better times" for Model Town. For example, Gossard Girl Dora Mussatto's wages helped her husband Ray expand a family grocery business. "I was a big help. I gave him *my* money to buy appliances—stoves, refrigerators, washing machines, and TVs—to sell at his business." As a wage earner, Dora continued, "it meant a lot. You could buy little knickknacks that husbands probably wouldn't want you to have . . . different things."

Gossard Girl Pearl Filizetti, who worked four years (1947–49, 1951–53), said, "I had to go to Ishpeming first for instructions and to learn how to use the machines, before they opened the Gossard in Gwinn." After her six-week training period ($5 per week rate to carpool twenty-five miles from Princeton), she operated a six-needle industrial machine and later a two-needle binding machine in Gwinn. Reflecting on this period, a quiet-spoken Pearl chuckled, "I could make my own money, I could buy extra things for my children." And if Pearl saw something she liked, she treated herself without feeling as if she had to consult with her husband. It was her money. Nevertheless, the circumspect Pearl acknowledged the factory's invaluable legacy. "The factory gave many, many women work. There were quite a few widows working here, and for some, it was their first job."

Pieceworker and mother Hilda Rivers preferred the rigors of an assembly-line environment over work on her childhood farm. "I never knew work could be so easy until I began working at the Gossard." A narrow and medium binder for seven years, Hilda worked on the second floor, her "dream floor" for their "smooth running machines." She enjoyed an employee benefit: making two personal bras from precut pattern pieces.

Seamers Aune Pelkie and her daughter Edna worked on the top floor in Gwinn's two-story factory. "The floors were all open, and machines were just in rows. The floor ladies placed a great big sack on the floor and a drawstring you had to tie. Whatever you were working on, you'd just take it out of there," said Edna. Twice a day (once in the morning and once in the afternoon) Edna took breaks from her "big black machine" to get a coke or "just get up and move," especially during her first pregnancy. She enjoyed "being with the other ladies" and earning as much as $40 a week, "good money in those days [1947–49]."

The September article predicted Gwinn would show "that small town workers can turn out the goods of mass production if machinery is taken to them. And they needn't be far from trees and sunlight."

1947 Gossard Picnic

Food—the great socializer—was included in workplace social gatherings whether in the factory or in public places. After the Gossard Company opened Ishpeming's plant in 1920, food was integral in company-sponsored festivities such as dances, holiday parties, and summer picnics. Evidence of these events can be gleaned from *The Gossardian*, the monthly employee newsletter for Gossard factories during the 1920s, when representatives from each factory submitted photos and accounts of their social gatherings.

Though the newsletter had been discontinued by the 1940s, social get-togethers endured. Some workers held fond memories of Gossard summer picnics usually held in early July. Gossard Girl Elaine Peterson attended picnics during the 1940s, where everyone—young, married, single, divorced, or mature women—appreciated "good eats, time to eat, and time to mingle."

The Gossard picnic of July 1947, however, was particularly festive and large, according to the *MJ*. "The H. W. Gossard company will be host to its 700 Ishpeming and Gwinn plant employees at their annual picnic this afternoon and evening at the Ishpeming Winter Sports Club's area." The Gossard picnic had a variety of overlapping games, such as an egg toss, old clothes and old sack races, a watermelon-eating contest, and Scotchman's Pastime. (Scotchman's Pastime is not the name of a specific game but more likely a reference to games played over the centuries in Scotland, Wales, and perhaps England. One such game is called quoits: a ring toss game. Without a photo from the Gossard Picnic or a reference from a Gossard Girl, there is no way to know with certainty if quoits was one of the games. What is known, according to the *MJ*, is that "Gossard Girl Viola Prin was in charge of Scotchman's Pastime.") Afternoon and evening festivities began with "an introduction and the crowning of the Gossard Queen" followed by two lunches and a dinner. At 4:00 p.m., Ishpeming's women's baseball team squared off against the team from Gwinn.

Decades later, Elaine, who played first base and shortstop for Ishpeming, proudly shared photos from "the clash between Gwinn and Ishpeming girls." The victorious team of ten, Elaine mused, had beaten their Gwinn rivals and garnered a trophy: a box of Brach's candy. The winning team posed in a field of daisies, perhaps thinking about the stories they'd be telling their families and coworkers. Later that evening *and* after the second lunch and wiener roast, the winning team joined others for dancing. For those without cars, management provided buses to transport Ishpeming and Gwinn workers home. Most assuredly, seven hundred workers returned tired, full, and armed with lasting memories of good food, good fun, and good camaraderie.

Major Factory Facelift

In March 1948, the remodel and enlargement of Ishpeming's Gossard plant began. The plant remained open throughout the extensive renovation, closing only for two weeks in late July and early August for annual inventory and workers' vacations. Unionizing efforts by the ILGWU also continued.

High school graduate Audrey Bergman used skills from courses in bookkeeping, shorthand, and typing to create "tickets" for cutters in a room nearby where "eight or nine men cut fabric and four women cut ribbon." An older Audrey said, "I received orders from Mr. Nyquist. And then the tickets would have to be typed out [onto cardboard-like paper] that went onto the bundles that went upstairs . . . to tell [pieceworkers] how many to sew or put together. There were other things I did, but that was the basic." The teenage office worker had fond memories of her brief tenure (two years). "The cutters were a very happy crew. They kidded around all day and laughed a lot. And Gloria [unknown last name], who worked there before me, was so helpful to me. I was a young woman who didn't know what she was doing," said Audrey with a smile.

Meanwhile, ongoing renovation included "construction of a fourth floor on the building, erection of an elevator shaft and loading shed on the south side of the structure, installation of a complete new steel framework, replacement of some small windows and larges [sic] and a new main entrance and exit," reported the Marquette *MJ* on March 26, 1948. Once completed, the process for manufacturing undergarments would begin on the top floor while the assembly of the undergarments remained on the second and third floors. Postproduction work—boxing, inspection, and shipping—was confined to the first floor where offices were located.

Gossard pieceworker Cecilia Jafolla described her workplace on the third floor: big clean aisles and large industrial machines in between workers. She sat next to one of the many large windows, convenient when she took advantage of cooler outdoor temperatures to mitigate the factory's warmth from the constant whirring of industrial machines.

The white noise did not distract pieceworker Bertha "Bert" Boase. Instead, it was "a new floor lady who showed favoritism," when she gave "certain girls the good bundles," those with "higher coupon values than other bundles." Bert "loved working with the girls," but helping her family was essential, especially when her miner husband was laid off or when his construction work wages were less than Bert's. Decades later, the pieceworker mused, "I learned how to get along on a little bit and always put a little bit away."

The 1940s was a decade of progress and change in the H. W. Gossard factory's history. For hundreds of Gossard Girls who made up the bulk of Ishpeming's plant, the company's commitment to employees during the war enabled them to help provide for their families' daily needs. The Gossard's prosperity following the war brought a second U.P. plant and gave the women reason to seek greater workplace equity. The push for a union would bring about something the U.P. communities had not seen before—a strike that had women on the picket line fighting for their own jobs, not those of their miner husbands. Despite the impact of unionization efforts, the Gossard and the women who worked there continued to be a vital economic contributor to families and communities of the region.

....

MADELEINE DELBELLO, GOSSARD GIRL

Madeleine DelBello was born in 1918 in Montreal, Quebec. Her parents, Frank and Maria Barbiere, immigrated from Rippabottoni, Italy, to Canada. A sister in Ishpeming, Michigan, would lure Frank from Montreal to Ishpeming in 1920. The family's move coincided with the opening of Ishpeming's Gossard factory. Decades later, Madeleine mused, "When I was little, my brother was always carrying me. It was so cute. This lady always had come and see him on her way to work at the Gossard."

It was love that lured Madeleine away from completing her high school education. She described herself in 1935 as seventeen and "green as grass." However, the young bride enjoyed seventy years of marriage to a man eleven years her senior. Once married, the DelBello couple settled in Gwinn, Michigan, where Madeleine's husband found work in the mines and later with a railroad company.

In 1947, Madeleine joined the long list of Gwinn Gossard Girls, who collectively would contribute a "quarter million wages" to their families and their small communities. Madeleine could not have been more pleased. A job at the Gwinn plant in 1947 was "a big help" for her family and for many others in what used to be a rich mining area. "The mines are closed—whether permanently isn't known but at least indefinitely," a *Mining Journal* article reported on September 13, 1947. Madeleine's husband was fortunate he had a job with Lake Superior & Ishpeming Railroad, but it was "just seasonal work" for the summer. And in 1947, railroad workers "didn't get no compensation or nothing," Madeleine said. Most assuredly, being one of the first hires at the Gwinn Gossard plant meant the world to Madeleine.

Madeleine learned of a meeting regarding Gwinn's new business in 1947 through word of mouth. "The word was going around that they were going to have like a town meeting." When Madeleine and other community members packed the clubhouse, she heard Mr. Miller, caretaker of the Gwinn Clubhouse and a local basketball coach, extol the work ethic of Gwinn women. "He [Mr. Miller] told us all about it, that they wanted to send the Gossard here. He says, 'All the Gwinn women are very hard workers.'"

Madeleine was thrilled to learn the location of the undergarment plant: just three blocks from her house. She walked every day of her eighteen years at the factory, a significant savings in transportation costs, thereby increasing the value of her weekly wages. "I was there the first day," said Madeleine, and "I was assigned to the seaming department on the second floor, where ladies from the Ishpeming Gossard showed us the ropes."

Although Madeleine's first and only job was seaming, the work distribution process for all pieceworkers was similar. "They bring you your work. You had bags. They were something like a canvas bag, maybe a cloth bag. That's where the work was. On the end of it [the bag] where you opened it, there's a big tag. And we all had numbers. My number was 47. That's your work." Assigning numbers to employees served two functions: convenience and maintaining standards. When an undergarment "went to a different department, and there was a flaw or something wrong with it, it would come back to 47. That's what they went by. It was more convenient instead of putting a person's name. So that was it."

Madeleine was content to work on seaming for almost two decades. Starting with a daily minimum piece-rate of "sixty cents per hour," an amount she used to measure her basic wage, Madeleine came to understand the wisdom of working in the same department on the same machine. Time meant money, she learned. "That's the only way you can make money, by being on the same machine. You can go faster and faster." Sometimes though, being a fast seamer could be a problem. Madeleine laughed as she recalled one such incident when some pieceworkers in seaming accused the floor lady of favoritism. "We had a floor lady that would give us our bags, and I can remember there was one [bra]. You could make pretty good on that bra. I was making pretty good on it, but then everybody didn't get that bra. Well then there was a squabble, and everybody got them."

Perhaps a similar incident would have surfaced over the assembly of black bras. Madeleine knew the piece rate for these was higher than for white or pink bras because black bras "were harder on the eyes." Not a problem for Madeleine who wanted to make "just a little more" for the DelBello family. "Maybe some did not need the money, but we did. We tried not to have any bills. That is the way we was."

One might describe the relationship between pieceworker and her machine as intimate. Madeleine prized her machine, in part, because she understood the connection between a well-maintained machine and making money. She knew oiling her machine was the most important preventive measure. Each morning Madeleine did just that. In return, she expected her industrial machine to perform almost seven hours a day. The second most important preventive measure took place in the afternoon. That's when the shaft's motor (one motor powered multiple machines) was turned off. Machine operators took a short break (about fifteen minutes). Before leaving her machine "to have a coke or something to drink," Madeleine brushed the dust and lint from her machine. She respected her seaming machine. It performed well, so Gwinn's two mechanics, Peterson and Bray, were rarely summoned to her machine.

Helping her family financially was vital, certainly more important than making time in the workday for humor or fun. Decades later, Madeleine reflected, "Well, we didn't have time to have fun. You don't talk. You sew." She described her work while also pointing to a permanent dent on one of her hands. "Piecework, that's what you got paid for. Like if we put the two pieces together like for the cup, you know the top, the left in the front and the top of the bra. Well, that's what we would do. When you'd sew it all in one like that, and you'd take scissors when you are done and, as you can see, I still have dents where my scissors went. You just think every day you used the scissors. Every day you went there, you'd cut. I worked there for eighteen years. That dent doesn't hurt anything." Neither did her knee hurt after many years of operating the industrial machine's presser foot daily for up to seven hours.

LAILA POUTANEN, GOSSARD GIRL

As a retired entrepreneur, Laila Poutanen hadn't strayed far from her childhood roots in Palmer, Michigan, a small unincorporated community in south Marquette County rich in natural resources: minerals and water. Over the years, deposits of magnetite and hematite from the area's two mines, Empire and Tilden, have fed the world's appetite for iron ore.

Work in the mines drew Laila's American-born parents to Palmer, but in 1945, there were scant employment options locally for their teenage daughter. "The Gossard was the only option for girls in 1946," said Laila. On the day of her seventeenth birthday and armed with a working permit, she became a Gossard Girl. It was exciting for a teenager raised in a small community (less than five hundred people) to work in the bustling city of Ishpeming (eleven thousand). "It was a fun place to work at that time," because the undergarment factory "was centrally located." She lived three blocks from the factory, ate "very good free hot lunches" in the basement cafeteria, and spent the remainder of "the noon hour shopping downtown and bumming around the stores." Most of her beginning piece-rate wages in 1946 were spent on weekly groceries.

Laila not only enjoyed making her own money, but also excelled in seaming; "I went over what the expectation was, so I got more pay." The end of a workday signaled the end to a "loud, noisy environment," especially if one worked near the zigzag department, where vibrating sounds from these machines were more pronounced. Even so, the white noise from the machines did not deter Laila from having "lots of fun during work hours." Years later, she recalled making miniature bra knickknacks from leftover Gossard material. "We used to make replicas out of our scraps, you know, tiny little bras. And we'd give them to our boyfriends so they could hang them in their cars."

This workplace, Laila said, also functioned as a space to receive sex education. According to Laila, she and other young girls "learned a lot from the older women. When the young girls were about to get married, the older women gave us sex education and things like that." Laila appreciated "these really nice ladies," and she enjoyed the diverse makeup of her coworkers, like the woman with an English accent who sat next to her.

Like many of her peers, Laila stopped working at the factory when she started a family. And like many of her peers, she returned to the Gossard when the Poutanen family of five (three sons) needed the income. It was in the 1960s when CCI began closing their underground mines, and her miner husband Hank was one of many who lost his job. Laila found work at Gwinn's plant in seaming and binding. She would have preferred to work in Ishpeming; nonetheless, she was pleased to have a job in piecework. "I always made above my rate, so I took home a little bit more than others."

There were differences between working in Ishpeming and Gwinn. In 1960, the Poutanen family lived in Palmer, and Laila would need to carpool with four Gwinn workers. It was a long commute from Palmer, and even longer during a typical Upper Peninsula winter, often stretching six months. Even so, Laila was glad for the job.

There was a sizeable difference in the quality of some of Gwinn's industrial machines, the former pieceworker insisted, "Oh, there was a big difference. We had some junky machines the mechanics couldn't even fix. They were cast offs from Ishpeming's plant. I'm sure." A circumspect Laila observed, "So, it wasn't much fun sewing on something you had to keep having a mechanic the whole while there. But that's the way it was." Health issues, not the second-rate industrial machines, forced Laila to quit shortly before the small factory closed.

Meanwhile employment opportunities took the Poutanen family from their roots in Palmer's mining community to lower Michigan where Laila's husband, Hank, began a career in the corrections department. When Laila and Hank returned to Palmer years later, Laila transferred her sewing skills into a successful upholstery business in the basement of her home.

Looking back, Laila was grateful for the experience she received from both undergarment factories. "I was thankful I got good at sewing for my business. We did Hank's Upholstery for thirty years." It was so successful their customer base would extend beyond Palmer to K. I. Sawyer, an air force base near Gwinn, to Cleveland-Cliffs Incorporated, to Northern Michigan University's president, and to customers as far west as California.

Laila "never regretted going" to work for the undergarment factory because it helped her become a successful entrepreneur, and she was grateful to some older Gossard Girls. Five days a week, Laila worked alongside and ate lunch among workers who treated her like their daughter and taught her "a lot about life."

Lucy Tousignant, Gossard Girl

Sixteen-year-old Lucy Grasso lied about her age when she sought full-time employment in Ishpeming's plant because she wanted to help support her family. Lucy, the sixth of seven children, was five when her father died, leaving her mother, Italia, to support the family. In the beginning, Lucy's older brothers helped support the family.

Lucy, like her brothers, quit school early, although her reasons were different. Every high school student was required to take mathematics to graduate, but math was the one discipline in which Lucy struggled. "I couldn't get algebra." Two months into her freshman year during the late 1930s, the teenager quit. Decades later, Lucy reflected that there were few occasions in her life where she needed algebra. Certainly not during the twenty-six years she worked as a Gossard Girl. In her retirement, the mild-mannered Lucy said, "I am very bad at math even now."

The teenager didn't need algebra when her neighbor hired fourteen-year-old Lucy to help with household chores in 1938. "My mother saw our neighbor hanging clothes, and she was crippled with arthritis, so [my mother] told me to help her." Lucy earned $1 per week, which she gave to her mother Italia, "a hard worker and a very, very good cook."

In 1940, Lucy wanted a full-time job. Working at the Gossard factory sounded appealing, especially since she had experience sewing on a peddle machine. But in 1940, the minimum age for working at the Gossard was seventeen. Lucy was sixteen. "A friend of Lucy's mother" knew Gossard manager Claude Tripp, who approved her hire. The underage Lucy (employee #282) would operate one of the industrial sewing machines in seaming.

She earned thirty-five cents an hour, a significant wage increase from her previous job. On payday Fridays, "I would give my mother the check because she was a widow." Lucy lived at home for eight years, which meant her wages went a little further. In 1944 when the Gossard Company provided free midday meals, she extended her wages even more, and she walked from the family home on West Superior Street to the factory. Lucy never missed work in the eight years she lived at home, not even during Ishpeming's worst snowstorms.

Now retired, a modest Lucy chuckled when she described the quality of her work. "Was pretty good, I guess. They always hired me back. They must have thought I was okay." For this, Lucy credited her training under "one of the best instructors, Carmella Tasson, a very nice and very helpful woman. She showed people how to put the bra pieces together."

A good instructor was beneficial, but good seamers like Lucy learned the value of organization in assembly work. Decades later, Lucy revealed a strategy for earning above the minimum piece rate. "You had to have a box next to you so a floor lady could throw the work in for you to do. When you sewed, you just left everything on the string, and you left about three inches of thread in between. Then you sewed that far [Lucy demonstrated with her hands]. When you had to do another part of the bra, you just took it, sewed the other half, and opened that little thing. Then you had to cut the threads in between so you could sew the edges, the bottom part, and the top part." Lucy's method worked smoothly most of the time except when she accidentally sewed her fingers. It wasn't serious, and besides workplace accidents were handled differently years ago. "It isn't like today," Lucy observed.

Lucy worked hard at the Gossard factory, and she made time to socialize. Prior to getting married in 1949, three Gossard Girls—Lucy, Pat, and Rose—had their routine. After work and before heading home, the threesome often ate hot fudge sundaes at the ice cream shop. "Before we were old enough to go to taverns and dance, we returned to the ice cream shop after supper. When we were of age, we tried to go dancing every night." During the 1940s and 1950s Marquette County was home to a number of supper clubs. Lucy, Pat, and Rose usually frequented "the Venice Supper Club or the Casino Bar," which had dancing every night.

Some of Lucy's fondest memories were social gatherings in the factory, especially Christmas parties in the basement. There were other informal socials such as when pieceworkers on her shaft regularly shared homemade treats. "We brought stuff, goodies to eat even on our shaft." Lucy shared her homemade sweets, cakes and cookies, with coworkers from outlying towns such as Marquette, Champion, and Republic, women who helped make the factory "a very good place to work."

Lucy worked at the factory long after it was an economic necessity. After she married and raised children, she returned because she wanted additional income. "I didn't want to be on the take, and I never minded working." However, her husband Louis looked forward to his retirement at sixty. Lucy supported his plan in no small measure because Louis "was very good around the house," which she valued immensely. When he worked afternoon shifts, Lucy went home to delicious hot meals prepared by Louis. Even their children ate hot meals at noon. When Louis retired before his wife, "he did everything but ironing," and on occasion, Louis was known to host coffee and conversation with a few neighbors. In retrospect, Lucy's husband was ahead of his time. "Everybody told me how lucky I was," she said smiling. "Louis was very, very good."

Lucy hoped historians would learn about the influence and contributions of hundreds of women in Michigan's Upper Peninsula in the twentieth century. Many women, some like Lucy who struggled with math, exercised their economic power to advance opportunities for the next generation. The H. W. Gossard Company "was a very good place to work for many, many women. A lot of them said, 'I am working so I can put my kid through college.'"

CHAPTER 4

Considering Unionization

U NION ORGANIZING APPEARS TO have begun in October 1941 when the International Ladies Garment Workers Union (ILGWU) targeted three factories in Michigan's Upper Peninsula (U.P.). "Founded in 1900, the ILGWU was one of the first U.S. unions to have a membership consisting of mostly females, and it played a key role in the labor history of the 1920's and 1930's," according to ILGWU Organizational History Local 105 Records at Cornell's Kheel Center for Labor-Management Documentation and Archives.

Union-organizing in the U.P. was part of a national effort by the ILGWU to improve conditions for garment workers and to increase union membership at local, state, and national levels. Information about early organizing efforts in Marquette County can be found in correspondence between Midwest ILGWU organizers in Chicago, ILGWU organizers in Michigan, and garment workers in Marquette, Negaunee, and Ishpeming.

ILGWU organizer Winifred Boynton traveled to Marquette County in late 1941 to assess conditions at several garment factories: Upper Peninsula Dress Company in Marquette, the Satin Shop in Negaunee, and the H. W. Gossard plant in Ishpeming. During her first fact-finding trip to Ishpeming, Boynton posed as a prospective worker and as a "research worker for the A.F.L. [American Federation of Labor]."

The undercover Boynton spoke to five factory workers, including one former Gossard Girl, at the Senate Bar and learned "if any organizing were done it would have to be an outsider as [workers] would be fired if they put their neck out." Even so, Boynton was optimistic in a letter to Abe Plotkin, ILGWU's Midwest general organizer, and sensed support from "the very friendly" workers who would be valuable "when the time comes."

According to Boynton's October 1941 report, employment in Ishpeming's Gossard plant ranged from five hundred to six hundred workers. "Non-Productive workers [were] on straight salary. Production workers on piecework earned 40 cents per hour. New hires earned 35 cents per hour

51

during their [probationary] six-month period. Employees had a 40-hour workweek, eight hours a day, Monday through Friday, with no overtime. Experienced workers and married women were preferred," she stated.

Boynton sent the results of her undercover research project to Joseph Zukerman, Michigan state organizer, who questioned the veracity of her report. "I hardly believe that the [Gossard] plant employs the number of workers Winifred gives in her report, and hope the rest of the report is more accurate," Zukerman stated in a letter sent October 24, 1941, to Plotkin.

Two months after Boynton's report, the meaning of "when the time comes" became apparent in a letter Boynton sent December 1941 to Plotkin. Gossard factory workers in Logansport, Indiana, went on strike, "and an attempt by the company to ship unfinished corsets to the Gossard factory in Ishpeming, Michigan, was blocked by workers without violence," reported *The Daily Banner*, a Wisconsin newspaper, on December 2. News of this strike was not carried by newspapers in Ishpeming or Marquette, according to Boynton. In her December report to Plotkin, Boynton wrote, "Give my regards to the workers in the Gossard plant at Logansport and tell them that we will see that the girls here will be their sisters in the I.L.G.W."

Thus began efforts by the ILGWU to unionize Ishpeming's Gossard plant. Campaign efforts by ILGWU organizers would require healthy doses of patience, determination, and secrecy. The path to a unionized shop would take eight years and require combined efforts by many individuals, including Gossard Girl Ruth Craine and Geraldine Gordon Defant, an ILGWU organizer from Chicago.

Organizing the Wives of Miners

The exact date Gossard Girl Ruth Craine, who worked in the seaming department, signed a union card and agreed to work in the factory's first union campaign is unknown. What is known is that in 1941 ILGWU campaign officials secretly enlisted pieceworkers like her to provide information about the factory. These undercover Gossard workers had to be discreet and with good reason. Plant manager Claude Tripp was adamantly opposed to a union, ILGWU organizer William Davis reported in a December 1941 letter to Plotkin. Davis's meeting with Tripp was cordial, but the manager told Davis "in no uncertain terms that it would be a fight." In a previous letter dated December 11, 1941, Davis had informed Plotkin "the people of this city" were "not in any way Union-minded" due to "the beliefs" of the area's ethnic and religious composition: "Swedish, Finn, Catholic and Lutheran." The struggle for a union shop, Davis assessed, would be long and hard.

The ILGWU representatives quietly formulated a strategy to unionize up to 672 factory workers (552 Gossard workers and 120 workers at two other Marquette County dress factories). A three-page "Memo to A. Plotkin," from Davis sent December 11, 1941, identified concerns and offered strategies for what would be the first unionizing campaign for Ishpeming's workers. Davis reported, the "Gossard Co. [had] not allowed" news of the Logansport strike "to become public." Moreover, an undercover "local helper" who applied for work in Ishpeming's factory reported she "[had seen] between 500–1000 orders from the Logansport plant."

Based on his findings, Davis proposed several strategies. He recommended having ILGWU organizers Boynton and Ma Dunham target their contacts among specific religious groups. Sister (a term used to address female union members) Boynton would work with her Lutheran contacts, while Sister Dunham would work with her Catholic contacts. Davis would work his "connections with the War Veterans." The ILGWU organizer also wanted three local helpers, who'd work on the inside. "If these 3 people are successful in getting into the plant to work you can readily realize what it will mean to us," wrote Davis. Lastly, Davis informed Plotkin that local organizer Mr. Peter Martell "was placed on the payroll at $20.00 per week."

A publicity campaign targeting media—radio and newspaper—was critical to address "the fear in the minds of [workers]," Davis wrote in his December 11 memo to Plotkin. Costs for a radio format, which interspersed "question and answer programs . . . with 13 five-minute broadcasts would be $125," and local newspaper advertising rates "will be 60 cents per inch under contract for 500 inches or more with no time limit for the full-fillment of the contract." The coordinated efforts by ILGWU union organizers, local prounion helpers, and media advertising, Davis stated, would "help create favorable public sentiments" and perhaps lead to a swift and successful campaign.

Davis met with stakeholders at local, state, and national levels, including with Tripp. However, Davis's meetings with representatives from the Upper Peninsula Chamber Board, the National Labor Relations Board (NLRB), and the AFL-CIO were promising. Mr. Devoe, secretary of the U.P. Chamber Board, "was well pleased that we are in here to organize the plant. He is cooperating one hundred per cent." He viewed the ILGWU as an asset, which "can increase the earning power of the Gossard employees," while also benefiting local businesses. Mr. Pascor, a representative from the AFL-CIO for Upper Peninsula mines, saw an opportunity to help organize "the wives of miners," while Mr. Brophy of the NLRB pledged full cooperation toward an election at Ishpeming's plant.

In a postal telegraph sent December 22 to Davis, Plotkin outlined additional campaign strategies to inform Ishpeming's Gossard workers about the Logansport strike. Plotkin would send Davis five hundred copies of the ILGWU's most recent newsletter, *Justice*, articles from Logansport's newspaper, and "individual letters of strikers." Perhaps the multipronged media blitz might crack the wall of fear Davis, Boynton, and others sensed in the workplace. If their strategies worked and 30 percent of the factory's workers signed union cards, a NRLB election would be scheduled in the near future.

Tensions Run High

How effective was Davis's strategy for educating Gossard workers about Logansport's strike? How many radio shows did he host? What local veteran groups did Davis visit? What prounion contacts did Sisters Boynton and Dunham cultivate through their religious connections? How did Gossard management respond to ILGWU organizing efforts? Answers are elusive because there is no correspondence between Plotkin and his organizers between 1943 and 1944. Nonetheless, the first NLRB election on May 27, 1943, was "struck down by a vote of 251–159," according to reporter Erin Elliot in the *Marquette Monthly.*

Correspondence between Plotkin and ILGWU organizers resumed in 1944. The Midwest organizer expanded the scope of ILGWU's territory to include a fourth factory in Delta County, and he hired Marie Gernet and Ruby Dingman to replace Boynton and Dunham. With 550 workers, Ishpeming's Gossard factory was still the largest, while the combined total of factory workers in Escanaba, Marquette, and Negaunee numbered less than two hundred. Gernet's letters to Plotkin in January 1944 underscored her challenges with prounion factory workers who were focused more on their pay instead of organizing. She wrote, "I deliberately stayed away from the office. I simply couldn't meet the money demands made on me and they were all hounding me for it. Three Gossard observers were here several times. Gert Vial was peeved. Mrs. Craine stopped in twice a day until I was nearly frantic," reported Gernet in a letter sent January 30, 1944. Additionally, organizer Lucy Rivard from Marquette had accused ILGWU organizer Gernet of "running around the state with PAID ORGANIZERS and ignoring the Satin girls."

There is no mention of Craine in correspondences between ILGWU representatives until Gernet wrote in 1944 of Craine's good work and union spirit. "She is working hard, and in the last two weeks has brought me 21 cards. Narcissis Suardinni [*sic*], my little Italian friend has 15 and 20 signed in the office totaling 56 for Gossard," Gernet reported to Plotkin in January 1944. Shortly after, Plotkin received what may be the first of many letters from Craine. She wrote on February 9, 1944, about an unpleasant incident where Gossard management used fear tactics to curb her unionizing activities. "I had a dozen which wasn't perfect seaming and both he [Mr. Harold Peterson] and Mr. Clifford Perry [were] present. Something they never do." Initially, management threatened Craine with a two-week layoff, but she knew her rights and refused to be intimidated. Manager Peterson and Superintendent Perry withdrew their warning. Craine left "the unpleasant meeting" feeling confident, but also aware the Gossard manager understood she was "out after members, and he knows I get my share of them." Craine was less concerned about the identity "of the leak" and more interested in a successful campaign, sooner not later. "We must act now as fast as possible to build up our membership," Craine reported to Plotkin.

The Gossard pieceworker and organizer pledged to increase union membership. "I am getting many new cards and I will pledge at least 75 [union] cards on this campaign. If Dorothy and Lester [Gossard workers] will do that with what the office gets we should have 300 members." Given the size of Ishpeming's plant (552 workers at the time) three hundred members would be a good target for a vote to unionize the plant. Securing seventy-five cards would not be easy because management was antiunion, and organizing activities were not permitted in the undergarment factory.

Gernet's challenges with prounion factory workers in two factories—Marquette's Upper Peninsula Dress Company and Ishpeming's H. W. Gossard factory—would persist. In a letter sent February 22, 1944, to Plotkin, a frustrated Gernet reported pieceworkers from Marquette's dress factory were unhappy with pay, frustrated with new pricing on shaded bundles (the rate of pay for sewing dark-colored garments tended to be higher because it was harder to see one's stitching), and irritated with the ILGWU, which appeared to be backpedaling on an agreement to subsidize a portion of workers' union dues while "[workers] waited for their back-pay [to come] through" from the War Labor Board (a reference to Gossard's petition for back wages from January 25 to June 25, 1943, according to Craine's February 9 letter). At Ishpeming's Gossard factory, Gernet wrote, it was piecework organizers' lack of trust and respect in her, Plotkin's newest appointee. Organizers appeared to have "lost all interest" in the Gossard campaign. In her letter sent February 22, Gernet accused three individuals (two were Gossard workers) of trying to "get rid of" her. It was a rumor she had heard regarding two previously ousted organizers. Frustrated, she directed Plotkin to "tell Dorothy off once and for all. This would certainly put an end to her dirty tricks." Gernet then informed the general organizer of her plan to bring Gossard worker and union organizer Narcissus Suardini to Chicago, the *one* person who'd "tell the truth" and who was "well respected by ALL the Italians."

Plotkin responded quickly and forcefully. "Please do not bring anyone to Chicago until I authorize." The general organizer was also "disappointed" Gernet had ignored his directive. "Instead of attending to your work in Escanaba, you seem to be paying more attention to the one thing I wanted you to leave alone for the present and that was the Ishpeming situation. That could work itself out in time if you would leave it alone," he said in a letter sent February 23, 1944.

Gernet's challenges in Ishpeming persisted. A letter sent in March 1944 to Plotkin reported that a disgruntled male Gossard worker questioned her authority. Not only did he refuse to sign an affidavit, but he also accused Gernet of lying about the number of Gossard workers who had signed affidavits (cards) to call for an election. She pushed back, reminding the Gossard worker that it was Plotkin, not Gernet, who had first provided the number (285) of signed cards. He countered, accusing Gernet of being "just like the rest" of them: untrustworthy. Furthermore, Gernet wrote he had refused to "take orders from a woman." A puzzled Gernet was also frustrated with Plotkin because this wasn't the first time he had "put her on the spot."

Two letters written by Craine to the general organizer suggest the tensions between Gernet and Gossard union organizers were serious enough that she considered pulling back from union-organizing activities. Frustrated by the pettiness among some of the union organizers, Craine began her undated letter (possibly written in February), "I really didn't like much of our conversation today." Though she did not reveal many details of their conversation, she was adamant about her support of the union and her hard work.

Craine's frustration over excessive jealousy between some Gossard union organizers had reached a critical point. In one incident (an undated letter), she tried to avoid the appearance of secrecy when she turned in signed union cards to ILGWU organizer Gernet. "I went to her desk and said loud enough [so] anyone could hear me, 'I have cards for you, some good ones' [that] previous organizers never could get. Even Marie herself was pleased when she saw them," wrote Craine. The second incident she described occurred at a union-sponsored dinner at "a Royal Neighbor Lodge supper for 100 members [that included] many anti-union Gossard women." Two Gossard workers in attendance observed Craine standing next to Gernet and assumed Craine was "whispering secrets to Marie." She wasn't. She had turned in "two cards that night," signed her pay voucher, and left. Later, Craine would learn these two Gossard Girls "raised hell with Marie after [she] left." Though Craine felt powerless to dispel these and other misperceptions, she did not waiver in her commitment, asserting "I know my whole heart back[s] the union."

Her feelings hurt, Craine defended her actions in the undated letter. "I think each person has a right to hand their cards in and be proud of a person's card that was hard to get without any foolishness." She then offered to stop working on the campaign. "Even though my inactivity will cause comment, many will never sign a card, people who would be a credit to the Union," she wrote to Plotkin. The forty-seven-year-old wanted no recognition if the campaign succeeded, only a check for the work she had done and to retain her pieceworker position in seaming.

In Craine's second letter (March 7), she defended her request to Plotkin for three weeks of missing back pay during January and her commitment to the present campaign. "I will cooperate and respect your campaign, and if things are run fairly and honestly, I will do my share of work." And she hoped for "a little team work" among organizers because with "one horse pulling one way and another the other way, you won't travel very fast."

Possibly Craine's candor and passion resonated with Plotkin, as the Midwest general organizer responded to her handwritten six-page letter quickly. He began his letter sent March 10, 1944, "Dear Sister Craine, I read your letter very carefully," and in doing so, acknowledged a conundrum. "It is hard to draw the line between the rights of an individual and where the rights of a Union organizer stop." Plotkin also informed Craine that Ruby Dingman would replace Gernet as head organizer in Marquette County. The change was necessary, in part, because Gernet felt "someone was after her job," and because Dingman understood "the mechanism of piece prices," Plotkin wrote. Moreover, the personnel change would bode well for "smoother sailing for the campaign." While no documentation of the vote count from the second failed campaign was found, reporter Elliot from the *Marquette Monthly* stated "employees voted again in 1944 . . . to remain independent."

Perhaps buoyed by Plotkin's optimism, Craine continued working as an organizer though the struggle for a successful campaign would take four more years. To be sure, workplace issues such as pay, favoritism, and seniority would not go away. Neither would Craine. Along the way, she would broaden her understanding of the ILGWU, organizing, and office politics.

Although Dingman concentrated on two unionized factories in Marquette and Negaunee, the recently hired organizer kept a watchful eye on the Gossard factory in Ishpeming. In her letter sent in April 1944, she informed Plotkin about the Gossard's new basement cafeteria. "Gossard's have [*sic*] opened a lunch room and are feeding the help at noon free. This has done a lot to hinder the girls from getting cards. They will have to lay low," Dingman wrote.

"The new lunchroom is a drawing card," Craine, too, wrote in a letter to Plotkin. She felt free meals would hinder union campaign efforts. Free meals might demonstrate management's concern for workers' well-being, and workers might view the free meals as a way to increase their earnings. Both viewpoints, Craine felt, might stall ILGWU's campaign.

Dingman's letters to Plotkin over the next five months suggest she was focused on issues such as pay, timings, fairness, and a potential strike in Marquette and Negaunee's small dress factories. An adversarial relationship between the manager of Marquette's Upper Peninsula Dress Company and the ILGWU was so strained its manager threatened to close the dress factory and open a small business where he controlled the hiring, not a union.

Not until fall 1944 would Dingman's letters include a report on issues in the Gossard factory. "Things were popping," reported Dingman and Craine in a joint letter to Plotkin sent October 2, 1944. "He is starting to pick on the Italians." The unnamed man would position himself at the plant's front door by 7:00 a.m., "to see who [came] late, [and he also walked] around the shop inspecting the work, something no other manager has ever done," said the two organizers. The increasingly hostile work environment would help Craine motivate seventy-five Gossard Girls to sign union cards.

With Plotkin's approval, the ILGWU sponsored a dinner party and dance in early November 1944 for local ILGWU membership. More than one hundred union members attended, including a chartered busload of sixty female union workers from Ishpeming's Gossard factory and workers from Negaunee's Satin Shop. Two weeks later, Dingman sent Plotkin an updated union membership list from the Gossard plant, which had grown to 161 members. While Dingman was busy with issues in Marquette's dress factory, prounion Gossard workers Craine and Suardini wrote to Plotkin about a Christmas celebration sponsored by Gossard management "for the first time in 10 years." Christmas festivities commenced at 2:00 p.m. in the basement where workers listened to an orchestra and two choirs, ate a turkey dinner with all the trimmings, exchanged gifts, and received bonuses ($3 to $25) "for all the girls."

The new year (1945) ushered in union-organizing challenges from Gossard workers previously employed at Negaunee's Satin Shop, said Dingman and Craine, who sent separate letters in March to Plotkin. Craine wrote, "The Satin girls [were] sure causing a lot of trouble in talking up here. There is one on every shaft who is anti-union." Dingman reported in her letter sent March 27, 1945, "Everywhere [Narcissus] went they [Gossard Girls] made reference to the U. P. shops and would not sign a card." These were serious concerns for Dingman, who was also dealing with a duplicitous manager in Marquette's dress factory, workers' grievances, and days of lost work in the "single needle departments."

Forbidden to campaign in the workplace, Gossard union organizers made home visits during April and May 1945. Such visits meant union organizers could speak freely in the privacy of workers' homes, free from the eyes and ears of management and other Gossard workers. But organizers Dingman and Craine often left frustrated. Whether through media (radio and newspaper) or local gossip, many Gossard workers had heard stories from Negaunee's unionized factories. Workplace grievances—favoritism, harassment, and pay at Marquette's unionized dress factory—motivated workers to picket. Sensing the inability of ILGWU organizers to help its union membership in Negaunee and Marquette, Gossard workers refused to sign union organizing affidavits/cards.

Meanwhile, "something [was] exploding at Gossard's," Dingman wrote in a letter sent May 26, 1945. A rumor had surfaced about short work hours for "some of the girls" and a heated argument between the "production manager and the superintendent," she reported. Three days later, Craine fired off a letter to Plotkin as the manager at Marquette's Upper Peninsula Dress Company announced the dress factory (a union shop) was "being dissolved." The announcement triggered more talk and more confusion among Gossard workers, who peppered Craine and Dingman with questions as to why "the union can't make the manager of Marquette's Dress Factory behave." Meanwhile, Craine was optimistic "for organizing at the Gossard not [because of] the lack of work, but poor prices and favoritism, [which] is causing a great deal of dissatisfaction."

Amid doubts, questions, and fears as to the strength of ILGWU, summer brought forth "pleasant news." In a letter to 215 Gossard union members on June 26, 1945, Dingman wrote, "We want you to know that while your shop is not under contract; nevertheless, it is getting the conditions that come from having a Union within our shop." ILGWU's petition to the War Labor Board to increase wages for *all* Gossard workers was expected within a few days. There would be "an increase of five cents per hour for all piece workers, and from three to seven and one-half cents per hour for time workers," Dingman stated in her letter. Surely good news for workers.

For August and September of that year Dingman did not mention the War Labor Board's ruling in letters to ILGWU leaders Plotkin or Morris Bialis. Regardless, Dingman was busy with union grievance issues at factories in Marquette, Negaunee, and Escanaba.

Dingman and Craine attended Local 293 dinner at Marquette's Hotel Clifton on August 16. In her August 10 letter to Plotkin, Craine wrote, "Our invitations to the dinner at Marquette is going to help bring out some of our young girls. Also will help me get more cards, I know." Six days later, Dingman expressed regret that Plotkin and Bialis were unable to attend Local 293's dinner but she was pleased fifty members from "the Gossard shop" would go. Both organizers in their individual letters urged Plotkin to visit Ishpeming. Craine, however, wanted to speak privately to him. "I am the only one who is in contact with all the girls and know the general opinion of all the girls."

Craine sent a letter on August 17, 1945, to report on a number of issues: "piece work price raise," workers' back pay, campaign progress, and job security. Of special note, for the first time, Craine's letter began with the salutation "Dear Brother Plotkin." She stated Gossard workers had not received a price raise, despite an unverifiable story of a check girl who received "a slip stating what her raise was to be." Craine questioned the story because such notifications would have been through "a notice on the bulletin board." Next, she asked Plotkin whether workers in Logansport, Indiana, had received back pay when their "plant closed last Friday" in observance of the death of "the Pres. of the Gossard." Ishpeming's workers had not. While issues of back pay were important, so too was job security. With the end of World War II, "the new girls" were worried about their factory jobs when "the girls return from the cities."

Craine pressed Plotkin again in a letter sent a month later. While she discussed some of the challenges and successes of the 1945 campaign in this and other fall letters to him, she framed her position more pointedly. "Right now we need letters mailed to every girl in the plant and actions in the form of mail as well as my collecting cards. I know the girls who are with me feel as I do. 'Plotkin or no one.'" It wasn't just because Plotkin oversaw the Midwest region. It was his strong character, she argued, that resonated with the union Gossard Girls. "You are sincere and a square and fair person. That and that alone is what we want." Furthermore, a plain-spoken Craine hoped the general organizer's remarks would be couched in "facts and sincerity" not "soft soap approaches" should he come to Ishpeming. For her part, she "promised to bring a group of girls."

Craine's sense of urgency was due in part to what she saw as deteriorating conditions in the factory. Management, she informed Plotkin, "was raising hell" with the union girls and discouraging "the new girls from signing cards." Even Craine, who was very good in getting cards signed, had a difficult time recruiting. "Ruby and I went to several homes tonight with no results." And she blamed some of the plant's cutters who "had gained so much from the union" yet had done nothing to support the women workers.

In his brief letter to Dingman sent August 22, 1945, Plotkin outlined his next steps. "Within the next thirty days or so I shall start moving in the direction either of obtaining a contract or forcing an election in Ishpeming." Plotkin directed Dingman "to start calling at the homes" of Gossard workers and "to enroll as many as you can." Presumably, Plotkin's directive was also intended for others on the union organizing committee. Those who followed Plotkin's directive may have met with resistance in getting cards.

When Dingman sent her report on August 30, Plotkin would learn about the challenges in getting signed cards. "Things [had] been rather slow lately. Everyone [was] talking about the raise," she reported, although her letter offered no further details about this raise. What she and Craine knew was that Gossard pieceworkers were confused by piece rate changes, scare tactics targeting new workers, and lost wages.

Craine predicted in her September 12 letter positive results in the campaign *if* Plotkin were "to straighten out a grievance" from two seamers who were unfairly discharged. "Every seamer was 100% union," and they were monitoring the situation closely, reported Craine.

A few days later, a frustrated, angry, and confused Craine fired off a four-page letter to Plotkin. The progress of the campaign seemed to come to a crashing halt she wrote. A confusing new pricing had irritated seamers, and "no one was satisfied." Machine operators peppered the Gossard organizer with questions for which she had no answers. "Why weren't we getting an election, why don't Plotkin come so we can have a meeting and do something, and why can't we all get together and demand what Logansport got?"

Complaints about a hostile work environment had surfaced again, Craine stated in her September 17 letter. Manager Peterson fired a seamer for "poor work on *one* bundle," she reported. Coincidentally, the pieceworker was fired after she questioned the new pricing, which reduced seamers' piece rate from $7 to $5. Peterson defended the new pricing saying, "$5 is enough for any girl to make. When they make over that, they do sloppy work," Craine reported in her letter. The unsympathetic plant manager also reminded the complainant, who had quit once before, that the company had rehired her because she was "a good seamer." Peterson would not have rehired her, Craine stated, had he known she'd "be joining that organization." In a separate incident, she informed Plotkin, the plant manager refused a Gossard mom's request to spend a few days with her son who was home after three years serving in World War II. Peterson had reportedly said, "The war is over, so is the fun."

These and other workplace issues weighed heavily on the mind of the union representative in the fall of 1945. "It's hard to keep up this way with 500 girls," Craine said in a letter. Vowing not to panic, she was "dam angry . . . the way things went sometimes" and pledged to continue updating Plotkin with facts. "Only one seaming bundle changed to a one-cent raise. One new bundle which was underpriced was raised 8 cents." Seamers were frustrated. These and other issues fueled Craine, who worked secretly amassing "179 signed union cards and still going strong."

Three days later (September 20, 1945), Craine reported more perplexing facts. Pieceworkers "received a one-cent raise" earning forty-nine cents instead of forty-eight cents an hour. Craine said, "We can't understand the back pay. Seamers all rec'd $15–$16. Zig zag dept. was paid funny. One girl rec'd $52, one $51 and one nothing. Narrow binding checks were as high as $25 and $30. Girls who worked less than a year didn't get a thing." Craine again suggested the Midwest organizer visit Ishpeming, but for an evening meeting rather than in the afternoon since "after work so many can't come." Collectively, these and other factors had created a "good fighting spirit" in the workplace, which would bode well if only "the election were tomorrow."

Plotkin did travel to Ishpeming in fall 1945, according to Craine's letter to Plotkin. Only a small number of prounion Gossard Girls attended. "I felt sorry to think you came for a meeting with such a small group," she stated in her October 3, 1945, letter. Even so, Craine's spirit was lifted by Plotkin's skills "to put the union spirit into the girls." She "reached her goal of 26 cards in two weeks."

Betty Fosco, one of thirteen siblings, followed two sisters to the factory in the 1940s. Like her older sisters, Betty became a pieceworker for many years. Decades later, she reflected on the day Ruth Craine, "the head one," visited her (presumably in her parents' house). "I don't really know. It was just the idea they wanted you to join the union, and then, I had a sister who belonged to the Gossard, and she was there many years. So, I just didn't join until I really had to join. I had nothing against it [the union]. I didn't know what it was all about. I had just started the Gossard. And so, they wanted everybody to join."

Plotkin was anxious to bring ILGWU's third campaign in 1945 to a swift and successful conclusion. Securing more signed cards was critical, but so were other media tools, such as radio and the newspaper. Craine and a few unnamed Gossard Girls received union training in Madison. After attending union school, Craine felt more empowered. "Your radio talk and the knowledge I received at school certainly came in handy Monday evening." In her October 3 letter, she discussed her toughest assignment at "a home that was so against the union." Determined yet patient, she spent ninety minutes educating a family about the ILGWU. It was hard work, and the union organizer left with a "nice headache . . . but knowing the family was no longer against the ILGWU."

In a postal telegraph sent October 19 to Craine, Plotkin directed her to have Dingman publicize about union activities at two Gossard plants in Indiana. "Both Logansport and Huntington are now drawing up their demands for the coming year. We invite you to join them and to help map out a unified program for all of the Gossard plants," wrote Plotkin.

Within a short time, Dingman reported in a letter to Plotkin sent November 9, 1945, "the girls in the Gossard shop [were] becoming very bold." She "gave all [her] Union buttons" to workers who "wore them in the shop [when] some big shots [visited] from Chicago." Dingman also requested a new supply of union buttons and membership cards since "more girls [had] asked for buttons."

A week later (November 16, 1945) Dingman reported on her meeting with Mr. Clarence Meter of the NLRB, who informed her that Manager Peterson would agree to an election, but only after January 1. Meanwhile, workers were frustrated because Peterson was hiring only antiunion workers. Dingman wrote, "He is putting new workers in the shop and also some of the old ones who have been definitely anti. In fact, when an application is made, the worker is asked if she is in favor of Unions." Peterson's strategy had already contributed to a declining morale "among many workers" who were now "thinking of quitting and [were] only waiting for the election," reported Dingman. A further delay would allow the manager to continue hiring antiunion workers.

A third attempt to unionize was tried in 1945, according to reporter Elliot of the *Marquette Monthly*, who noted the year but not the vote count. "Employees voted again in 1945 to remain independent."

A Final Attempt

How Plotkin responded to the third failed election is unknown. A search in Cornell's labor archives for his efforts to unionize Ishpeming's factory yielded no letters during 1946–47. The next correspondence was Craine's letter dated February 23, 1948, in which she informed Plotkin that Gossard management had laid off ten prounion workers, including one worker with seventeen years of experience. In describing the unpleasant work environment, Craine reported, "two stooges . . . [were] going around to each girl and examining her work," while Manager Peterson "picked up their work," intimidation tactics that sent workers to "a boiling point," reported Craine. Despite being sick, Craine worked diligently in two weeks, amassing "over 300 applications," well above the minimum of 250 cards. When Plotkin read her letter, he sent a letter dated March 4, 1948, to ILGWU vice president Morris Bialis. "I still fell [*sic*] that [first name unknown] Bovshow ought to be assigned to cover this territory. He has had more than eight months in which to break in the new locals and should have enough time to cover this vitally important area."

Bovshow would not be selected, and Dingman would not retain her head organizer's position in the U.P. Plotkin tapped an ILGWU employee who, until now, knew little of the Michigan's Upper Peninsula. Her name was Geraldine Gordon.

Geraldine, the youngest in her family of six, had grown up in Chicago during the Great Depression where "it was impossible not to be aware our society was crumbling," she recalled decades later during her 1990 interview by Jennifer Grondin. Geraldine's interest in and advocacy for improving workers' conditions were nurtured by her mother, who "had a political background," when the Lithuanian native immigrated to America from England. While in England, Geraldine's mother was a "child worker in a cap-making factory," working "seven days a week and ten hours a day," said Geraldine. After immigrating to America from England, her mother again worked in a cap-making factory where she helped organize a union.

Geraldine's family settled in Chicago, and she recalled a childhood where political ideas were regularly discussed in the family home. In addition to family discussions, there were newspapers and relevant political books "around the house," which helped shaped the future union organizer and advocate of social justice.

As a high school student, she witnessed images "of a crumbling society" traveling each Saturday to a job in a Chicago suburb where she earned one dollar (minus twenty-five cents for two car fares) for twelve hours of work. En route, Geraldine observed people in breadlines, people selling apples, and families who had been evicted from their homes sitting on the street, pervasive signs of a disintegrating society, which no one could avoid seeing.

In addition to these ubiquitous Great Depression images, the high schooler participated in a strike supporting public school teachers during the early 1930s. At issue were teachers' salaries. Chicago's Board of Education "was out of money" so public school teachers received scrip (a form of credit) in place of cash. After graduating from high school in 1933, she attended college at night while working days at the Chicago Relief Administration (CRA). The clerical worker took "case histories describing how people were living" and became "completely immersed in the symptoms of a crumbling economy." And Geraldine became more active in union organizing.

She helped organize "the union at the CRA." Next, she helped Chicago's taxicab drivers organize. In the mid-1930s, Geraldine was volunteering at a labor law firm, where her brother worked. One day "a group of about a hundred cab drivers came into the lawyer's office asking for help, 'We're on strike. We need help to organize a union.'" Geraldine took time off from her clerking job at the CRA and worked nights at her brother's law firm, answering phones and helping those who'd been arrested. "If a driver was picked up, a report was made and what station he had been taken. I instituted a bond securing procedure to get them out of jail," Geraldine recalled. Once police became aware of this, they moved strikers "from precinct to precinct" to delay their release. Countermeasures were implemented. "We had people watching each precinct as much as we could, so we could start to get them out. Very exciting times," she said.

Geraldine returned to her former job at the CRA until she traveled with her parents to visit relatives in California. She returned to Chicago, got married, and worked at various jobs while attending night school.

Tangentially, Geraldine would gain more union organizing experience. When calls went out for support of picketers, Geraldine showed up on picket lines. None of the jobs she held during this period interested the socially conscious woman until she "heard about a job opening with the garment workers union." It was an appealing idea, so Geraldine applied at the Midwest office of the ILGWU in Chicago. Her union job consisted of organizing "runaway shops or the shops that had never been organized."

Perhaps her ILGWU superiors from the Chicago office recognized Geraldine's strong organizing skills because within three years, Geraldine was promoted to business agent. In her new position during the 1940s, she oversaw "a group of local unions and trained workers in collective bargaining and in grievance procedure techniques." Public speaking was an important element of her work as business agent. Whenever Geraldine attended union meetings, she "would speak before meetings" informing workers about national events, economic news, and political news. The meetings were avenues to build workers' trust and respect for unions. While public speaking was important, so too was her work addressing workers' grievances and contract negotiations. It was one thing to talk about the whys of unions, but it was another thing to act upon one's ideas on behalf of workers, whether it was resolving workers grievances or collective bargaining in union contracts.

During one of Geraldine's meetings in the early 1940s at ILGWU's Chicago headquarters, she informed ILGWU officials about an open shop in Ishpeming, Michigan. Geraldine had learned about the open shop because she had been servicing two undergarment plants in Indiana; one was a Gossard plant in Logansport, similar in size to Ishpeming's plant, which had been in operation for twenty-one years. Perhaps it was Geraldine's intel that sent ILGWU representatives, including Winnifred Boynton, in late 1941 to organize Upper Peninsula garment factories, including the H. W. Gossard factory in Ishpeming. Neither Geraldine nor the ILGWU representatives had been in the U.P. Until 1948, the furthest north Geraldine's union work had taken her was New London, Wisconsin, a city she described as on "the edge of the country."

Unionizing efforts at the Ishpeming factory began in 1941, but it wasn't until 1948 when Geraldine was attending an ILGWU meeting in Chicago that she would be asked "to take a crack" at organizing the Upper Peninsula plant, where she also learned of "three or four efforts to organize and none of them successful." This was also a time when the Gossard Company had recently moved from a money system to a point system for piece-rate work. The new system meant "bundles were priced in minutes or points rather than pennies," said the ILGWU business agent at Gossard's Logansport and Huntington union shops. "In the union shop, this created a burden and a whole procedure of grievances and time studies, both by the company and by the union, of . . . how many minutes it actually took to do this operation, and then negotiating, bargaining with the plant manager on the final payment." This was a tedious and confusing process, according to Geraldine. "We knew then that if they were doing this in the union shop, [that] all hell must be breaking loose in the Northern shop which was [why] it was timely to attempt to organize them."

Though the exact month and day are unknown, Geraldine and two additional unnamed ILGWU organizers headed to the U.P. in 1948 and "organize[d] by going home to home and attempt[ed] to get people who were friendly, if possible to get a few workers from that department together and to visit them and to talk about the advantage of working in the union shop . . . and get union cards signed," said Geraldine.

A self-described timid Pauline Toivonen enumerated how a "very shy" pieceworker would support the idea of a union. "When I graduated from Ishpeming High School in 1946, I didn't want to go to college because I was shy. Marriage was not an option. Grams taught me a lot of things on sewing. I filled out an application at the only place where all the women worked." In three years, "I got to know some of the girls sitting around me little by little, but I also held back just a little bit." A year later and with mining layoffs affecting her husband and stepfather, twenty-year-old Pauline joined frontline picketers who "were out there in force, just being a little bit noisy, trying to state their opinion, and singing songs." These were complicated and stressful times for the shy newlywed.

After nearly eight years, three failed elections, and under Geraldine's leadership, a majority of Gossard workers voted in favor of a union "by nearly two to one," according to Geraldine. In his undated *Report on Michigan and Indiana*, Plotkin stated, "Certification election won on November 12, 1948." Election won by nearly two to one. Now in process of negotiating. 600 workers employed." Negotiations commenced in Chicago; meanwhile, Gwinn Gossard workers voted against union representation in their plant in December 1948.

Decades after the strike, Gossard Girl Ruth Webb Fagerberg said, "I wasn't old enough to realize what a union was." Workers refrained from union discussions at work, and the teenage worker did not attend union meetings outside of the factory. She "just did her work and listened." Moreover, whatever Ruth would hear did little to change her thinking that Gwinn workers "were doing fine." While Ruth and others in Gwinn's factory did not want their factory unionized, "there was a group of women there who wanted it, desperately wanted it to be unionized," said Ruth.

Geraldine set in motion her next steps: assembling a committee and hiring an attorney. "At that time, I looked around the community for an attorney. There were some technicalities, and standard procedure was to have an attorney represent us," Geraldine recalled. She hired Michael Defant, recognized by local unionized steel workers as "the union lawyer in the communities of Negaunee and Ishpeming." (In the early 1950s, she married Defant after divorcing her first husband.) Ninety percent of negotiations were conducted in Chicago, home to corporate offices of ILGWU and the Gossard Company.

Contract negotiations between the Gossard Company and ILGWU carried over into 1949. The issues, according to Geraldine, were whether the Ishpeming shop would be a union shop and adopt a contract similar to those at undergarment plants in Indiana. Manager Peterson was "vehemently anti-union" as well as "a small, very local anti-union group in the shop," she said. Gossard Company management in Chicago was equally adamant, even though Logansport and Huntington were union shops.

From the outset, company officials viewed Ishpeming's plant differently from its unionized factories. Essentially, the Gossard Company considered Ishpeming's factory "an experimental plant to try things [the Gossard] couldn't do easily in a union plant, to try out new methodology, to try out lower rates," an older Geraldine recalled. When union plants made the similar garment, company management used "rates in the non-union plant as an example and the production levels as a bargaining point."

On this issue, the ILGWU was adamantly opposed. Nonunionized plants might jeopardize the union's relationship with the Gossard Company. Nonunion workers would receive the same benefits as union workers, yet nonunion workers "would be playing a company role rather than cooperating with their fellow workers," Geraldine recalled decades later, a situation she characterized as "unfair . . . unsound . . . and a sore point that would never go away." Ultimately, it was a situation that would undercut the credibility of the ILGWU. Each side remained locked in their respective positions for five months, until union workers voted to strike. It would take another four months, but Geraldine's dogged commitment to social justice for all workers would prevail.

Months of failed arbitration and threats of a strike failed. So Geraldine asked workers to authorize a strike, not an easy decision for the ILGWU or for workers. Supporting strikers at one of the company's largest plants (550 workers) would be very, very expensive. Geraldine knew feeding strikers and their families, providing emergency funds, educating strikers, and providing educational classes was costly. And a significant number of Gossard Girls were sole providers in their families. The undergarment factory was recognized as the best paying job for women in Marquette County. These and other issues weighed heavily on the Chicago native and social activist. Gossard workers may not have known Geraldine's early years advocating fair wages for workers, but in 1949, they would watch a strong, confident woman fight tirelessly for social justice in *their* workplace.

Gossard Strike

Before the sun rose on Tuesday, April 12, 1949, the H. W. Gossard factory was bustling with activity. Marquette's *Mining Journal* (*MJ*) reported a crowd "of 200 women, some carrying signs," had been at the Gossard plant since 5:15 a.m. Under the watchful eyes of head union organizers, Geraldine Gordon and Gossard Girl Ruth Craine, picketers positioned themselves around the factory to prevent "anyone from entering the plant." Picketers maintained a peaceful presence despite attempts by nonunion Gossard employees to enter the building. Gordon said in her interview with Grondin that nonunion workers entered the factory. They took "some of the cut work to other plants either to Gwinn to be completed, or to subcontract it to other corset manufactures in the Middle West who would then finish the product so . . . the company could continue to fill its orders, or at the minimum complete the orders that were already in process." Meanwhile Ishpeming's city police and Marquette County's sheriff's department stood by "to see that order was maintained," reported the *MJ*. The orderly first day soon shifted to a week of rising tensions between nonunion workers and picketers.

Passionate pro- and antiunion sentiment gave way to "pushing and name calling," an activity Gordon considered "nonviolent . . . tussles." Despite picketers' best efforts, several management employees entered the factory. For example, Gossard Girl Elaine Peterson witnessed her boss, Ida Santamore, drop bundles from the second-story fire escape while Manager Peterson snuck cut work into the trunk of his car.

Because of this, a plan was devised to help picketers monitor and hopefully stop management from taking assembly work from Ishpeming's factory to Gwinn's. According to Gossard Girl Rose Collick, who lived across from Ishpeming's factory, picketers asked to use her porch and garage for this purpose. Rose, who had left her pieceworker's position to raise two young children, "liked the idea of a union," and in the ensuing weeks, to demonstrate their appreciation, picketers pooled their resources and "purchased a buggy" for Rose's baby.

A week later (April 19) the *MJ* front-page headlines announced, "Picket Lines Set Up around Gwinn Factory." Gossard Company officials estimated a crowd of "150–200 ILGWU members" had set up picket lines at the Gwinn plant before 6:30 a.m. Gwinn pieceworker Ruth Fagerberg saw pickets when she entered the factory. Once inside, management discouraged workers from observing the pickets, but management could not muffle their chants, she said.

"Eight supervisors from Ishpeming plant" entered Gwinn's factory "with the help of Sheriff Jacobson, one of his deputies and plant superintendent Kenneth Strengberg." Manager Peterson reported picketers had threatened the eight, shouting they "will never get home tonight." It was a tense morning as he felt the union had no right to picket the nonunion plant, while Gordon countered saying pickets would not interfere with Gwinn's workers.

Car Injures Picketers

Tensions spilled over the following morning, and Marquette's newspaper reported on an accident outside Gwinn's factory. Up to nine Gossard pick- eters had been injured by a car, the *MJ* reported. Wednesday morning, April 20, when Gordon and picketers arrived at the nonunion plant, they found the plant already encircled "with hundreds of . . . local Gwinn people." Also present were six to seven members of Gwinn's sheriff's department. The presence of Gwinn businessmen and others, Gordon felt, was meant to intimidate and frighten away picketers. Decades after the incident, she reflected on underlying tensions, which she felt had contributed to the car accident early Wednesday morning. "The Gwinn community looked at that plant as the only place for women to work . . . and they felt the picket line coming down from Ishpeming was threatening . . . the one industrial plant in the community."

Picketers encircled the plant before the start of Gwinn's workday. They sang union songs, a common activity, "to bolster their courage and give them[selves] a feeling of camaraderie," Gordon said. Gwinn's 140 employees would enter their plant that cold Wednesday morning without any interference before 7:00 a.m. Forty-five minutes later, reported the *MJ*, "the women [picketers] were standing on the edge of the road (Maple Street) in front of the Gossard factory when [they were] hit." Both local papers—the *Mining Journal* and the *Iron Ore*—reported on April 23 that three women sustained serious injuries while six received minor injuries.

Picketer Elaine Peterson, who drove a carload of strikers to Gwinn, arrived soon after. She quickly retrieved an army blanket from her car to keep the injured warm while they waited for medical personnel. Anger spread quickly among the rest of the picketers. "They were really mad. They were going to tear everything apart, I guess. But we settled us down, and we came home," said an older Elaine.

Shortly after this accident, a group of nonunion employees from Ishpeming entered Gwinn's factory without incident. Then Wednesday evening local Congress of Industrial Organizations (CIO) membership "gave assist[ance] all of Wednesday night," reported the *Iron Ore*. It was an unusual show of support, said the newspaper, "when CIO members enter picket lines of the American Federation of Labor, but this has been going on for a week." The *Iron Ore* reported "the unfortunate accident" occurred when the driver "became excited and stepped on the gas pedal when she thought she was applying the brakes." The "Princeton housewife" was charged with felonious assault, and the case would be dismissed in early December 1949.

Gossard Girl Shirley Terzaghi witnessed the accident. The image, she said "was like bowling balls or ten pins or something." On the ride back home she said, "I felt ill. It was tragic" for the injured picketers, including one she knew very well. Despite the tragedy, Shirley continued to picket, but only at Ishpeming's factory. "I remember the camaraderie of everyone, going for coffee, and keeping each other's morale up and playing many, many card games of Rummy and Smear." To this day, Shirley has maintained her vow to never play cards again.

Countywide Protest Meeting

Five days after the car accident, Gordon organized "a county wide [protest] meeting," said the *MJ*. Hundreds of people from Marquette County attended including mayors from Negaunee, Ishpeming, and Marquette, as well as local labor union representatives. Plotkin, the evening's main speaker, urged strikers to persevere. "They will get what they want if they remain unfaltering in their fight," he said in the *MJ* article. In return, Plotkin promised strikers that they "won't go hungry," and the ILGWU would disperse "$5,000 in relief payments" each Tuesday for the duration of the strike. Blame for the strike and injuries to nine picketers, he insisted, rested with Ishpeming's manager and a company lawyer for misleading the company. Subsequently, the ILGWU head organizer read a resolution, on behalf of those citizens present, that listed five demands, including a demand for no interference from state police, a demand that Ishpeming's factory remain closed, and a demand for Manager Peterson to stop transporting work and machinery from Ishpeming to Gwinn.

Mediation Fails to End Strike

Meanwhile, efforts by a new representative from the State Labor Mediation Board failed. James Greenfield, representative from Lansing, assigned blame to labor and to management representatives who refused to change their positions. In a statement to Ishpeming's *Iron Ore* paper, Manager Peterson said Plotkin "had no intention of attempting to reach an agreement with the company," inasmuch as he would not have attended had there not been a request by the State Labor Mediation Board. But neither had the undergarment company's demands changed. Peterson argued against a wage increase and a union shop, citing "present economic conditions" in the undergarment industry, as well as in other Upper Peninsula industries.

The strike persisted. Most strikers picketed 24-7 at Ishpeming's large four-story factory. Some women, according to Gossard Girl Dorothy Baldini, "played cards on the steps of Ishpeming Theater to pass the time," while "some men from the mines stood on the corner." A smaller contingent picketed Gwinn's two-story factory during morning work hours. Picketers often used humor and satire to pass the time. Gordon spoke about these antics. "Some of the young women would come to the picket line dressed in a costume and they would entertain themselves." Another time the group dressed in costume and "put on a mock wedding [and] they had a local choral group accompany the[m]." Such antics, she said, were meant "to have fun and make use of the camaraderie" during the strike.

Editorial Opinions

A series of May articles in Ishpeming's *Iron Ore* weighed in on the ongoing strike. On May 7, in its weekly column "Direct from Division Street," the editorial board printed a letter mailed "by the Negotiating Committee, on April 29, to Gossard workers who have not and will not join the strike movement." The letter accused the company of not keeping its promise to help nonunion workers with unemployment during the strike, while strikers received weekly benefits of $10–$30, as well as free meals "in the Union Hall on Second Street." In a separate article on May 7, "Gossard-Union Meet[ing] Ends in Failure," the newspaper reported an impasse from a recent meeting between union and company representatives. Manager Peterson issued a statement to a representative of the *Iron Ore* stating the union "had no intention of attempting to reach any agreement with the company," while also reiterating his company's position on wages and a union shop. "The company feels that this is the most it can do and that any other course would be ruinous. In our own general area, we have seen companies close all operations in the Copper Country and in Delta County, and we have seen some layoffs and some reduction of working hours in both mining and logging industries."

Seven days later (May 14), the *Iron Ore*'s "Direct from Division Street" column updated its readership on what it felt were some of the underlying issues behind why the ILGWU had "selected the H. W. Gossard plant as ripe for a strike." Unions had helped elect "Governor 'Soapy' Williams." Family members of Ishpeming's Mayor Mark Willey (brother of Ruth Craine) were "deeply involved." Michigan State Police, which the editor viewed as "nothing more than a township traffic patrol," and "the head union office in New York" would benefit financially (union dues) from a union shop. Finally, citing an incident in Lower Michigan where a clothing factory closed because of "the tactics of [the] union," the newspaper warned its readership that the Gossard factory might leave Ishpeming.

"Nothing of an encouraging nature to report on the local strike situation" from the second mediation conference held in Cleveland, reported "Direct from Division Street" a week later (May 21). "Not one concession." Furthermore, the newspaper added, "there were fewer picketers with most of them sitting in cars in preference to wearing out shoe leather on the pavements. Maybe a sit-down strike."

Strike in Stalemate

The month of June 1949 began with no discernable end to the strike. Frustrated business groups such as the Ishpeming Chamber of Commerce, Rotary, and Ishpeming Town Club joined forces to pressure Ishpeming's mayor and local law enforcement to enforce national, state, and local laws, laws they felt would allow those Gossard workers who wanted to go back to do so. No doubt local businesses felt the effects of the Gossard strike, now in its eighth week. Weekly payroll from Ishpeming's five hundred idle workers was felt in downtown businesses and in families.

The Ishpeming Chamber of Commerce sent copies of their resolution to the mayor, city council, and chief of police asking them to "make a renewed and determined effort to enforce the laws of the United States, the state of Michigan and city of Ishpeming," reported the *MJ* in June. Rotary Club and Ishpeming Town Club had also drafted and mailed similar resolutions denouncing picketing. If local officials were unable to enforce these laws, the resolutions urged Ishpeming's mayor and city council members "to petition" Michigan's governor to send state police to Ishpeming. Mayor Willey again refused.

Meanwhile, company and union officials pressed forward with their respective strategies, and Gossard strikers continued picketing 24-7. Gossard management from Ishpeming's factory also continued its production efforts. The *MJ* reported that on June 2 and June 7, pickets blocked Peterson "from entering the plant with his automobile." Peterson filed a complaint. Twenty-five strikers were arrested on June 7 and charged with "alleged mass picketing."

Two perspectives of the June 7 incident would emerge. The *MJ* reported on June 8 that "the arrests resulted from an accident at the plant," though the paper offered no details. The union, on the other hand, viewed the incident as another "obvious entrapment" strategy to break the strike, the Chicago-based ILGWU head organizer informed the newspaper.

Ishpeming's local paper supported the arrest of the strikers. In its "Direct from Division Street" column on June 11, the editor stated, "The law has finally caught up with the civil rebellion which has been in progress on Ishpeming's Cleveland Avenue for the past two months." Essentially, twenty-five strikers had violated the "state's labor law on mass picketing." A week earlier (June 4), the *Iron Ore* editorial board had blamed illegal mass picketing on outsiders. "A lot of citizens who have the welfare of Ishpeming at heart have been thoroughly disgusted with the antics of a lot of male and female goons sent here to foster disrespect for the laws of the state."

On June 8, twenty-five Gossard strikers entered not guilty pleas through their attorney, Michael Defant, and the union posted $2,500 bail for the twenty-five strikers. Two days later (June 10), Defant was back in municipal court to respond to conspiracy charges against fifteen Gossard workers stemming from a June 8 incident where the fifteen Gossard strikers allegedly "prevent[ed] entrance into the plant. An additional bond of $500 was set for each. An absurd charge, Chicago ILGWU union representative Geraldine Gordon said to a *Mining Journal* reporter. "No one was injured, no one was threatened with injury, no property was damaged. In fact, no person was denied entry to the plant. The whole charge reduced to its utter absurdity is that (Harold) Peterson's car was refused admission. We think the car should have signed the complaint."

In the meantime, mayors from Ishpeming, Negaunee, and Marquette hatched a plan "to protect and further the rights and objectives of labor in Marquette County" at a June 11 meeting in Ishpeming's Winter Sports Area (now known as Al Quaal Recreation Area). "Attendance was difficult to estimate because many persons listened to the speakers from their cars. There were several hundred cars," reported the *MJ*. Negaunee Mayor Hampton read a resolution authorizing the three mayors to appoint individuals to the Committee to Preserve Rights of Labor in Marquette County. Its members, the mayor said, would have the authority to ask Michigan Governor Williams "to refrain from sending the state police to help the Gossard company to break the law." Others spoke including "Michael Defant, Negaunee city attorney for the striking ILGWU, who termed the meeting 'the most significant meeting in the history of Marquette county,'" the Marquette paper reported.

The month of June would end the way it began: no discernable end to the strike. Gossard company leadership would meet with "executives of the Ishpeming plant" during the week of June 12, "but there is no change to the situation," reported the *MJ*. On June 23, union and company representatives convened a conference with Gossard President J. L. Varley and Vice President Savard. Again, no agreement was reached, and the strike, now in its tenth week, continued. No movement on negotiations, no movement on the mass picketing charges for twenty-five strikers, and no movement on conspiracy charges for fifteen strikers. Not a comforting future for workers whose salaries benefited their families. Not a comforting prognosis for local businesses whose bottom line suffered. And not a comforting situation for an international undergarment company saddled in 1949 with 1,200 workers in three idled factories: Ishpeming, Michigan, and Logansport and Huntington, Indiana.

Amid the growing uncertainty, the *MJ* printed a letter President Varley had sent to all Gossard employees. He wrote the letter after spending two days (July 22–23) visiting with different stakeholders in Ishpeming—city officials, "civic-minded people who had lived in Ishpeming for years," and some Gossard workers. Whether each employee received this letter, as reported in the *MJ*, is unknown. Henry Morissette, Gossard employee in shipping, received a letter, while Elaine Peterson, prounion Gossard Girl, did not.

Nonetheless, Varley's letter reported on his two-day visit and urged workers to return to work. He described the Gossard Company not as "bricks and mortar, plants and machinery" but rather as an "ever-growing Gossard family" comprised of "human beings, customers, employees, management, and stockholders." Inasmuch as family members depend on each other, so too, the president felt, should each member of the Gossard family. "Teamwork" between its members could resolve differences "without the aid of outsiders," wrote Varley.

The Gossard president then reported on his discussions with different stakeholders. "Most working people did not want to be forced to join a union if they did not want to." While they were "glad for their job and the money they [could] earn," some workers, said Varley, complained about management "not being considerate or listening to their complaints." Even so, the president acknowledged "the most vociferous complaint" targeted Gossard management in Chicago who "had neglected" workers in Ishpeming's factory. "This will not happen in the future," wrote the president, but his position on a union shop and wage increases was unchanged. Varley again urged workers "to return to work at once" while he continued negotiating with the union.

The strike continued despite the president's pleas, and Varley took his concerns to Michigan's governor. On June 29, the *MJ* reported President Varley had "for humanitarian reasons . . . urged" Governor G. Mennen Williams "to intervene personally." It's unknown whether economics and/ or humanitarian concerns drove Varley to seek help from the governor. What is known is that the company had more than one thousand workers idled in three plants and two states. The Ishpeming and Logansport plants were the largest plants within the company. Governor Williams would agree to intervene.

Noel Fox, the governor's special legal advisor and commissioner of the State Labor Mediation Board, would bring together business and labor interests in the ensuing weeks. The first of these conferences, with ILGWU representatives and the Gossard Company, took place in Ishpeming around July 4. On July 13, Fox then convened "an all-day meeting" in the governor's Detroit office with two representatives from state and national labor mediation boards, two Gossard Company representatives, and two ILGWU Midwest representatives, reported the *MJ*. Following a third meeting in Chicago during the week of July 25–29, ILGWU organizer Gordon reported to the *MJ*, "Some progress already had been made in negotiating on company-union differences." Hopeful remarks in advance of a fourth meeting on Monday, August 1, from the head organizer.

Meanwhile, picketing continued 24-7 in Ishpeming and Gwinn, the ILGWU continued serving free meals to strikers (and qualified families), and the ILGWU helped qualified families with pressing economic needs such as groceries, medical bills, or utilities. Decades later, Gossard Girl Evelyn Corkin, looking intently at a newspaper photo from the strike said, "We were all punctual ladies. There were so many people and women standing from the corner all the way to the door. I was standing in front of the building."

On Tuesday, August 2, the sixteen-week strike ended. "The company submitted an offer which has been accepted and ratified by the union members" at a meeting in Ishpeming's American Legion, Geraldine reported. "Token picket lines" would continue outside the factory while company and union lawyers reviewed settlement documents for the "three strike bound plants."

On Friday, August 5, employees returned to Ishpeming's factory on a seniority basis, in accordance with the new union contract. Those who had worked the longest would return first. Within six months, all production workers, except for those in management positions, were required to join the union. Employees received an average pay increase of six cents an hour, a ninety-cents-per-hour guarantee for operators, and an eighty-cents-per-hour guarantee for other hand workers. The union pledged to train a "time study person [in each department] who could recheck company's figures [on] a department average." This new policy gave voice and power to workers when they felt the company's time-study rate was faulty. Looking back, Gordon would say this new policy "raised earnings in the plant by 25 percent." Where disputes occurred involving workers, the union contract provided arbitration through one's shop steward. According to a *Mining Journal* article, after the strike was settled, the mass picketing charges against twenty-five picketers and conspiracy charges against fifteen picketers were dismissed.

Employees returned to work Friday, August 5, 1949, with mixed emotions. Prounion, antiunion, and the undecided were working side by side, a testament to their ability to move past personal differences. After sixteen weeks, this commitment by a wide variety of women with disparate political knowledge and attitudes persisted in pursuit of fair wages and working conditions for *all* workers. The eight-year journey for a union shop ended, followed by a celebration of the collective efforts by hundreds of women. All Gossard workers and CIO members were invited to a "Victory Dance at the Rendezvous" with live music from "Frankie Flowers Band and dancing."

Satisfied without a Union

Gossard Girl Madeline Kaupilla, who worked sixteen years at the factory, did not live in Ishpeming during the strike, so it wasn't easy for the medium binder to join the picket line in 1949. While picketers "wanted a union shop," Madeline "was satisfied with the way it was." She found employment at a local party store for the duration of the strike.

Teenage Betty Fosco did not support the strike, yet she "needed money" to help her family during the four-month strike. She "did housework and that," though her wages were significantly less than that of her lucrative piecework in seaming and end finishing.

Similarly, nineteen-year-old Dona Lenten, a pieceworker on two-needle zigzag machines, did not support a union shop. Decades later, Dona spoke about her father, James Johnson, who "crossed the picket line when the mines were on strike." He also walked "the [railroad] tracks and picked up bits of coal to make the house warm, for his newborn twin boys, and my dad did just fine." Dona worked "at a local drive-in near the outdoor food market" until the strike was over.

Six months after the strike, Madeline, Betty, and Dona, and others who did not support a union had to join and pay monthly union dues. Dona's wages increased, but there was more pressure "to make a certain rate," the skilled pieceworker said. There was also pressure to curb socializing while one worked. Chuckling, she described the day management "came over and said, 'Dona, you can't talk as much.'" But other Gossard girls supported the strike and felt empowered by it and by union membership.

....

Elaine Peterson, Gossard Girl

"We took charge in a small town." Not an easy task for women in the late 1940s. Cultural expectations for women like Elaine Peterson did not include working outside of the home let alone going on strike. Decades later, this is what the retired Gossard Girl hoped future generations would learn from the history of the H. W. Gossard in her hometown, Ishpeming, Michigan. Elaine was one of many Gossard Girls who made history in the Upper Peninsula, when they took charge in the bustling town of ten thousand.

"The struggle to become a union shop wasn't easy," Elaine said. The H. W. Gossard Company had agreed to a wage scale settlement, vacation, work hours, and seniority. However, the company would not agree to a union shop. While the four-month strike would strain the social, political, and economic fabric of the bustling town, the strike also empowered some Gossard Girls in ways they never imagined. For Elaine, the struggle taught her to "make your point and stick to it. Never give in."

For Elaine, taking charge also included becoming more than a picketer. Elaine would be asked to join the Gossard negotiating committee. Initially, she hesitated because of her age; she'd recently turned twenty-two. Too young, she thought. Yet the more important issue of favoritism by some department heads was something she could not and would not ignore. Department heads distributed bundles in their own areas, and "all [their] friends would get the job [good bundles]," she said. Operators were paid by the unit, so the more good bundles a department head gave her friends, the more money her friends made. Before the strike, "nobody would speak up for the operator," so Elaine agreed to join the negotiating committee despite concerns about her age.

As a child growing up on a farm in rural Ishpeming during the Depression and a world war, Elaine learned to take charge. The eldest of three children, she grew up working on her family's country farm of pigs, chickens, cows, a vegetable garden, and hay fields. There was plenty of work for each member of the Millimaki family. Elaine enjoyed growing up on a farm with no electricity or phone, "Oh we had a lot of fun. We had a lot of fun playing kids' games." And even though her father, a diamond driller for a mining company, owned a car, "money was scarce."

When Elaine graduated from National Mine High School in 1944, she chose a separate path from her peers. The male graduates joined the military, and some female graduates went on to school. Elaine, however, had a different goal: to find a good-paying job in Washington, D.C. She did. With the help of an older cousin in D.C., Elaine quickly found work in the Navy Department in June 1944. Her employer greeted the wide-eyed high school graduate, "Am I glad I got a Northern girl." Many people believed that Northerners were harder working than people who grew up in the South. Elaine enjoyed her top-secret work environment until the day she watched her boss pass sensitive drawings to some ordinary-looking men who turned out to be spies. After three and a half months, Elaine quit her job, took a train home, and became a Gossard Girl.

Becoming a Gossard Girl

Elaine's parents were enthused their eldest wanted to work at the H. W. Gossard where they "had heard so many good things." Elaine was equally excited. She'd be earning forty-four cents an hour, a lot of money in 1944.

Thus began Elaine's twenty-two years (1944–50, 1960–76) with the H. W. Gossard, a company with an international reputation. By the time Elaine retired, she had worked in at least ten different areas in Ishpeming's plant. "Zigzag operator, cut repairs, print tags/labels, check girl, department head, stockroom, production manager's assistant, molding machine operator, and company tour guide." Over the years, Elaine worked side by side with women, she supervised women, and she worked side by side with men. Collectively, the jobs furnished her with a unique lens into the inner workings of the undergarment assembly environment, a place where one had to be there to comprehend the myriad of interconnected steps to produce top-of-the-line undergarments.

In 1944, new hires like Elaine started in a training unit where she learned to operate industrial machines. "It was simple work at first. When you got out of the training department, then you got moved to the other department where all the seamers were." Elaine said a seaming operator did "a very simple operation on what we called 159 garter belt. Just went all around the garter belt and put four pieces together and joined four pieces and flipped them over and made a garter belt out of it. Then when you got to do that pretty good, you got a little harder model."

Perhaps Elaine's superiors observed her take-charge attitude as well as the quality of her work because she was quickly transferred to cut repairs. When machine operators found flawed material in bundles, they tied the material "onto the tag with their [employee] number on the back and put in a box." Cut repair workers, like Elaine, retrieved the material flaws from the box, matched the material, cut good material with a special knife and guide, and returned the good material to the machine operator. Though the cut repair job seemed simple, Elaine knew she needed to work quickly and efficiently. A sharp knife and weekly application of linseed oil on her wood block made the cut repair job easier.

Whether Elaine worked as a machine operator in seaming, zigzag, or molding, she knew accuracy and speed were a machine operator's best friends. Topnotch operators like Jennie Melka, Rose Collick, and Marjorie Ketola also understood this, said Elaine. Too humble to place herself among this group, Elaine said, "Well-maintained industrial machines were critical. You can imagine running a machine steady. Your machine was pretty hot by ten o'clock, since it had been running steady for three hours. Time to give the machines a rest, and the operators, too." Every morning at ten o'clock, a mechanic switched off power to industrial machines connected by a long metal shaft.

Then Elaine conducted routine maintenance on her industrial machine. If her oil can (each operator had her own oil can) was empty, she walked to the mechanic's bench and pumped a fresh supply of oil into her "little Singer can." Mechanics, she insisted, *never* oiled machines powered by a common shaft. "Every day. Ten o'clock. Shut off the power. Turn your machine up. Take a dust rag and clean all the lint out from under the machine around the bobbin case. Clean it all up. Couple squirts of oil. Put it down. Couple of squirts of oil on the top. Put your can back and wipe it all off." Power remained off long enough for all workers to go downstairs for a coke, coffee, or even a sandwich. However, Elaine knew speedy machine operators, those who made $30–$35 a day, replenished their oil cans before the start of each workday and before power to the machines was turned back on. Lastly, weekly scissor maintenance—cleaning and sharpening—was also necessary, she added.

Elaine's routine continued after the plant was unionized in 1949 and until the Gossard replaced many of the machines by 1961. Self-oiling machines, Elaine explained, eliminated the need for the power to be turned off, but this new technology did not eliminate preventive maintenance. Mid-morning breaks continued, though plant managers Kenneth

"Chick" Strengberg and Roy Peterson instituted separate policies for the midmorning break. Under Manager Strengberg, workers did not go downstairs for their 10:00 a.m. break, but under Manager Peterson they did, according to Elaine.

Holding Many Positions

Prior to the 1949 Gossard strike, Elaine was moved from machine operator to check girl where she prepared finished undergarments for shipment. Attention to detail, speed, and efficiency were necessary skills for this job. Elaine prepared girdles and combinations for shipment. At least once a week (usually on Tuesdays) she received a list that included, among other things, the shipment date and the exact number of girdles and/or combinations for shipment: no more, no less. She transported girdles and combinations in a truck (wooden box on wheels) to the building's only elevator and down to the loading dock. Use of the elevator was reserved for the male-only shipping department; however, Elaine and her supervisor "snuck" onto the elevator on occasion to meet the company's shipment deadline.

At times Elaine would describe her former work environment as organized, yet she also felt it was impossible for anyone "to visualize the factory unless you were there," including the job of instructor. Working ten positions over her twenty-two-year career, she, more than most, understood the inner workings of the organized factory.

A skilled instructor, one who demonstrated strong work ethics, leadership skills, and workplace fairness, was invaluable. She supervised twenty-five operators (i.e., seamers, binders, overcasters, lace edge girls, etc.). "I had a great group of girls. They were cooperative." Cooperative workers were important in a piecework environment where time meant money and where all finished garments were inspected. Elaine understood this; she had worked as an operator. But as an instructor, Elaine had to be alert to the complexities of the entire assembly process. For example, Elaine supervised assembly of two different bras, no. 3400 and no. 2725. One was a simple assembly, and the other, a heavy rubber-padded model, was more labor intensive. Elaine explained, "When one operator finished her step, she'd pass the garment on to the next step. Maybe you'd have three people that would be doing one operation, because it was a costlier one, and it took more time. Now maybe [in] the next operation, that girl could do a very small operation, and she could do as much as those three girls on her operation. And maybe the next would be two and maybe again it would have to be more." Consequently, Elaine had to be more vigilant during the assembly of the rubber-padded bra.

Elaine expected quality work from her twenty-five operators. She worked hard, and she expected those around her to work hard. Except for one unexpected incident when Elaine took an operator to the hospital to remove a needle, there were no other accidents on Elaine's shaft. But there was plenty of laughter and camaraderie. "We had a lot of laughs. They brought me goodies. Some would make my favorite sandwich (ham and cheese) or cookies (oatmeal raisin). We had lots of fun together."

Supporting a Union Shop

Economics, not social justice issues, attracted Elaine to the H. W. Gossard plant. Money was scarce in the 1930s and 1940s, and jobs even scarcer for young women like Elaine. During her first year, she saved "every penny." She limited her expenses by living at home ($5 room and board) and carpooling (50 cents a week). The rest Elaine saved because she dreamt of owning her own car. She fulfilled her dream within one year (1945) when the nineteen-year-old bought a Model A for $100 cash. Yet four years later, workplace issues caused Elaine to join a chorus of others in a struggle for a union shop. And the Model A, a symbol of Elaine's economic power, transported Gossard picketers to Gwinn's nonunion factory, twenty-six miles from Ishpeming.

According to Elaine, favoritism by some department heads prompted her to sign a union card by 1946, three years prior to the 1949 strike. It didn't matter that Elaine was no longer an operator but a time worker. At issue was the inequitable method department heads used to distribute bundles among their operators. Bundles, according to Elaine, were grouped in several categories. "Some were classified as excellent bundles. If you had them all day long, you could make money. Some were classified as mediocre bundles." But, Elaine emphasized, "some were *very poor* bundles. I'm talking about the units that operators would be getting doing the garments." In other words, the more units an operator finished, the more money she earned above the minimum rate. Complaints were made, but "not much was done because there was no one to back them up or verify it."

In the absence of help from Gossard management, concerned Gossard Girls, like Elaine, would begin to see union representation as their only form of redress. During organizing efforts during the 1940s, "we signed union cards secretively," she said. Secrecy was paramount because management was against the union. "If [management] ever found out, [prounion operators] were either given very poor bundles or let go," she recalled. In fact, production manager Ida Santamore was surprised in 1949 to learn "the girl just out of high school" had "signed a card in 1946 to back the union." Ida mistakenly assumed this young check girl wouldn't have risked her job to join the union. Ida also mistakenly assumed Elaine was indifferent to department heads' favoritism.

The path to a union shop, Elaine reiterated, was shrouded in secrecy. "Until the day you went out on strike, you did not know who was for the union. You didn't know who to trust." Secrecy stretched beyond Gossard management (i.e., department heads, instructors, managers, or super-intendents) to family, neighbors, and best friends. Elaine's parents and siblings did not know she had signed a union card. Elaine and her best friend, Dorothy Sari—both check girls—never discussed unions. They respected the code: trust no one. "I didn't know my best friend signed a union card until the first day of the strike." How surprised the two friends must have been on April 12, 1949, a spring day "colder than hell."

Joining the Negotiating Committee.

Much work was needed in advance of the first day of the strike. The first step in the process, Elaine recalled, began with a vote by Gossard workers who had signed union cards secretly. Though Elaine did not recall the date of the vote (November 1948) or the exact count, she knew the results; a "very low margin" had voted for union representation.

The second and more tenuous step would be another vote, this time to go on strike. The margin to call for a strike wasn't huge, but results were all that mattered, Elaine said. Headlines in the *Mining Journal* on May 4, 1949, reported the results of a strike vote in April: 335 yes votes and 173 no votes. The negotiating committee was now empowered to set the strike date, Elaine said, unless last-minute "conferences between union and company representatives on questions of pay increases and union shop" would avert a walkout.

The call for union representation set in motion a third step: activating guidelines, procedures, and responsibilities of the Gossard negotiating committee, and forming the committee. In late 1948, union membership at the Ishpeming plant selected seven Gossard workers, including Elaine.

Serving on the negotiating committee would be a rare opportunity, one that would teach Elaine two lessons. Lesson one: "Never give in. Be stubborn. Make your point and stick to it." Lesson two: "When you are all unionized, you have a lot going for you." Years later, she considered her position on the negotiating committee within a larger historical context: the women's movement. Elaine stated, "At that time, there weren't many women who stuck up for themselves. Look how far we have come instead of scrubbing and cooking. It's a woman's world." When viewed through the lens of history, the Gossard strike is not only historic in the narrative of the Upper Peninsula's history, but also a relevant story within the national story of women's struggles for equal rights.

And so, Gossard Girls took charge. Of the seven Gossard workers on the negotiating committee, at least five were women, according to Elaine. "The girls start[ed] putting what they wanted: so much an hour, this and that, and union shop. There was some union representatives: Geraldine and others. Then they came up to negotiate with us against Harold Peterson and the representatives out of Chicago for Gossard. We met at the Mather Inn. We had all our meetings there to negotiate. Then we had a man [mediator] come in to decide. We didn't get anywhere with that either. We went on and on and on and on, and finally we weren't getting anywhere. We [Gossard workers who signed union cards] had a union meeting and decided to have a strike. So we went out on strike."

The decision to strike set in motion additional planning by members of the Gossard organizing committee and ILGWU representatives. No small undertaking, but it had to be done. Elaine said, "We organized pickets. We had shifts. Those that worked in the kitchen at the Gossard [factory] volunteered to cook for the picketers. The union paid for all of the food. We never paid a penny for it. It was all donated. If you picketed or, like the cooks, [prepared and served meals,] you got paid for that."

Elaine served on a committee for picketers in more severe economic conditions such as large families, single households, or divorced Gossard Girls. "We would okay tickets for them to go to the stores and get more food or whatever. Beyond the picket and the meals," she recalled. In these situations, the Gossard worker would file an appeal before the subcommittee. "If they needed something, if they needed fuel or they needed a light bill paid or they needed some bill paid, we would okay it." Monies for these extreme situations came from ILGWU. Local towns and businesses, who had come to depend on the economic power generated from weekly paychecks of over 550 Gossard workers, were affected. Grocery stores, clothing stores, barber shops, hardware stores, restaurants, and churches were impacted.

But there were other hardships. Often, relationships within families, between friends, and among neighbors were tested. There were multiple times when Elaine was berated by those in the community who did not support a union shop, but she remained committed to a more equitable work environment for *all* Gossard workers. At the end of a challenging day on the picket line or in a negotiating committee meeting, Elaine went home knowing her parents supported her 100 percent. "They said, 'You know what you are doing. Stick to your guns.'"

And she did stick to her guns. Decades after the Ishpeming plant closed (1976), Elaine remained grateful to be part of a historic movement in the Upper Peninsula where women workers won the struggle for a more equitable workplace environment. Without hesitation, the prounion Gossard Girl spelled out the benefits as if the struggle had occurred yesterday. "Work was divided equally. Nobody was nobody's pet. You were all on an equal basis. You had a voice to speak. If you didn't like the units that were on the bundle, you could write up a complaint, have it retimed to see if you could get a better timing on it to get more money. I mean you *had* a voice in what you wanted. That was the main thing, not to take what they offered but what you thought was fair."

To be sure, there were times when picketing wasn't easy. In early June 1949, for example, Elaine was one of twenty-five strikers arrested and charged with mass picketing. She also faced conspiracy charges for blocking the entrance to the Gossard garage. "Well . . . the policeman took us over to the jail. We all stood before the judge. We were called over picketing. Too many people were picketing in one spot. We should have been moving faster or walking faster than standing around talking with the signs." The union posted her $600 bail ($100 for overpicketing plus $500 for conspiracy), and when a union contract was settled, both cases against Elaine (and others) were dropped.

But once the strike was settled, the joke telling and laughter resumed, Elaine said. Many friendships returned to prestrike times.

Picket Line Proposal

The 1940s were formative years, and Elaine's involvement in the strike helped forge lasting memories about never giving in. Coincidentally, this was also a time she dated a man five years her senior with life experiences in never giving in. It was a typical late evening shift when Elaine, a shift captain, might be playing Smear (also known as Schmier) with her picketing crew. Smiling, Elaine mused, "My fiancé came at midnight and gave me a diamond on the picket line." When the Gossard strike ended in early August, the newlyweds traveled to Niagara Falls for a two-week honeymoon. A year later, Elaine left the Gossard to rear their newborn son.

Returning to the Gossard

Ten years passed before the thirty-four-year-old wife and mother returned to the unionized plant in Ishpeming. "Lots of things had changed," Elaine observed. Perhaps the most significant change was the assembly line. The change, Elaine said, meant that "the garment is sewed from beginning to end and finished right there in that department. It's not brought to second floor. It's not brought to third floor. It's what you call an assembly line. The garment is finished right there." Much better for machine operators, she observed. "If you do the same thing over and over and over and over and over, you'll get faster and better and better." Though Elaine would hold other positions from 1960 to 1976, she saw the benefit of sewing the same garment over and over. Put simply, she said, "You can almost do it with your eyes closed after a while."

Another change was an opportunity to break a gender barrier. As far back as Elaine could remember, men had worked as cutters, mechanics, and stockroom workers. Never women. Whether it was an official Gossard policy is uncertain. Elaine was moved from assistant production manager to the stockroom, where she remained. Stockroom workers were responsible for delivering "findings" (i.e., elastic, zippers, lace, snaps, etc.) to all the departments in a timely manner.

Elaine's new position came about when Ida Santamore, production manager, became concerned when the all-male stockroom was even slower in delivering "items on the delay list." Delays slowed production. Lower production levels reduced pieceworkers' ability to meet or even exceed the rate. Delays cost the company.

Ida complained, "things are not getting done," and proposed moving Elaine into the all-male department. Ida knew her take-charge assistant would get things done and the findings would be delivered swiftly. More importantly, the former pieceworker and production assistant would bring a wealth of experience to the stockroom. Despite her qualifications, Gould Lawry, head of the stockroom, was not enthusiastic about a female worker in his stockroom. Not at first, according to Elaine. Years later, Elaine reflected on Gould's hesitancy, "When he got to know me, he didn't want me to go." He didn't want her to go because he learned she made sure departments "got their stuff quickly," especially items on the delay list. When shipments arrived at the plant, usually several times a week, Elaine headed to the truck's loading dock, located items on the delay list, and delivered these items to the right department. Elaine remained in the stockroom until the plant closed in 1976.

....

Helmi Talbacka, Gossard Girl

Sisu, a cultural construct in Finland, when translated into English means "strength of will, determination, perseverance, and acting rationally in the face of adversity." One need not be Finnish to demonstrate *sisu*, but Helmi Talbacka was of 100 percent Finnish heritage. This concept best typifies Helmi, first-generation American who grew up in Michigamme, Michigan, a small mining community twenty-five miles west of Ishpeming. It would take the income of both parents—her father a miner and her mother a tailor—to raise ten children during the 1920s and 1930s. Years later when Helmi married, it would take two incomes to raise her family.

Becoming a Gossard Girl

It was lucky for Helmi that in January 1947, the Gossard factory in Ishpeming was hiring. "I had two children. That seemed like work. Where my husband worked, the wages were low. So it took two to work, which it does nowadays, too," Helmi said in recalling her Gossard start.

It was boom time for the factory with employment expected to reach six hundred and with workers injecting "four-fifths of a million dollars" into Ishpeming's community. The Finnish pieceworker, who worked in two departments—hooks and eyes, and corset zippers—made very good money, and in doing so, her wages helped her family. Yet, by her own admission, Helmi did much more than helping her family. "I helped get the union in."

The Fourth Unionization Campaign

Helmi did not remember the month or year (1947 or 1948) she signed a union card, nor did she recall who asked if "she'd join the women." Such requests occurred in secret. Once she signed a card, Helmi agreed to help recruit Gossard workers in what was then the fourth campaign. "They'd asked me go and see this woman or this girl to see if she'll join the women. Some would, some wouldn't." Sometimes Helmi recruited alongside Elaine Keto and Wilma Sparks. Helmi would speak to potential recruits during work or lunch breaks, but *always* outside of the undergarment factory.

"Now it's up to you or not," Helmi would say in trying to persuade workers. "But I think you should, you know. It's coming to that all over." Other times, Helmi would say, "I think we should join, all of us. A lot of the girls are. We'll get better wages and seniority was a big thing. They probably shouldn't be monkeying around with the prices on the bags that was similar to others. It should be the same." Meanwhile, Helmi continued to educate herself about unions and organizing. She attended union meetings locally, and she was also selected to attend union organizing meetings in Wisconsin. "We went to Madison, Wisconsin, for a week and listened to some boring guy talking," Helmi said humorously.

However, there was one person who wasn't boring when it came to talking about unions. Pausing briefly, Helmi specified pieceworker Ruth Craine. "Oh yes, she's a doll." When pressed to discuss what Ruth had done to receive high praise, Helmi said, "Oh, oh she knew what she was talking about. When she talked, you listened. She was usually one of the speakers at the union meetings." Helmi liked Ruth, but Helmi's nuanced explanation also suggested a level of respect and admiration for her coworker.

Going on Strike

What memories Helmi has of the four-month Gossard strike are few but telling. Collectively, her memories may suggest she understood the value of strength in numbers. "I remember one time, there was a garage where the boss would keep his car. So one day we thought, 'Well, we'll fix him.'" Helmi said nonunion workers were using the Gossard garage to load raw material into the manager's car for transport to Gwinn's plant, a nonunion facility. The fix, Helmi said, was simple. She and a small group of picketers "piled in front of the boss's garage and wouldn't let him put his car in there." It was a tense moment, Helmi recalled, when the boss and car faced picketers. "He was so bold. He went right up. They [picketers] had to move or he'd hit them. But nobody got hurt." The incident would send an important message to their boss and the undergarment company. But the incident also emboldened Helmi, an ethnic Finnish woman with *sisu*.

To be sure, many families knew about strikes. Their husbands, fathers, or other relatives were employed in the local mining industry. The difference with the Gossard strike, Helmi noted, was women were on the picket lines advocating for their rights.

In the coming weeks of the strike, Helmi and fellow strikers continued to picket in front of the Gossard garage. To help pass the time during her two-hour shifts, she learned to play Smear, a popular card game in 1949. Decades later, she couldn't remember how to play the game. She did, however, remember the lifesaving support from the ILGWU, earning $15 each week for picketing. Qualified families like hers ate free meals—breakfast, dinner, and supper—in an upstairs makeshift room across from the Venice Supper Club on Second Street.

Holding Back Coupons

Helmi was glad the factory became a union shop in 1949. More than anything, she believed a union shop would help everyone, including her. But the picketer recalled two separate instances when she felt the union didn't or couldn't help her. Whether she sought help from the union is unknown. She felt shortchanged because the union wouldn't and didn't fight for pay equity. In those days, the culture believed men should make more than women. Helmi remembered the day management said she would never earn more than the Gossard men. "He definitely said *no woman* is making two dollars an hour like the men," Helmi said unequivocally. Two dollars an hour was a lot of money in those days, she observed. When asked to explain how it felt when management said she couldn't make more than the men, a somber Helmi replied calmly, "You listen and keep quiet."

Angry and disappointed, Helmi fought back in the only way she could. She said, "So, we'd hold back coupons and kind of relax the next day and wouldn't have to work so much and use those coupons that we should have put on. We'd put them on the next day. We cut coupons off when we finished with the bag and then at the end of the day, we'd figure out first to see how much they were before we glued them on, and if it was over two dollars an hour, we didn't put all of them down." It was a risky practice if management caught one holding back coupons, according to Helmi. If one was caught, a pieceworker might be assigned to work on "a certain new model, and it might be identical to sew on," but with one difference: the units on the new model were valued less, so a pieceworker actually earned less for the same assembly step. Helmi disapproved of management's method to prevent this unauthorized practice. "Oh, they had dirty ways," she stated.

The next time Helmi felt the union let her down happened after she'd been employed for at least fifteen years. For health reasons she took time off from the factory, about three to four months. She worried her recovery time took longer than expected, but Gossard officials assured her that she'd have her job. When she did return, Gossard officials refused to reinstate her seniority. Helmi said, "They told me I was going to start as a new girl because they said I had been out a year." Helmi did not agree. But management, who "got kind of snotty," refused to reverse their decision. Helmi returned, but her earning power was greatly reduced.

Not long after she returned, a resolute Helmi hatched a plan. "At three o'clock," Helmi said, "I picked up my things [and] left" the factory." Her actions would be more powerful than words. Management dispatched Gossard pieceworkers to Helmi's house to convince her to remain an employee because she was so fast and accurate. She agreed to return if management reinstated her seniority and paid her what she made before she took time off for health reasons. Next, management visited Helmi, but her response was the same. Unless management agreed to her conditions, her answer was "NOPE." The manager said, "Well we can't do that," and

Helmi again reminded him that she took medical leave for three to four months, not a year. Neither Helmi nor management budged. So Helmi did the only thing she could do: she left, never to return to the Gossard. It wasn't an easy decision. She had invested more than fifteen years at the factory. She was fast, she earned very good money, and she enjoyed the camaraderie of her coworkers. But management had "really ticked me off."

In 1965, she found "an old tablet" and began writing "a day-by-day thing [she] did for the day." Helmi was bored and needed work, so she cleaned houses and local businesses until she was hired "at the best place": Bell Memorial Hospital. Forty-seven years later, the woman with *sisu* still keeps a journal. Her only regret was she did not discover her love of writing when she was a Gossard Girl. Nevertheless, Helmi mused, "the Gossard Factory was important to me. This was the first big job I had."

Denise Anderson, Gossard Girl

Denise Dussart, one of seven siblings (three sisters and four brothers), was born in Esneux, Belgium, on November 11, 1924. Denise's journey from Esneux to Ishpeming, Michigan, had its roots in World War II, where in 1945 she met Allied soldiers involved in the Battle of the Bulge (also known as Battle of the Ardennes). Esneux, today a small town of thirteen thousand, was situated less than fifty miles from the Battle of the Bulge. "On Sundays we were allowed to go after the dishes and the dinner into town for a couple of hours. We could sit on those chairs there and watch the people," said Denise. These people, she said, were American soldiers.

On one of these Sundays, Denise met Kenneth Anderson, a soldier who fought in the Battle of the Bulge. Little did Denise, then twenty-one, realize her "odd" encounter with a man from Ishpeming, Michigan, would blossom into a journey across the Atlantic Ocean. Laughing, Denise described that fateful Sunday. "So, ah, I was the last one because I always had to finish my sister Suzanne's work doing dishes and all that stuff. And I came last, and there was a glass of beer on the table outside. I said, 'Who is that for?'" Denise's sister quickly responded, "That's yours. If you like it, drink it." Denise, still annoyed with her sister, said, "Well, I don't want that." Suzanne countered, "Yes you do. You like beer." Laughing again as she remembered the details of her odd encounter, Denise continued, "So I sat down and drank the beer. It was from Kenny."

The two Dussart sisters accepted the two American soldiers' next offer, to go to the movies. Suzanne orchestrated the theater seating, directing her twenty-one-year-old sister to sit next to the tall soldier. Denise said, "So ah . . . my sister says, 'You can have him.' She says, 'he is too tall for me.'" Denise complied, "I went and sat by him and ever since then we been together."

In the absence of a common language the two soldiers and sisters talked with their hands. "We couldn't talk English, so we talk with hands," Denise would recall when she was nearly ninety years old. The nonverbal communication succeeded; the twosome would continue seeing each other in 1945. Within six months and with the help of a French and English dictionary, Denise and Kenny became closer. She observed, "In six months, I could understand. We had a book between us: French and English. So, we get along pretty good."

Coming to America

The affection between Denise and Kenny grew stronger. They got engaged, and Kenny was shipped back home, leaving his young fiancée behind to arrange her travel. The journey to Ishpeming would not be easy.

In 1947, Denise secured the last spot on a large freighter bound for the ports in New Orleans, Louisiana. Reflecting on her eventful transatlantic trip, Denise remembered traveling in the company of a Jewish family and the seventeen-year-old daughter of the woman who had helped Denise secure passage in Antwerp. Denise said, "Boat ride took twenty days." Midway through their Atlantic crossing, a massive storm rocked the freighter and its passengers. Denise, who had never been on a freighter, became sick. "When we were in the middle of the Atlantic, there was a five-day storm at sea going back and forth, left and right, and I got sick to my stomach." The storm persisted. It rocked the freighter vigorously and ripped open the drawers in the girls' room. Denise laughed in describing the next scene, "We were full of lemons in our room." So ill was Denise, she had forgotten about the medicinal benefits of lemons. "They put lemon in all the drawer. You could chew lemon when you were seasick." Denise found relief in the lemons.

She slept, and her appetite returned. "'I feel pretty good.' I say, 'I am going to go downstairs and eat.'" How swiftly would feeling pretty good shift to feeling pretty disgusted. More than sixty years later, Denise had not forgotten the horror and disgust when she took her first bite of food. The feeling of disgust wasn't from being seasick, but from what she was served. "I sat there, and I sat there. I look down and they had a soup bowl. We had a soup, and it was a turtle soup. A little turtle. I put my spoon down my plate and I came out with a little turtle." Older now, Denise mimics covering her mouth and being sick at the sight of a dead baby turtle on her spoon. She returned to her room, escorted by a sailor. Fortunately, Denise did not encounter any more violent storms or exotic dishes during her twenty days at sea. She remained mystified years later that the baby turtle encounter did not spoil her love of soup. "I don't know how I like soup today," she mused.

The unexpected storm delayed the arrival of the freighter. Surely, a delay must have weighed on the mind of the young Belgium immigrant, already exhausted and weak from her journey to America. What if her fiancé wasn't at the dock? What if she could not find her way to Ishpeming from New Orleans? What if Kenny was unsure about a foreigner for a wife? What if he changed his mind? What if Denise never saw her Belgian family again? What if her twenty-day visa expired before she married, and Kenny's prepaid $500 bond would be used instead to cover the cost of her return trip by sea to Esneux? These and other thoughts weighed on Denise.

Fortunately, the what-if questions evaporated the instant Denise spotted her fiancé. "The first time I look on the quay I could see my [future] husband there." If Kenny entertained any what-ifs, they must have also disappeared when he spotted his fiancée. Kenny and Denise were reunited on the dock; he slipped a ring on her hand. The reunited couple remained in New Orleans long enough for Denise to get well before they traveled to her new home: Ishpeming, Michigan, a distance of almost 1,300 miles.

Becoming a Gossard Girl

When Denise moved to Ishpeming in 1947, she was impressed with her husband's hometown. The large town boasted a population of about ten thousand, and the H. W. Gossard plant, now in its twenty-eighth year, employed well over five hundred workers. Women comprised 90 percent of the Gossard workforce. The sight of countless Gossard Girls heading to and from the Ishpeming plant, located in the middle of town, did not go unnoticed by the Belgian immigrant. Denise recalled, "My husband and I would walk downtown, and I look at the girls go to work, and I was bored." How she longed to be one of those Gossard Girls. Kenny, however, did not support his wife's dream; he did not want his wife to work outside of their house.

Their impasse persisted until 1948, when good fortune crossed paths with the Belgian bride. One day while Denise was downtown without her husband, she met a special Gossard Girl. Not one of the pieceworkers, but one of two office girls, who "took the names at the window." Access to a job at the plant started with these office girls. According to Denise, one office girl encouraged Denise to become a Gossard Girl, "Why don't you come and apply at the Gossard?" Denise didn't need any encouragement; it was her inflexible husband who needed to be convinced. So Denise turned down the office girl's offer saying, "No, . . . my husband don't want me to work." But the office girls persisted saying, "Aw, apply, that'll do you good. You won't be here all the time." Denise agreed. She headed to the Ishpeming plant and filled out an application. Now the difficult part would be telling her husband. Denise knew Kenny would not be happy. "He was mad." He was not impressed that his wife was offered a job the day after she applied. Kenny did not intend for his wife to work anywhere but at home. Years later, Denise remembered her husband's firm position: "He say, 'No place. . . . I didn't get you up here to work.'"

But Denise remained steadfast with her decision. Another hurdle, a language barrier, was more difficult. Denise's first language was French. What English-speaking skills she had were rudimentary. Furthermore, the assembly-line environment would not make accommodations for any immigrant worker, whether she spoke French, Italian, or Finnish. Denise understood the challenge that lay ahead; "I couldn't even talk English. I didn't understand [what] they tell me to do." Despite the language barrier, Denise felt confident she could be a successful pieceworker because she knew how to sew. "I know I watch them sew. I know how to sew. They show me what to do." The determined and focused Belgian immigrant cleared those hurdles and many others that would come her way.

After her training period, Denise worked almost thirty years at the Ishpeming plant. She spent the bulk of her time (twenty-four years) in the zigzag department. Piece workers like Denise sat seven hours a day repeating the same operation. She did not seem bothered by the repetitive nature of this work. In fact, Denise earned the reputation of being fast pieceworker.

Going on Strike

Denise became a Gossard Girl in 1948, a pivotal year in Ishpeming's plant. In November, the Ishpeming employees voted to be represented by the ILGWU. Denise had no memory of voting; however, she remembered clearly the circumstances in which she became one of the picketers five months later. Initially, Kenny did not allow his wife to participate; he was afraid for her. One day Denise passed the strikers, and her friend Elaine Peterson urged the immigrant pieceworker to join the strikers. "You may as well come out with us. You get your $10 and your food." The timing of the Gossard strike for the Anderson couple could not have been worse. Kenny had been laid off from the mines. The couple had little means to pay their modest rent ($8 a month) or utilities or to purchase food. So a weekly payment of $10, as well as meals from the ILGWU, in exchange for two hours of picketing meant a lot to the husband and wife. Denise said, "Every Friday we would get $10; every day we would get food—breakfast, dinner, and supper—in the same place upstairs above Woody's Bar. That's where they [ILGWU] had their headquarters." Decades later, Denise was forever grateful for the safety net. Without union benefits of eating three meals a day above Woody's Bar during the strike period, "we wouldn't eat otherwise."

Presumably Denise's husband was grateful for the union's safety net, yet Kenny was also distressed. His wife would be required to participate in the strike. Only two hours per day. Not a lot of time. Still, Kenny's level of worry remained high. "He was afraid something would happen to me," Denise recalled. Perhaps it was a fear born from a common cultural belief that women do not belong on a picket line or a fear his immigrant wife wasn't fluent in English. Whatever the basis for Kenny's concerns, he took measures to protect his wife. Years later, Denise fondly recalled an image of her protective husband, chuckling halfway through her story. "I remember during strike we were walking the sidewalk in front of the building. I remember he came with the girls [Gossard workers]. He was all dressed up. And they were laughing because he came and watch[ed] me. He was right behind me."

Years later, Denise remained convinced with her decision to partici-pate in the 1949 strike, even if it meant going against her husband. When asked to consider a benefit of working in a union shop (the underlying reason for the strike), Denise said, "To me it helped, because we could apply our rights." In particular, workers' seniority rights. Before 1949, the allocation of work, particularly during slow periods, was not uniformly based on one's seniority. After 1949, according to Denise, seniority became relevant; she now had a process to challenge management when she felt her seniority rights were threatened.

There were other times, though, when she sensed the limitations of union membership. Denise, a fast worker, consistently earning above her rate, felt being fast and being good weren't necessarily the best thing for her. Being fast with high-quality work affected her relationship to both union stewards and management. Workers did not want to be caught between union leadership and their management bosses. Denise recalled periods when she (and others) purposely hid coupons (tickets) from management. "We didn't give them all those tickets. We held those tickets. We didn't want to tell them how much money we were making. Foolish eh?" If she didn't withhold some of her tickets, "they [management would] cut the price down." Cutting the price down referred to piecework rates set by management. Denise felt strongly enough she cautioned a pieceworker in Denise's area. "That girl in front of me, she used to brag about it. I say, 'Don't brag too loud. They'll cut you down to nothing.'"

A Lifesaver

Despite the plant's closure in 1976, Denise was resolute. "The Gossard was a lifesaver. It saved lots of people like the children and stuff." And during the four-month strike in 1949, the ILGWU had helped Denise's family. The retired Gossard Girl, wife, and immigrant understood the economic power her Gossard family brought to their families *and* to their communities for over half a century. She said, "They used to go out, and go to the A & P, and shop there, and cash your check, and shop." Gossard Girls—economic engines—kept their towns and families going.

Gossard Plant (formerly Braastad Building) in Ishpeming, Michigan. Unknown date. Digital file provided by Superior View/Jack Deo.

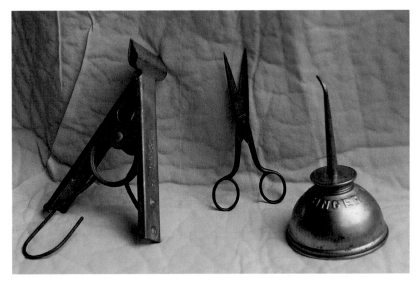

Workers' tools (clamp, oil can, scissors), 2014. A metal clamp used by cloth layers to secure multiple layers of raw material. Personal Singer oil cans used by machine operators for routine daily maintenance. Scissors (each worker was responsible for purchasing scissors) were sharpened weekly. Photo courtesy of the author.

Thread holders: plastic thread spools and a sewing bobbin holder. Gossard male workers fashioned bobbin holders from repurposed metal and six-inch metal nails. Bobbin holders were used for empty bobbins, a hazard if they were on the floor. Empty thread spools were repurposed for making homemade sausage. Undated photo courtesy of Sandy Arsenault.

Strikers picket in front of Ishpeming's Gossard factory, while nonunion workers observe picketers from the second floor. 1949. Organizer Ruth Craine, wearing a wool coat and hat, stands curbside. Photo courtesy of the author.

CCI Gwinn Hospital in Gwinn, Michigan, 1910. The building was renovated in 1946–47 for the Gwinn Gossard factory. Photo courtesy of the Forsyth Township Historical Society, Gwinn, Michigan.

Gossard workers attend a picnic in 1946. Digital file provided by Superior View/Jack Deo.

Gossard baseball team at Gossard Company picnic at Al Quaal Recreation Area in Ishpeming, 1947. Front row, left to right: Joyce Rock, Elaine Peterson (holding the game prize, a box of Brach's chocolates), Gossard Queen Dorothy Windsand, Jean Sandstrom, Dorothy Waters. The names of women in the back row are unknown. Digital file provided by Superior View/Jack Deo.

Gossard strikers in front of Ishpeming's factory, 1949. Digital file provided by Superior View/ Jack Deo.

A rectangular wood box (truck) mounted on three metal wheels *(left front foreground)* was used to transport bundles of unfinished and finished garments. Machine operators used wooden boxes with attached wooden handles *(right foreground)* to store their work. Undated photo courtesy of Sandy Arsenault.

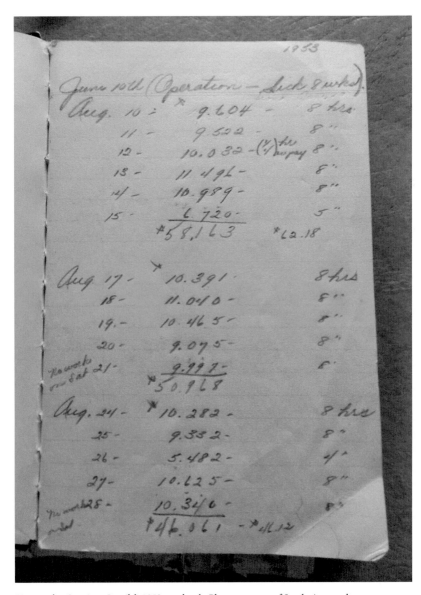

Pieceworker Lorainne Lassila's 1953 notebook. Photo courtesy of Sandy Arsenault.

Pieceworkers operate industrial machines on the second or third floor of Ishpeming's plant. Undated photo. Digital file provided by Superior View/Jack Deo.

Metal seam gauge used by roving inspector Betty Pepin to verify seam allowances, number of stitches per inch, or stitches per area on a garment. Photo courtesy of Sandy Arsenault.

Last days in Ishpeming's factory. Standing left to right: Betty Thurston, Borghild Thexton, Elaine Peterson, and Ruth Basto. December 1976. Digital file provided by Superior View/Jack Deo.

Edith and Clifford Perry, a health-conscious man, who sweetened coffee with honey and endorsed healthy outdoor activities. Undated photo. Digital file provided by Superior View/Jack Deo.

Henry and Alice Morissette, parents of Michael Morissette. Undated photo. Digital file provided by Superior View/Jack Deo.

Six Gossard Girls attend Gossard presentation at Northern Michigan University in March 2010. Back row, left to right: Elaine Peterson, author Phyllis Wong. Front row, left to right: Cecilia Kangas, Catherine Johnson, Marjorie Ketola, Rose Collick, and Evelyn Corkin. Photo courtesy of the author.

Eight Gossard Girls attend Gossard presentation at Gwinn Community Center (Gwinn Clubhouse), April 2010. Left to right: Pearl Filizetti, Judy Green, Edna Roberts, Madeleine DelBello, Ruth Nyman, Dora Mussatto, Ruth Fagerberg, and Nathalie Hutchens. Photo courtesy of the author.

Dorothy Windsand, seated wearing a crown and corsage, garnered the most votes to be crowned Gossard Queen at the 1947 picnic for Ishpeming and Gwinn workers. Digital file provided by Superior View/Jack Deo.

Gossard Memorial Quilt and quilt artists, from left to right: Esther Johnson, Gossard Girl Chris Wiik, Toyo Kaumeheiwa, and Judy Parlato. October 2010. The quilt was exhibited at the Autumn Comforts 2010 Quilt Show, Northern Michigan University, Great Lakes Rooms, Marquette, Michigan. Photo courtesy of the author.

Singer Sewing Machine. One of the first sewing machines used in Ishpeming's factory. Circa 1920. Photo courtesy of Sandy Arsenault.

CHAPTER 5

....

Transforming Fashions

FASHION BEGAN A SIGNIFICANT transformation in the 1950s. "Achiev-
ing the feminine ideal of the 1950's entailed a constant effort. Everything needed to be coordinated in an ensemble, including accessories and
underpinnings," wrote the authors of *Uplift*. Furthermore, they reported,
"technical details and interesting fabrics distinguished bras of the postwar
period." For example, vertical or circular stitching adorned some bra
cups. The split, branched, or tangent bra straps provided "more freedom
of movement." Fabrics such as eyelet, cotton broadcloth, and Dacron
polyester were some of the new materials, while "Gossard had several
lines with embroidery." Padding, which had a long history in women's
undergarments, was "all the rage in the 1950's."

New technical details and fabrics would offer undergarment companies
new marketing opportunities to promote the feminine ideal of the times.
For example, "manufacturers coordinated packaging with sales promotions
in newspapers, magazines, subway and bus cards, radio, television, and
store counter displays." And some companies used movie stars such as
Marilyn Monroe, Grace Kelly, and Lauren Bacall as examples of the ide-
alized figure: petite, curvy, and elegant, according to the authors of *Uplift*.

Meanwhile, in Michigan's Upper Peninsula, the second half of the
twentieth century opened with optimistic news about the H. W. Gossard
Company's two factories. As if to signal the important economic impact
of the Gossard factories within Marquette County, the *Mining Journal*
(*MJ*) ran two articles on its front page above the fold on March 25, 1950.

The first article, "Sun Clothing Produced at Two Plants," reported the
undergarment company was introducing a new product line in women's
wear: a two-piece bathing suit. The Gossard Company, like its national
peers, was producing "the new two-piece garment called the Gossard Sun-
Suit . . . in lots of between 40–45 dozen a day," Manager Harold Peterson
said in the article. The bottoms of the sun-suit were made in Ishpeming,
and the strapless bra tops were made in Gwinn. Furthermore, Ishpeming's

factory had added production in "special small orders of Gossard luxury line undergarments," according to the newspaper.

The push to meet the company's expanding products was felt on "truck days" said Gwen Skewis, who began in narrow and medium binding. Three days a week Gossard trucks transported finished undergarments to Gossard warehouses. On these days, management waited until 1:00 or 2:00 p.m. "to push workers" to increase their output. "We worked like crazy," and management "put a paper on the bulletin board telling the ones that don't make their rate. I made sure my name was never on the list." Even so, Gwen recalled "one girl . . . no matter how much they piled on that table, she would not go any faster. She had one speed." When Gwen was transferred to boxing, she still felt the push to increase her output on truck days but in a job with "very low pay. If I made seven dollars, it was a good day. My sister-in-law was on the assembly line, and if she made ten dollars, she said it was a bad day." Furthermore, she added, boxing required more steps ("open box, fold bras, place bras in box, put a lid on the box, and tie boxes together") when compared to binding.

However, narrow binder Evelyn Corkin felt the pressure daily. "Trying to make my rate everyday was fearful, and I had to push myself. I don't know where I would have gone to work from there." She focused on her piecework, forgoing socializing with those on her shaft. However, she would socialize during work breaks, during the "beautiful meals of roast beef, potatoes, and all the vegetables," and during union-sponsored trips to Chicago for union business. Helping her parents' family, later raising children as a single parent, and taking care of herself were paramount.

"Everybody wanted to work at the Gossard," said Gossard Girl Alice Haapala. "It was the only place you could make a little bit of money in 1949 because none of us had much of an education." Alice didn't like sewing, but she "liked the money" she earned "working on 2275 line of bras" for sixteen years, earning more than $3 an hour when she retired in 1965. Even so, the pressures of making money often made it "a hard place to work." The steady buzz from industrial machines, the pressure to sew fast, and the pressure to meet company deadlines weren't easy. The pieceworker went home tired, yet her persistence and hard work reaped big dividends. She used her wages to help build a home, supplement her husband's wages, and take the couple on nice vacations.

While family values—saving money and a strong work ethic—guided Dorothy Waters's eight-year tenure in Ishpeming's factory, so did humor and fun. She played on the "Gossard Girlies," a company-sponsored baseball team. During the holidays she "had a lot of fun" disguised in Santa attire during a Gossard Christmas gathering. When she learned a coworker "hated snakes," she made a rubber snake from material remnants, tied a string around the snake, and discretely hid it among her coworker's bundles. Soon a terrifying scream pierced Dorothy's work area.

Of course, she didn't mind being on the receiving end of a joke or prank. Decades later, Dorothy laughed recalling a special engagement gift from her coworkers. "One of the girls sitting across the row sauntered over to my station and said, 'Let me set this down for you now that you're engaged.'" Dorothy unwrapped her gift: tiny underpants made from fine rubber material used in ladies' bras. "You will have little ones. That's the little training pants for the little one," said her grinning coworker.

"We were actually a close family," said Gossard Girl Gloria LaFave who joined the Gwinn family three days after she graduated from Gwinn High School. There she joined her mother and a sister, and over her four years the young office worker observed workers "taking care of each other." It began with the factory's manager. Gloria's first job was "packing bras [in] boxes," not a secretarial job for which she had studied in high school. "I much preferred using my experience as a secretary," said the gutsy teenager to Manager Kenneth Strengberg, who agreed to her request. "I had to double-check the adding and all that kind of stuff and keep a book of each person's record of what they had done. How much they accomplished and what was owed them and so forth. It was a lot of detail."

Next, Gloria singled out two cooks for their attentiveness. "Mrs. Samuelson and Mrs. Raymile were extra nice to me. I was very young, and they took me under their wing. I visited with them in the coffee room during breaks." When office duties took Gloria regularly to the shipping department, shippers Bud Tousignant, Roy Peterson, and Roman Farquar welcomed her. "I got to know them very well. They were just *really* nice guys." Though Gloria missed the Gossard family when the factory downsized, she remained grateful to her Gwinn family.

With the economic boom of the 1940s spilling over in the 1950s, both factories increased their workforce. Gwinn, the newest and smaller branch factory, was near capacity at 130 workers, while Ishpeming's factory, which was "believed to be the biggest employer of women north of Milwaukee," operated a million-dollar payroll, reported the *MJ* in March 1950.

The second *MJ* article from March 25, 1950, "Ishpeming's Factory Gets Face-Lifting," reported on the "finishing touches" of Ishpeming's $300,000 renovation. Of note in the extensive remodel was an expansion and renovation "of the largest cafeteria in the Upper Peninsula." Not only was the footprint of the basement cafeteria area expanded by twenty feet, but the kitchen, which was "equipped with a new ventilating system," and pantry area were painted and enlarged. Though not finished, plans were underway to add a recreation room near the cafeteria. The enlarged shipping room on the first floor was equipped with "conveyor belts to the finishing and inspecting lines," reported the paper. Finally, by December 1950, the company would "replace [a number of] stationary line shaft machines." These machines (ten to twelve in a cluster) were connected to and powered by a common metal shaft. The shafts' replacement machines would now have their own individual drives.

Other factory updates included new wiring, additional electrical outlets, fluorescent lighting, an updated phone switchboard with two trunk lines, replacement exterior doors and fire escape stairs, windows, and a new coal bin setup. No doubt, the extensive remodel conveyed a sense of optimism for workers, downtown businesses, and Marquette County.

In April 1950, Manager Harold Peterson reported in the *MJ* that the "Gossard [Company] has planned a special advertising campaign" in response to a prestigious national award from the New York Fashion Academy. The company became the first foundation company to receive a gold medal award for outstanding style achievement from the academy, according to the Marquette newspaper. "Gossard foundation garments hold a place of first importance in the wardrobe of America's best dressed women," stated Emil Alvin Hartman, director of the academy.

Within three years, the company purchased a special "parts cutting machine" to increase production in both factories. The behemoth machine, housed in the basement of Ishpeming's factory, was known as the clicker. The 5,600-pound industrial machine, supported by "a foot thick layer of concrete footing," was capable of cutting through "96 thicknesses of some types of material at one time," reported the *MJ* in July 1953. Elaine Peterson recalled when the clicker was used in the production of a popular bra. "Both plants made the 1830. It was a nice simple bra, nothing fancy. The clicker was used to cut through 72 layers of cotton material." Perhaps the hydraulic machine would have also been used in cutting material for "the Perma-lift range of bras and girdles featuring the 'Magic Insert,' a cleverly shaped support within each bra cup to give permanent lift," one of the brassiere models listed on the history page of the Gossard website.

These were busy times for pieceworkers like Shirley Terzaghi whose first job in 1948 was check girl. Once eighteen, she made "good money on high-powered machines." Even so, "being good" could be viewed as a liability. "One time my supervisor overstepped her bounds. I did good and she kept changing me on different things. Because I did so good, she'd put me on something else. Well, I counted; I had ten different things." Shirley filed a grievance, which "was ironed out right away." What Shirley had fought for in 1949 was now benefiting her.

Even though both U.P. factories were considered stabilizers in their respective communities, the factories saw their employment decline during 1954. Peak employment in Ishpeming's factory, then in its thirty-fourth year, leveled off from 659 in the late 1940s to 500 workers in 1954. A year later, Republic High School graduate Elaine Maki wanted to help her family by taking care of herself. At first, Gossard Girl Elaine walked to Sarepta Rest Home where Oliver Heikkila picked up some Gossard Girls and brought them to the factory. Later she shortened her twenty-one–mile commute by renting a room at Mrs. Johnson's, a ten-minute walk to the factory. "I saved my wages because I was planning to get married."

"Everything I did was interesting," Elaine said referring to four areas (machine operator, boxing, inspector, and office worker) she worked in her brief tenure. As office worker, Elaine witnessed the camaraderie and helpfulness among her coworkers. "I was young, nervous, and intimidated, but Helen Drake was the nicest person," who helped "me manage the old switchboard." Decades later, a circumspect Elaine mused, "this factory was a valuable resource for women in small communities. Not everyone can go to college."

Employment at the branch factory in Gwinn, now in its seventh year, dropped from 147 to 75 workers, said the *MJ* in July 1954. Even so, to secure a position in one of the two undergarment factories was still valued. Gwinn's Local 286 membership was busy "conducting a campaign for books for the Gwinn library" that was being reorganized, reported the *Ironwood Daily Globe*.

After living away from her hometown of National Mine for three years, Marlene Kautz came back home and searched for employment at "the only place to look for a job in 1955," and the place where many of her friends and her Finnish relatives worked. Carpooling was convenient to Ishpeming except when Marlene finished her piecework before closing; then she walked home three miles. Marlene worked on two-needle binding and zippers, and she enjoyed walking "during the lunch hour" when she browsed Ishpeming's apparel shops such as Goldies, the Style Shop, Gatley's, the Dime Store, JCPenney, or her favorite store, Evelyn's.

Marlene, who regularly made above her rate, left the Gossard factory in 1959 for a key-punching job in Washington, D.C., at the Bureau of Ships for the Navy. When she returned to the area in 1978, two years after Ishpeming's factory closed, she was sad at the change but thankful the factory had provided jobs "for a lot of women" whose incomes were invaluable when miners "were on strike or laid off." And for some, like Marlene, a Gossard position became a jumping-off point to another job.

In 1956, Negaunee High School graduate Judy Green opted "to make money for a year" rather than attend college as her father wished. "It was just a very good job, especially for somebody like me who likes to sew." Judy recalled Gossard's high standards. "They were very particular. The inspectors wanted the binding to be *exactly* where they said it should be. They didn't want the first stitching to show at all from under the binding." Having sewed extensively in high school, Judy was comfortable fixing her industrial machine, since there was only one "maintenance person." Nonetheless, a year later, she left for office work in Negaunee where she would use skills she had trained for in high school.

Even with fewer workers, the undergarment company continued to support the Ishpeming community. For example, Sam Cohodas, local businessman and chairman of Ishpeming's Bell Memorial Hospital Fund, announced receipt of a check for $8,000 from H. W. Gossard Company. The check represented the final payment of the company's "1954 pledge of $16,000 on behalf of its Ishpeming plant," reported Sault St. Marie's newspaper, *The Evening News*, on Friday, June 11, 1954. Not only did the factory provide jobs for women, but the company also invested in the community.

Marjorie Ketola, Gossard Girl

In 1941, a teenage Marjorie Ketola and her girlfriends talked their way into Gossard employment with the promise they were fast at sewing and not nonstop talkers, the latter a bit of a fib. But the hiring began what would be almost thirty years on the assembly line at the best-paying job in Ishpeming.

Some pieceworkers worked in different assembly departments (i.e., seaming, binding, zippers) during their tenure. Not Margie. Whether working on bras or corsets, she remained on zigzag ends. Zigzaggers, as many in the department would call themselves, enclosed the ends of bras with zigzag stitching. Zigzaggers assigned to "the great big corsets" reinforced zippers with zigzag stitching. "Everybody hated them [the bigger corsets] because they were heavy, large, and difficult to manage," said five-foot Margie. Nonetheless, Margie could not escape such tasks.

Margie was considered very fast. What accounted for her ability to make $30–$40 a day? What special shortcuts or tricks did she rely on to earn this reputation? "No tricks," she said, "just work, go fast, and no talking." The latter, she admitted, "was very hard for me." Yes, Margie loved to talk, but her family's strong work ethic was more important. She'd work fast to exceed the minimum piece rate and confine talking to morning and lunch breaks.

Like many young women, Margie left the factory when she married "a local lad" who had returned from military service in World War II. The young couple moved to Chicago in 1946 for his work, but Margie returned to Ishpeming in 1950: unemployed, divorced, and pregnant with her second child. The difficult situation was made less onerous because the family of three would live with her parents until she remarried.

In 1953, Agnes Helstein, Gossard Girl and president of the local ILGWU, recruited Margie to return to the undergarment factory. It wasn't an easy sell, Margie recalled. Her second husband made good money, and parenting three children (two sons and a daughter) occupied much of her time. Nonetheless, a reluctant Margie listened to Agnes's pleas as they stood near Ishpeming's downtown JCPenney store. The president of Local 286 was persistent. "Marjorie, we have so much work. Why don't you come back? Just go sign up in the office. You come back. We need you on ends. We've got loads of ends," Agnes insisted.

Margie did return to the factory in 1953. The promise of loads of work translated into higher wages. Beyond that, Margie liked the new work hours for pieceworkers (7:00 a.m.—3:00 p.m.), so she could be home when her sons returned from school. Even though her husband had a good-paying job, Margie's income would go a long way to fund the family's wish list. Her daughter wanted to take dance and ballet lessons. Her youngest son, a talented athlete, could play baseball on a local Elks team. Another son wanted to attend college. The family could buy a new car and build a house on Division Street close to her parents. Collectively, these and other items would go a long way toward fulfilling the Ketola's desire "to better ourselves."

Making money and improving one's life motivated Margie to stay at the factory until it closed in 1976. And because she lived close to the factory, she saved on gas and lunch purchases, which helped reduce her weekly expenses. But there were times when living close to the factory wasn't a benefit. Blizzards are not unusual in Michigan's Upper Peninsula, especially in Ishpeming, the birthplace of organized skiing in the United States and the site of the current U.S. Ski and Snowboard Hall of Fame and Museum.

One day the intensity of a storm brought the town to a standstill. Whiteout conditions forced schools and many businesses to close, but not the Gossard factory. Margie received a pressing phone call from head floor lady Ida Santamore. Her voice animated and speaking rapidly, Ida said, "Marjorie, I know you live close by. You just live down the street here. We gotta get those bundles out. You gotta come. You come or I'm going to come and get you." Margie donned her coat, boots, hat, gloves, and scarf and began walking down the middle of the street, but whiteout conditions were so intense, she became disoriented. She didn't know which direction to walk. Frozen in place, she recognized two people walking down the street: "policeman Ernie DeCaire and his little Italian wife, Carmen." With Gossard Girl Carmen in front of Ernie and Margie clinging to the policeman's big belt, the threesome forged a path to the undergarment factory. Whiteout conditions subsided momentarily, long enough for Margie to orient herself. "I looked once, and we were over by the Royal Bar," said Margie. Whiteout conditions resumed, and Ernie knew they were within two blocks of the factory. Years later, Margie remained grateful for Ernie's help to plow through the seemingly impassable streets. "There was so much snow, the plows couldn't keep the streets or sidewalks clean. I *never* would have got to work that day if he hadn't helped me."

Margie enjoyed working at the undergarment plant not just because she had economic power, but also because "the comradeship was beautiful." She had developed important friendships over the course of her employment, spanning almost thirty years. The plant's closure would have a devastating effect on local businesses and many Gossard Girls' families. But the plant's closure would not sever friendships between workers. "Everybody took care of everybody else. Oh, they had their tiffs once in a while, but they took care of everybody," Margie said.

After Ishpeming's factory closed in December 1976, some workers hatched a plan to form what Margie referred to as the Gossard Club (also known as Golden Age Club). One hundred Gossard Girls became members. Initially members met at St. John the Evangelist Church. It was a tight squeeze fitting one hundred members, Margie recalled. "You had to get there early or else."

In the absence of today's digital technology, a phone tree was used to inform members about club meetings and activities in the 1970s, 1980s, and 1990s. Margie was responsible for contacting fifteen members. Union benefits came with membership in the club, according to Margie. "We got money from the union ($500–$600) in the beginning for a Christmas party." Years later when membership dwindled, the club would receive $200 for its last Christmas party. Margie, who "wasn't really 100 percent union," was touched by the ILGWU's holiday generosity. When the factory unionized in 1949, the Gossard Company scaled back on some employee perks (i.e., picnics, parties), and so the union's yearly contribution for former members, most on fixed incomes, was deeply appreciated.

Margie was conflicted about the benefits of a union shop. Even today, she wonders if the undergarment factory would have remained open if it had not unionized in 1949. She was pleased workers received more money as a result of efforts by the ILGWU, but there were consequences. Broadly speaking, she observed, "they [H. W. Gossard Company] weren't so kind as they were before because they had to pay out a lot more." Gone were the free midday meals, company-sponsored picnics, and other benefits. A circumspect Margie, who had lived in Chicago (1947–50) during the strike, was candid with coworkers on the union issue. "A lot of the girls kind of thought I wasn't right because I wasn't 100 percent union." But for the former zigzagger, exploring the merits and qualities of a union shop wasn't a black or white issue, but rather a gray one.

Rita Corradina, Gossard Girl

When Rita Roberts graduated from Saint Paul High School in 1956, she did not see herself working at the Gossard factory, even though it had been a mainstay of the local economy for thirty-six years. Aside from the 1949 strike when the factory lay idle for four months, the plant was one of the leading economic engines in the community. And by her own admission, Rita "couldn't thread a needle." Much of her high school curriculum had prepared the teenager for office work, not for work on industrial sewing machines. The adventuresome Rita set her sights on work as a telephone operator in Detroit, Michigan, close to relatives. Her parents, Carmen and Jack, may have been relieved their daughter would be close to family, but what her parents really hoped was their daughter would become a teacher.

Within six months of her graduation, Rita returned to Negaunee. She was homesick. The small-town girl missed her Upper Peninsula family and friends. Rita returned to Negaunee "around Christmas time 1956" and set about pursuing her parents' dream. In spring 1957, she had earned a coveted four-year scholarship at Northern Michigan College. However, before the end of her first semester, Rita would see a future in office work, not education. "I seemed to prefer office work. That seemed to be my forte rather than going in the classroom," Rita said. No amount of persuasion from her "heartsick" mother would persuade Rita to stay in college. Instead, she became a Gossard office girl in 1958.

"Ceil Conte was at the window when people would come in. She knew my parents, so that could have helped me get the job." Even if her parents had advocated on her behalf, it was the excellent training Rita received at Saint Paul's in shorthand, bookkeeping, and typing that caught the attention of the factory's manager and office personnel. "They felt I was very qualified," said Rita.

She enjoyed her job in no small measure because of her coworkers. Most of the women were much older than Rita, but she didn't mind the age difference. Instead she viewed the age gap as a benefit because Mildred Andrews and Ethel Lawer, "took me under their wings." It was a pleasant workplace environment, one in which "everyone got along very, very well." Additionally, it wasn't just women who contributed to Rita's great work environment. The factory's manager, Kenneth "Chick" Strengberg, made Rita "feel very comfortable." In doing so, Rita said, the factory's manager came across "as an employee, not one's boss."

Rita felt badly she had to leave three years into her dream job when her husband accepted a job in Green Bay, Wisconsin. She sincerely enjoyed her workplace environment, the exceptional camaraderie with her coworkers (including the manager), and the work hours (7:00 a.m.—3:00 p.m.), which were perfect. Even though the young bride left the area, she would stay connected to the factory through coworker Mildred. In fact, Rita remained close to Mildred and her husband until their deaths many years later.

The former office worker gave 100 percent to her job. That's how she was raised in the late 1940s and 1950s. Perhaps this is what her coworkers (Mildred, Ethel, Ceil, Helen) recognized. And perhaps it was one reason Manager Strengberg thanked Rita frequently "for doing a good job," even in those unassigned duties like modeling new bras.

Just as pieceworkers had a daily routine, so did Rita. Her workday began at 7:00 a.m. Rita left the office daily at 9:00 a.m. to pick up the company's mail. She always walked to the post office, a mere four hundred feet from the undergarment factory. She quickly "got to know all of the postal workers." Once Rita returned, opened the mail, and passed it around to the appropriate offices, Mildred and Rita worked together "to get out the undergarment orders."

After dropping off the orders, the twosome was often involved in timing one of the pieceworkers. Armed with a stopwatch, the young office worker sat next to machine operators selected by one's department head. Once the machine operator removed the bundle from her work box, Rita prepared to time the worker. "A machine operator would take a bundle out and either put on the back where your bra snaps went, or a strap or something like adding on a cup here, and we would watch her do this with a little stopwatch." When the machine operator finished her bundle, Rita and Mildred noted the time it took the operator to complete the bundle. Whether Rita timed machine operators on hooks and eyes, seaming, binding, or other tasks, "Mildred or someone else" computed the time into a value, in other words, how much an operator would earn for each completed piece.

When discussing the Gossard factory fifty years later, Rita was still impressed with the complexity and organization of the undergarment company. "Oh yes. Many people, many hands were involved in the project of putting a garment together."

The young office worker's duties often took her into different areas of the four-story factory where she observed "each person doing something different." Consequently, Rita logged more steps in Ishpeming's factory than pieceworkers, the bulk of the factory's workers. She never used the plant's one elevator as it was reserved for male workers who transported unfinished and finished garments from floor to floor. No, Rita used the factory's wide stairs. During her three years at the Gossard, she "walked up and down the stairs frequently during the day," but she avoided them "around quarter to three or three o'clock when the bell rang," signaling the end of the workday for pieceworkers. "You took your life in your hands when you punched out. It was *vroom* like a herd of turtles," Rita chuckled recalling the daily image of the four hundred Gossard Girls descending two flights of stairs, measuring 6½ feet x 11 inches, all at the same time. After four decades of daily use, thousands and thousands of shoes had sanded the wooden stairs, whose edges "got kind of rounded," she said.

Once traffic on the stairs emptied, Rita retrieved pieceworkers' time-cards from locked boxes on the second and third floor. Each timecard (also called a sticky) contained information for Helen Drake, the office bookkeeper who "kept track of workers' hours." Other afternoon duties included meeting with Manager Strengberg, who dictated letters and memos to Rita. She returned to the post office to mail these letters and other company correspondence. Designs for bras changed frequently, and so on occasion Rita also modeled a sample bra "to check how they were made or if the sample bra required changes."

Rita lived at home before she married in the early 1960s, which wasn't unusual for young single girls. Living at home was a way to extend one's wages, especially if one did not have to pay room and board. However, Rita did pay room and board: ten dollars a week. "That was the understanding, if I lived at home," Rita recalled. She "resented paying room and board to her parents." When she was married, her parents gave their daughter a check. "Here's the money you griped about every time you got paid," said her parents. They never used her room and board payments. As she reflected on this, Rita said her parents gave her something else besides the check: an important life lesson for the bride and future mother of two children. "Pay your own way when you are out on your own."

After paying room and board, Rita often used her weekly wages on discretionary items, such as clothing, entertainment, bowling, and travel. She owned a "hand-me-down" Ford from an uncle who worked for the Ford Company, which she and some friends used to visit Rita's relatives in Dearborn, Michigan, and Madison, Wisconsin. "I always drove. I always liked to drive." When she wasn't traveling for pleasure, Rita took four Gossard Girls to the undergarment factory. For this daily taxi service, each passenger paid Rita one dollar per week.

Rita's duties as a timer helped broaden her understanding of production costs for undergarments. In the early 1960s, there were many different styles of bras, including those made with delicate lace or wire. Looking back, she said, "It wasn't fair to workers on piece work if putting a wire in was going to take longer than it would be to sew on the back of a bra strap or something. So, I remember going up and trying to figure that out."

Rita earned an hourly wage; pieceworkers' wages were based on completed units. The faster they worked, the more they made. Rita's aunt, a machine operator, understood this. "Auntie Mae Roberts was very focused on her work. She wouldn't move her head, nor would she talk to me if I was in the area."

The former office worker reflected on the factory's legacy in Ishpeming. "It did so well with the economy in Ishpeming. We were a flourishing town in our time. We were booming." Rita would have continued at the factory had her husband not accepted an out-of-state job. Decades later, however, her hometown had yet to recover. "It was just like the company took the heart out of Ishpeming," when it shut the factory's doors in December 1976.

The most enduring legacy, however, was its impact on "the very hard workers," who not only played a major role in the town's economy, but also helped pave the way for today's young female professionals. "The Gossard Girls just kind of plateaued for the next working women. At one time, there weren't working women. I think the Gossard Girls were the starters of it. I think that was super."

CHAPTER 6
....

Changes Force Gwinn Closure

INITIALLY, BRA MAKERS IN the 1960s continued to produce the previous decade's "pointy-cupped bras with low-backs, low fronts or no straps," according to the authors of *Uplift*. Within a few years, "women's disdain for bras-as-usual" pushed those in the industry to create new designs, where bras appeared "less conspicuous and more flexible." The shifting attitude about women's undergarments coincided with a rise in political activity by women activists advocating for equal rights, equal opportunities, and entry to careers "traditionally reserved for men." Within seven years, "56.8 % of the roughly 27 million women in the labor force worked in white-collar jobs. Across all categories of age and marital status, one-third of American women engaged in paid work." Of note during this decade was women's access to birth control pills, which, among other things, gave them more control over their bodies. As a consequence of these and other factors, in 1967 advisors to the undergarment industry saw a trend toward the "no-bra no-girdle looks, a major shift . . . toward comfort and freedom in undergarments."

How did those in the industry, whose existence depended on women wearing bras and corsets, respond? According to the authors of *Uplift*, many in the industry turned to spandex, a stretchy fiber that could be "incorporated into their garments." In the 1950s, lace was "limited to occasional trim on the styles of a few manufacturers," but during the 1960s, spandex, if used in lace, "expanded the possibilities." Pointed bra-cups gave way to more rounded cups. The new bra designs "became seamlessly smooth to fit unobtrusively under sweaters, double-knit dresses, and even T-shirts. Molded cups held their shapes, and by implication the wearer's shape, through machine laundering cycles. Heat-shapable 'thermoplastic' polyester and nylon, along with spandex, became the mainstay of bra making." Bra makers reevaluated other features in bra construction: elastic, shoulder straps, buckles, and hooks to produce less bulky bras. "Girdles slipped into oblivion" in the late 1960s, and panty hose replaced girdles. Bright colors and kaleidoscopic prints in lightweight coordinated bras and panty girdles were popular, while "printed designs accounted for just 5% of coordinated lingerie sales, against 29% for brown-beige tones and blues," reported the authors.

Product design and development in the 1960s became costlier. For example, Warner "reportedly spent almost $1 million to develop a stretch strap." Companies responded to these and other factors differently. Some merged to survive. In 1962, a national trend in lingerie coordinates motivated Gossard to merge with Artemis, a lingerie firm, and then the Gossard Company "linked up with Wayne Knitting Mills in 1967 to become Wayne Gossard."

Some in the undergarment industry began recognizing and listening to new customer groups: preteens and black Americans. Bestform, Formfit, and Gossard advertised in *Ebony*, using "dark-skinned models routinely" in photos. Calls by some women to go braless did not gain traction, according to the authors of *Uplift*. Despite the myriad of fashion, political, and social changes of the 1960s, one thing did not change: "the vast majority of U.S. female population continued to wear bras."

Meanwhile, Gossard workers in Marquette County's two factories remained vital economic engines in their communities. Retired Air Force bomb navigator technician Bob Sihtala considered himself very fortunate to secure a job as a sewing machine mechanic in Ishpeming's undergarment plant. "You couldn't buy a job around here in 1961. Lots of unemployment and guys standing in line to get jobs. Jobs were *very, very* scarce," said the Ishpeming native.

Bill Lehmann, who taught economics in Ishpeming's high school in the sixties, also worked as a timer in the Gossard plants. "I did time studies on the process to determine how much they [pieceworkers] got paid." Timings were done with "three stop watches on the same lever and fixed to a clipboard." Bill submitted results from his time studies to supervisor Roland (unknown last name), who determined how much pieceworkers would be paid.

Joan Nelson, of Ishpeming, was also pleased to find work at the same factory in 1961, because she wanted to purchase new furniture for her home. To make well above the minimum rate on model no. 1830, she would hold the scissors by the tip *not* by the handle, a technique that enabled her to "snip the threads quickly," especially when sewing red-tagged bundles. In the 1960s Gossard Girls remained significant economic drivers, according to Joan. "Ninety percent of Gossard Girls went to town for lunch and to buy things. They returned to work with their purchases."

During her childhood in New Swanzy (a suburb of Gwinn), Virginia Ayotte gained experience in math and accounting, a talent that would be used in Gwinn's plant. The oldest of three siblings, Virginia helped her father who worked in the lumber industry. "He hired men to peel pulp. I was the little bookkeeper keeping track of pulp and each guy that got paid." How her immigrant parents managed to send their daughter to business college in Green Bay, Wisconsin, mystifies her even today. "I will never forget. At that time people didn't go to college like they do now. Green Bay was *far*. We had to take Train 400 out of Little Lake. That was *some trip*." She returned to the family home in 1948 and "fell into an office job" at Gwinn's plant, when Betty Thurston "gave notice."

For the next fourteen years she enjoyed her work: figuring out payroll deductions for bonds and for social security; verifying worker's hours and wages; informing the Gossard office in Chicago the amount of payroll to be deposited in Gwinn State Savings Bank; and working with a "nice boss who was never overbearing." Mindful of the factory's impact, Virginia said, "It was a lifesaving job for some women like my mother [Pierina]. Just being able to save a little bit to buy bonds. Boy, that makes you feel pretty good. You are not just a housewife. You've got some talents. You were a person."

On September 15, 1961, a *Mining Journal* (*MJ*) article, "Gossard Employees Awarded Citation by U.S. Treasury," reported on Gossard workers from Ishpeming's factory who received special recognition for their "consistently high participation in series E bonds." More than 50 percent of four hundred wage and salaried workers had been investing in the weekly payroll savings plan. While the national sales director of the U.S. Savings Bond Division acknowledged workers' "patriotic service," he also noted several advantages: "peace-of-mind, guaranteed rates, and protection against lost, mutilated or destroyed bonds." Michigan's state director of U.S. savings bonds hoped other Upper Peninsula businesses might emulate what the Gossard Company and its women-dominant workers had achieved.

More than a year later, the *MJ* reported on Ishpeming's "flourishing" factory. While the number of workers had dipped slightly from 400 to 389, the factory had for at least several months been "running at top capacity six days a week."

Moreover, for more than four decades, Ishpeming's factory remained the city's largest industry outside of mining. Reporter James Trethewey noted, Gossard workers' payroll generated $833,309 annually for the city's roughly nine thousand citizens. In similar fashion, the workforce in Gwinn's plant dipped to seventy-three workers in 1962. Even so, Ishpeming's manager Kenneth Strengberg extolled employee loyalty, their public spirit, and the factory's prodigious output in 1961: "272,808 combination garments and 1,001,668 bras."

Perhaps Trethewey's optimism in the face of declining workforces might be viewed within a wider historical context. Ishpeming's factory, which opened in 1920, distinguished itself among the company's ten Midwest plants, never closing during economic downturns or wars. Since the end of World War II, five plants had closed, but not the two way-up-north factories (Ishpeming and Gwinn), which were considered important assets within Marquette County. Gossard Girls' economic power kept their rural towns going.

George Romney, president and chairman of American Motors, also sensed the importance of the Gossard plants to local economies. In 1962, the businessman and Republican gubernatorial candidate campaigned at the Ishpeming plant. He may not have known about the history of the Gossard or the historic four-month strike by Gossard Girls in 1949, but his presence at the plant in 1962 signaled the significance of the plant in the Upper Peninsula (U.P.) and to the state of Michigan.

Presumably Ishpeming's manager escorted Romney around the plant. Elaine Peterson's photo from the *Milwaukee Journal* did not reveal this detail. The photo, however, did show Romney on the second-floor assembly line talking with pieceworkers. The businessman would leave with an increased awareness of the economic power generated by hundreds of rural women workers. Politics aside, a visit from a gubernatorial candidate to the U.P.'s largest women-dominated factory was a point of pride for many workers and local leaders.

Most workers took vacation during the annual two-week summer inventory, but not zigzag pieceworker Genevieve Valenti, whose wages helped her family of eleven. "I learned a lot. It was nice. We had inventory of everything." It was also time away from an industrial machine that required frequent repairs. "My machine hardly ever made ten stitches to the inch. It was impossible to make the daily minimum rate of $8 for zig zag." Only when Genevieve was temporarily transferred to feather-stitching—a decorative stitch used to join two pieces of fabric—could she make above the rate for this assembly step: $13–$15 per day. When the regular featherstitch operator returned from vacation, an easygoing Genevieve returned to her temperamental machine. More than anything, the fun-loving Genevieve enjoyed the workplace camaraderie. She liked telling jokes, and she didn't mind being the recipient of funny pranks. One day her supervisor said, "There's a lady at the door waiting for it." Genevieve believed her supervisor and began working faster. "There wasn't a lady at the door waiting, but I thought there was," said Genevieve with a laugh.

Ishpeming's factory was home to the Gossard Outlet Store, a popular retail business selling discontinued Gossard undergarments (bras, girdles, lingerie) and discontinued sewing notions (fabric, lace, thread, elastic). In the mid-1960s, Trudy Gray's mother, who did not work at the factory, upholstered her son's car with Gossard material. "My mother was always very creative. She went to Sidewalk Days in Ishpeming. She went by the Gossard and came home with a bolt of girdle material. It was durable, stretchable, and cheap. You could stretch it any way you wanted it." After dying the white girdle material, brother, sister, and mother used heavy cording to keep the repurposed material snug around the car seats. "It looked quite professional, and it wore like iron," Trudy said with a chuckle.

Meanwhile, Superintendent Clifford Perry, who had been transferred from Ishpeming to Gwinn in 1950, oversaw production of finished undergarments trucked to Chicago and then shipped to Gossard warehouses in New York, Atlanta, Dallas, and San Francisco.

The second time Gossard Girl Judy Green worked in Gwinn's factory it was an economic necessity. Her husband had been laid off from his construction job. When he did work, it might be for a few days, and then he would be laid off again. This uncertainty weighed heavily on Judy who informed her husband of her work plans. Neither her husband nor her father approved. Judy respected both men's "old country thinking"; a husband not the wife should provide for the family. Under normal circumstances Judy might agree; however, with two children, "things being too uncertain," and her husband's "unemployment too low to make ends meet," she "had to go back to work." Judy worked until Gwinn's factory closed, declining an offer to transfer to Ishpeming's factory. Absent a pressing economic reason, "the perfectionist sewer" saw no benefit in traveling sixty miles roundtrip to the remaining factory.

Wife and mother Alice Vallier also worked at the Gwinn factory in its final years of operation. With two children in middle school and a third child in high school, the forty-year-old sought part-time employment. "It was something to do," said Alice, and "my children always needed something for school, such as a prom dress or something special. . . . We left the house at the same time each day. I walked, I worked part time only, and I was always home when the children came home from school."

A pieceworker, Alice worked in the seaming, zipper, and boning departments where she "never made fabulous money. Some girls could whip up the garments in no time." Not Alice who remarked, "I was too fussy." Management, she continued, also felt she was too fussy. Decades later, she could enumerate Gossard's standards as if it were yesterday. "You were supposed to ease the material, not pull the material. You were supposed to feed the material correctly, so there would be no seams hanging over. You weren't supposed to use scissors for trimming the fabric. Scissors were only to be used to cut your thread. The pieces were cut to the right size and you had to feed the material through the machine just right. Inspectors made sure there were so many stitches per inch (something like six stitches per inch), and if not, you had to rip out the seam. When you redid the stitches, they had to follow in the same line."

When Gwinn's factory closed in 1964 (the years of operation, 1947–64, are written on a list of Gwinn workers provided by Madeleine DelBello), Alice said, "I remember helping lower the heavy metal H. W. Gossard Company sign. It was a big, big metal sign on the building facing the boulevard. I got a rug burn from helping lower the sign off the wall." Though her tenure was brief, Alice fondly remembered Christmas potluck parties and free lunches (usually sandwiches) made by Mrs. Selina Sarasin, the cook who lived one block from the factory.

At the time of the Gwinn factory closure, many of its workers had the option of working in Ishpeming's plant, though few chose to transfer there. Many of Gwinn's Gossard Girls had walked or carpooled from neighboring villages, short distances compared with the thirty to forty miles to Ishpeming's factory.

Paulette Nardi, Gossard Girl

Paulette Denofre grew up in Ishpeming, attended St. John's grade school, and graduated from Ishpeming High School. She remembered her childhood years with great fondness. It was a childhood she wished many of today's children might enjoy. "I loved it. We had all four seasons, and of course when I was growing up, it was nothing to go out and cut our own Christmas trees. They weren't artificial trees back then." The former Gossard pieceworker smiled as she reflected on the family's "month-long holiday celebration [that] brought together everyone for Christmas." Everyone included visits with aunts, uncles, friends, grandparents, and neighbors. Winter "was most fulfilling," said Paulette who "skated, played hockey with boys, played in the snow drifts, and shacked cars. I did it all." She thoroughly enjoyed the Upper Peninsula's five to six months of white.

Unlike her mother, Barbara Kelly, who installed 3–3½ foot metal bones in corsets at Ishpeming's factory right after high school in 1943, Paulette was not interested in working at the Gossard or any other place after her high school graduation in 1964. She was, however, interested in addressing persistent health issues. "I put off surgery until I couldn't any longer. I was turning eighteen and going to be off my father's insurance. I figured I am just going to lie around home and milk this for all I had." And so the teenager did just that. But her father had other plans.

Without his daughter's knowledge or approval, he "put her name into the Gossard." It wasn't until Paulette received an unexpected phone call from her family's neighbor, Gossard worker Cecilia "Ceil" Conte, that Paulette knew "she was stuck." Ceil informed Paulette her interview would be postponed until the following year after her surgery.

In May 1965, Paulette went to the unemployment office in Ishpeming to complete a required test for Gossard applicants. Under the supervision of an unemployment office person, each applicant received a cloth bag of wooden shapes (circles, triangles, squares, etc.) and a covered board. Apparently, the speed with which Paulette placed the wooden shapes in their corresponding holes was excellent because she went right "from the test to the factory." Paulette was amazed since she had "flunked sewing in school," but Paulette's father was "tickled pink" and perhaps pleased he "had pull."

Despite Paulette's initial disapproval with her father's intrusive action, she absolutely loved her job. Her first piecework job was basting. She described this simple but important first step in bra construction: "When a bundle was brought to me (there were about thirty of us doing the same job), and I took a piece of nylon tricot, which would have been the fabric back then, and attached it to a home, the bottom of the cup. And I was the first person to do it. The stitch of course had to be six to eight stitches to an inch back then. In other words, if you had say twenty stitches to an inch, you'd have a puckered effect, and there is no way it would pass inspection. So, you had a bigger stitch so that the fabric—nylon tricot—wouldn't pucker."

By her own admission, Paulette was not a seamstress, yet she excelled at the Gossard, whether she worked in basting, cup-to-band, or zigzag applique work. The piecework environment at the Gossard benefited pieceworkers like Paulette who wanted to "set the pedal to the metal" to maximize their pay. "We worked for units. There was a card [coupon] that was attached to your bundle, and all your units were on there. In other words, there was 3490 basting stitch; 350 units is what you'd get. So when you completed your forty-eight pieces, you would clip that 350 unit off, and you'd attach it, lick it and attach it to your sheet of paper."

According to Paulette, in the early 1960s, the minimum pay for a Gossard Girl working as a baster was $1.10 per hour or $7.70 per day. Paulette's "need for speed" and her aptitude "to figure out the science of things" propelled her well beyond the daily rate for units completed. She made $200 per week, a hefty increase over the minimum weekly rate of $38.50, and much more than her husband who worked at the A & P store in Ishpeming.

Not all basters on the second floor shared Paulette's appetite for speed. In fact, Paulette noted, "I had a lot of people that did not like me because I went very fast. I mean I had it down pat. They went so far as to put me on my own little island. I had to sit by myself because I had so many ladies angry at me." Some basters refused to talk to Paulette, which further isolated her, but she was not bothered by their silence. She loved working at the Gossard.

Still others believed that Paulette's swiftness would jeopardize their ability to make their rate. According to Paulette, "They [the basters] claimed that the faster I went, they [Gossard management] would cut the units down." Cutting units down suggested that the rate of pay for each unit could be reduced. Paulette did not agree, "There is only a few of us that can do this. Go this speed. They can see when you hand in your sheet at the end of the day and I hand in mine, the majority of the ladies were not going to cut the units. They are going to understand that there's two or three of us that can really, you know, go fast and put them together a little faster. Call it nervous energy; call it whatever." Others took their "bellyaching" directly to a union representative and to the basting instructor. Paulette remembered on occasion Borghild Thexton, her instructor, "would come over and pretend she was giving me hell in plain English. She wasn't. She just said, 'I gotta make out [that] I am reprimanding you.'" This reprimand did not bother Paulette, who simply remarked, "I said that's fine." More than anything, Paulette loved her job because she could work at her own pace, a very fast pace.

As a baster, Paulette also worked on the third floor where corsets were assembled. It was here that she may have been challenged the most, not because of the difficulty of corset work, but because the work environment was ill-suited for someone her height. Height mattered for pieceworkers engaged in the assembly of large undergarments like corsets. These third-floor worktables were higher than those on the second floor, a significant issue for Paulette, who stood four feet, ten inches tall. "The very, very high tables may have almost come to bust level, and I could not navigate that big piece of undergarment. So back downstairs I went."

Paulette fondly recalled another challenging job on the assembly line for bras where delicate materials and a narrow zigzag stitch threatened the Gossard Girl's speed, as well as the safety of her hands. "It was the first time we put attached lace, little flowers, to the netting. And you needed a zigzag stitch. That was really enjoyable because when you went too close, you had two fingers poked at all times. You worked with bandages until you realized what the distance was between the needle going back and forth and back and forth." Figuring out the most efficient technique, or "getting it [zigzag applique] down to a science," was Paulette's goal. Once she "put the needle in the hole," she did not stop her machine until the small lace flowers and netting were completely attached to the bra. Paulette enjoyed figuring out the most efficient techniques, she enjoyed working at her own pace, and of course she loved speed.

A reliable sewing machine was the lifeblood of Gossard Girls involved in piecework, and so maintenance-free machines were highly valued. One might think about the relationship between a pieceworker and her machine as highly personal. Paulette characterized this relationship, saying, "if you respected your machine, that machine performed for you. Hmmm. That was my baby, my machine." This bond tended to remain strong as long as a pieceworker oiled her sewing machine and kept her machine's foot in proper alignment. Paulette oiled her "baby," a Singer machine, daily at 9:30 a.m. "You had to be very careful how much oil you put in there, because when you were working with such delicate fabric, you didn't want oil blowing all over the place." At one point, Paulette's close relationship with her Singer was almost severed, when "the second-floor boss lady" denied Paulette's initial request to keep her trouble-free machine. When Paulette was unable "to break in" the new machine—a Union Pacific—she was reunited "with her baby."

The plant's location in downtown Ishpeming benefited local businesses enormously, Paulette said forcefully. Gossard Girls brought "a lot of life to the town because every one of these women purchased from down-town." During her years of employment (1965–76), Paulette typically ate lunch—a hot dog—at her favorite lunch place, Woolworths. And like many other Gossard Girls, she spent the remainder of her lunch break shopping in many downtown businesses such as JCPenny, Montgomery Wards, Sears, J.J. Newberry, and the Style Shop. Paulette purchased a car from one of the five car dealerships. The close proximity of department stores, grocery stores, women's specialty dress shops, shoe stores, and car dealerships was ideal until the factory closed in 1976 and she would witness "businesses close one by one by one."

Despite the closure, a resolute Paulette holds fond memories of her eleven years. "I don't think I can say an ill thing about this place, what-soever. Nothing. I enjoyed it. I enjoyed a lot of the people I worked with, even though I was on my own little island. I never had trouble sleeping knowing I had to get up the next morning because I loved what I did. I made money at it. I was good at it. It just piqued my interest. And I don't care what Ida [the production manager] may have wanted me to do, I was willing to try it. Plus my husband worked next door at the A & P store. We had virtually the same hours. We were both off on the weekends. I mean what more could you ask for?"

The factory, she observed, was more than a place to earn good wages. "It was one of the best places on earth to work. It was your own little family. You developed friendships. Even to this day I still have friendships that started there. There were girls who weren't quite fast enough. But if I bumped into that person today, that's exactly what we'd talk about today: the Gossard and the good times we had at the Gossard," Paulette said unequivocally.

Anita Lehtinen, Gossard Girl

High school senior, Anita Kestila read a newspaper article about an undergarment factory coming to downtown Gwinn, less than thirty miles from her home in Rock. Employment opportunities in small unincorporated communities like Rock, Perkins, and Princeton were nonexistent for teenage girls and older women. News that a reputable company with its international reach would employ 150–200 female workers was viewed as a huge windfall in 1947 by the Anitas in these small communities.

Like many of her high school peers, Anita applied to the new Gossard plant, but age and inexperience threatened her chances at the new factory. Anita, then seventeen, would not turn eighteen until after she graduated. Looking back, Anita observed, "it must have been the law in 1947." Additionally, her mother had advised Anita against working at the Gossard because the teenager had limited sewing skills. Yet Anita remained hopeful. When she received a card from the Gwinn plant about her starting day, her mother cautioned Anita, "You'll never make it. You may as well stay home." Surely, her mother's well-intentioned comments caused her to question the wisdom of her plan, but Anita's desire to work overshadowed her mother's worries. All Anita knew was that she wanted to try, even knowing "it was hard work." She knew the apprenticeship period would be challenging, but the promise of earning seventy-five cents an hour at her first job was just as important. With perseverance she could "get used to the machine" and position herself to earn more than the minimum rate as a pieceworker. It was worth a try.

Anita persevered not just because she was determined, but because her good friend from Rock would also be a Gossard Girl. The friends would support each other. They did not own a car; nor did they live close to the newly opened plant. Affordable lodging two blocks from the plant was their only option. Anita and her friend rented a room with kitchen privileges, a basement toilet, and a basin for daily washing. Plus, their short commute would be ideal during the town's lengthy season of white.

Although rent included kitchen privileges, Anita and her friend were more excited about the company-sponsored lunches. When the factory opened its doors in 1947, it offered free midday meals for all employees. These substantial meals, according to Anita, were "very good hot lunches," and they were a money saver. "It was good for us because then we didn't have to fix such a big meal when we went back to our rooms." In Anita's case, the money she saved from groceries and from walking to work was budgeted for her wedding in 1949 as she planned to marry Leslie W. Lehtinen.

It wasn't unusual for Gossard Girls to interrupt their employment due to a marriage, pregnancy, divorce, illness, etc. Many who did return to the workforce did so because it was a necessity. Anita left in spring 1950 for the birth of her first child. She intended to parent full time, but pressing economic conditions in her family forced her to return ten years later (1960). "I returned to work when my son was in the first grade because my husband was unemployed. He was working in Olson Motors in Marquette. He would have unemployed winters, and he wasn't working, and his unemployment ran out a week before I returned to the Gossard," Anita said.

Anita did not recall the length of time her husband remained unemployed, but it was long enough that he worked at home doing household cleaning including washing dishes. Later on, her husband worked for the mines. Of course, the mining industry was subject to slowdowns and threats of strikes, but the mines offered year-round employment. Olson Motors did not.

Employment at the Gwinn factory was year-round, at least during Anita's early years (1947–50) in seaming, when she worked forty hours. Ten years later when her family depended on her income, the climate for selling women's undergarments had shifted, and not for the better. Pulling out her pay stubs from this period in the 1960s, Anita reflected on the changed times. Some workers might be temporarily laid off, if only for a few days. Some workers, like Anita, had reduced hours: twenty to thirty hours a week. Gossard standards and making one's rate remained. When pieceworkers failed to make their daily rate, the Gossard still paid these operators. Looking at one of her weekly pay stubs, Anita pointed to the column designated "Make Up." "The Gossard made up the difference because I didn't sew as much as the average, I suppose. I wasn't as fast as they thought I should be." The daily pressure, whether overt or hidden, did not go unnoticed by Anita, who, by her own admission, was not an experienced sewer.

One frustration for pieceworkers, Anita said, was working with timing engineers. When new models were introduced or when there was a dispute over a set rate of an existing model, timers were used. Anita did not approve of or enjoy participating in these timings. She sensed the engineers were more concerned with speed over quality, and the timing process made her nervous. "They had engineers who stood over your shoulders." Anita, who now worked in two-needling binding, ordered timers to move. "If you choose me, you stand over there. You don't stand over my shoulders. I don't want to sew my fingers," she said. The timers did. More than anything, the pieceworker felt the engineers' timing procedure was an example of "doing their work the wrong way."

Despite reduced work hours, despite weeks when she did not make her rate, and despite her displeasure with the timing process, Anita remained at the Gwinn plant until it closed. Her modest income had become a benefit to the family. And her modest severance pay ($250) from the factory's closure was no trivial amount. Anita used the bulk of her severance as a down payment for her son's upcoming dental work ($700). "That's how poor we were. Humble beginnings."

When asked to advise future generations of young women, Anita drew upon a story of her perseverance. "Go for whatever you think you would like to try, and if it doesn't work out, why you can always look for something else. I know when I started at the Gossard, my mother cut out an apron, and she told me to sew the bias tape on the apron around the pockets. She looked at it when I got done and said, 'You'll never make it.' She said, 'You don't even have to go.' But I did go, and I tried it, and I made it. I even went back a second time." Anita's persistence reaped economic, social, and personal dividends. A fine legacy for a Gossard Girl from humble beginnings.

G. Mae Kari, Gossard Girl

"I gotta help out," said Mae of her decision to become a Gossard Girl in 1962 due to her husband's health issues. Helping out was part of her DNA. When she was younger, "my parents had fourteen head of cattle that were milked twice a day and delivered to residents of Palmer and Ishpeming." Fourteen-year-old Mae (she didn't have a driver's license) drove the family car to deliver milk to Palmer residents. She also helped tend and harvest fruits and vegetables from the family garden.

When Mae started at Ishpeming's plant, "there would be rush periods and they would ask her to only take a half hour for lunch." Sometimes, she worked Saturdays due to "the extra workload." Surely, the extra pay helped the Kari family. In 1967, when the mother of five reevaluated her family's situation (her youngest enlisted in the Marine Corps), she reasoned, "I may as well keep going to help." The pieceworker stayed until Ishpeming's factory closed, and her wages "helped with daily living and whatever we needed, mostly groceries."

After her training period, Mae worked in simple seam binding and double-needle seam binding. Later, she was moved to underwire bras, where she would have remained had she not witnessed a serious accident. "There was one incident involving one of the girls close by where I was sitting. She hit the wire and the needle broke and landed in her eye. That made me a nervous wreck. I got so nervous, I ended up going to the hospital." Unable to move past the unfortunate accident, Mae told management, "I have to quit or get off of underwire bras." She moved to double-needle seam binding *without* the wires until her lucrative position was discontinued in the 1970s, and she was reassigned to lace edging.

"I wouldn't say I was good. One time I had to redo an entire bundle," Mae mused reflecting on a time when her instructor failed to provide important directions. "When I started at the Gossard, the instructor said, 'Always remember the seam goes up on all our bras.' Well, on one model it did not. It was first seam down, and they didn't tell me that." Her instructor, not Mae, would fix the mistake.

Whether working in seaming, double-needle seam binding, underwire bra, or lace edge, Mae would visit with seamstresses seated near her. In the beginning, they faced each other on the shaft, and the old timers teased her because she "didn't talk so much." The soft-spoken Mae responded, "Maybe not, but I am a good listener." Sometimes she would listen to them speak about when "it [was] more pleasant years ago to work at the factory." And on occasion, she would say, "Well, I think the atmosphere is pleasant and cheerful."

Fourteen years at the factory benefited the Kari family. Mae observed that it was also a vital resource for single women. "The Gossard factory was a livelihood for many single women for many years, and it was a good clean place to work. We could buy discounted items at the Gossard Outlet Store, which helped my family."

....

CHAPTER 7

Signs of the Time

THE 1970S BROUGHT WITH IT more upheaval within American society and the domestic undergarment industry. An energy crisis, a political scandal known as Watergate, and the environmental movement were but a few of the national issues. The Vietnam War ended as did antiwar demonstrations, but not postwar effects such as "posttraumatic stress syndrome, movies, and public debates." The U.S. Senate passed the Equal Rights Amendment on March 22, 1972, but marches and other lobby efforts failed in their attempts for thirty-seven states to ratify the amendment.

Meanwhile, *Uplift* authors observed, the American undergarment industry "was reactive rather than proactive," while large corporations looked to absorb small companies. Several factors—technology, costs, and cheap labor—contributed to the industry's general upheaval. More "computer-aided design" significantly reduced the time to design new undergarment models. Additional automation "expedited cutting, assembly, and packaging," while some tasks "formerly carried out by the parent company were contracted to outside sources, both domestic and foreign." Containing costs in the domestic piecework environment, where some brassieres might be composed of as many as forty to sixty separate pieces, drove more companies to "into third-world venues." These and other factors led to a declining workforce in the Gossard Company's Midwest factories, including the remaining Gossard factory in Ishpeming.

In 1970, a Middle East oil embargo, rising gas prices, and gas rationing threatened the trucking industry, which was responsible for transporting up to 75 percent of the nation's goods. Ishpeming's Gossard factory, now in its fiftieth year of operation, relied on truckers who delivered raw materials three times a week and who then transported finished garments to the company's Midwest warehouses.

Donald Merrill, a World War II veteran, was a Gossard hand cutter who was pulled into trucking duty during the 1970s national trucking strike.

Initially, Don transported merchandise to the local airport in Negaunee, but "that got to be pretty expensive. So I rented a rental truck. I loaded the truck, and I took off in the afternoon and went to Logansport, Indiana, where they [the undergarment company] stocked everything from the different factories. I worked six days a week for two months. I was paid overtime for everything over thirty-five hours because that was the workweek. So one week I worked sixty or seventy hours."

The national trucking strike coincided with one of the hottest summers in the Midwest and Upper Peninsula. "It was so hot there were breaks in the highway. I'd hit some bumps, and sooner or later a bracket would break on the generator. And there I'd be. The temperature would go up. I'd have to pull off to the side of the road." Don persevered, driving six days a week and never missing a day.

Perhaps the stress of working six days a week during the hottest summer was to blame for an incident in which Don thought someone had stolen his rental truck. An older Don recalled the panic he felt after stopping for coffee to keep him alert. "I go out to continue my trip and no truck. Somebody stole the truck. So what am I going to do now?" The problem wasn't simply a missing rental truck, but one loaded with thousands of dollars of Gossard merchandise. The panic-stricken driver returned to the truck stop café, where he noticed another entrance. "I went out. There's the truck. You talk about a scare," he said with a chuckle.

Six-day workweeks, potholes, truck engine problems, a health scare, and the possibility of a stolen truck weren't the only challenges Don faced. Looming even larger were the union and striking truck drivers. Union workers were supposed to support each other; they did not cross picket lines. Decades later the former union member pondered his decision. "If the strikers knew what I was doing driving a truck, I'd be in trouble. They'd be after me. It was a dangerous job."

Employment continued to decline in the company's domestic factories, and Ishpeming's head mechanic Bob Sihtala occasionally traveled to factories in Logansport and Sullivan, which were "shorthanded to help them prepare machines." He was also sent to factories in Poplar Bluff, Missouri, and Piggott, Arkansas, factories that had been absorbed by Gossard in 1967 into the Wayne Gossard Company.

Management flew Bob to Culver City, California, where he hauled a state-of-the-art bra cup molding machine in a U-Haul to Ishpeming's factory and installed it on the fourth floor. Elaine Peterson, the first woman to run this machine, described it as transformational. "The machine had sixteen cast iron cup molds (for example, A 32, A 34, B 34). The molds were so heavy I had to ask Bob to change them. I placed twelve layers of square-shaped polyester material on the bra molds. Three operators used hot wire coming down from the top of the machine to burn out the polyester bra cups. They treated the hot wire as if were a pair of scissors."

The addition of this high-tech machine, however, did little to dispel what Bob felt were ominous signs of the factory's decline. "I saw the handwriting on the wall. There were a lot of layoffs. Production orders were diminishing. Imports were really hurting the company. And there were talks . . . rumors of closing this plant. In 1974, I had a chance to get a good job with Cleveland-Cliffs, so I thought I better get out while the getting's good. I didn't want to stick around until the last dog was hung here."

On the other hand, in 1972, Ishpeming High School graduate Debra Lucas was thrilled to become a Gossard Girl. She knew little of cheap imports and diminishing orders. Securing a job at the factory was a golden opportunity to pursue her passion: sewing. She learned from the best, her grandmother, she took sewing in high school, and she sewed all of her own clothes.

As a pieceworker working on one-, two-, and three-needle machines, Debra said, "I was fascinated with the different operations that went into making a bra. And each style had different operations."

Debra also worked shipping where Alice Morissette—"a sweet and patient woman"—made Debra feel welcomed. She enjoyed learning new jobs, but not the damage her fingers endured from handling shipping tape and cardboard. Debra said, "The tape went through a thing with a sponge with water. As you pulled it out, it wet the glue and strapped it down on the cardboard boxes. Well, between the cardboard boxes and the paper tape, my fingers would just get raw."

Another sign of the declining times occurred in 1975, when Gossard officials visited Ishpeming's plant. As department head in boxing, Rose Collick was asked to teach workers from a plant in Wisconsin how to fold and box a new bra model. Typically, multiple bras were placed in one cardboard box, but the new model was boxed in a clear plastic bubble, one bra per bubble. As such, each bra required precise packaging to fit in the transparent container, according to Rose. Within a few months, Ishpeming workers stopped manufacturing this bra.

Gossard Girl Pam Nault witnessed the decline when she became a pieceworker in 1975. "There weren't many guys around to fix broken machines, so I had to fix my machine." The twenty-two-year-old seamstress from St. Ignace, Michigan, was interested in "earning her own spending money . . . at the place that produced very, very good quality work." Earning well above the minimum ($2.85 per hour), the newly hired pieceworker quickly acclimated to her industrial environment noting "the noise from sewing machines was peaceful, like white noise."

Meanwhile in August 1976, when Debra Lucas, now a twenty-two-year-old wife, was out on maternity leave, she began hearing "the Gossard factory was winding down. Even when I returned to the factory in October, I kept hearing the buzz. The more I talked to my supervisors, union reps, and other employees, the more I realized it was possible the factory might close. I was newly married with a new baby. To me this was a new job. I had been here not quite four years. My husband worked here, too. We had no idea what we were going to do."

On November 1, 1976, E. J. Tipton, vice president of manufacturing in Chicago, told the *Mining Journal* (*MJ*), "We definitely plan to close the Ishpeming factory effective December 31, 1976." Tipton cited Michigan's "general business climate" and high transportation costs between Ishpeming and Gossard plants in Illinois and Indiana. Other factors included Michigan's higher unemployment and corporate tax rates when compared with Gossard factories in other states. This was a weighty shift on the horizon for Ishpeming's economy, considering "the Gossard Co. is one of Ishpeming's largest employers," stated the *MJ*. Indeed, Ishpeming's economy relied on the economic power generated by Gossard Girls' wages, wages that had recently helped offset a decline in local mining jobs. Once closed, Ishpeming's Gossard workload would shift to four Indiana factories, and the company's four-story Cleveland Avenue building would be sold.

Manager Roy Peterson said the announcement "hit home and it really hurt. The atmosphere here is pretty despondent." He pointed out that until a few years ago, "the annual payroll averaged some $1.5 million." Rumors had been circulating for some time, yet few imagined the city's half-century fixture would actually close on December 31. In the meantime, the holiday season—Thanksgiving, Christmas, and New Year—would be tough for laid-off workers.

Gossard worker Josephine Barry was not surprised. She recalled a three-month period where the plant operated on a reduced production schedule. "First, we stayed home one week. Then we went one week on and one week off, and spent a couple of months working three days, then going home. Then one day they told us the Gossard was going to shut down," said Barry in the *MJ* three days into the new year. The fifty-eight-year-old Gossard Girl knew finding a job would not be easy. "They say after you're 40, they don't want you. Even waitress work. We just don't have the legs for that kind of work anymore." She needed to work until she turned sixty-two to collect her Gossard pension. Medical coverage was another worry; Barry didn't know if she'd be able to keep the company's hospitalization plan.

The closure affected management and nonmanagement workers differently, reported the *MJ*. Some in management, including Manager Peterson, were offered transfers to other Gossard plants, a difficult situation since he had recently returned to his hometown. "I don't want to leave the area again," Peterson was quoted in the November 1 newspaper, and yet he wasn't ready to retire.

Nonmanagement workers—the vast majority of workers—were not offered transfers to Gossard plants in Indiana. Instead, the dominant female work force would receive benefits in the form of severance pay and supplemental unemployment, reported the *MJ* on December 30th. Benefits were based on the term of service each worker had with the union, according to Harold Schwartz, regional director of the International Ladies Garment Workers Union (ILGWU) in 1976. Laid-off workers with a minimum of two years were eligible to receive $20 per week for up to six weeks or $120. Those with more than twenty years of employment were eligible for up to twenty-six weeks of supplemental unemployment or $520.

However, "the rules for administering the benefit fund had changed," Schwartz informed *MJ* reporter John Bauer. Now "eligible workers would receive benefit checks . . . in one lump sum at the end of their benefit period . . . or a maximum of 26 weeks after they completed the application." Prior to October 1976, laid-off workers would have received two checks: supplemental benefits and severance checks. But due to numerous plant closures during the past three years, "the union's benefit fund was at risk, and being depleted faster than it could be replenished," reported the ILGWU representative in the December newspaper. The new application process for receiving benefits would not begin until three months after a union shop closed. For workers, especially sole wage earners, a three-month wait meant another added stress.

Evelyn Corkin, president of Ishpeming's Local 286, summarized the feelings of her coworkers in the November 2 newspaper. "What with all the years this plant has been here and the closing announced just before Christmas and all, everyone is just pretty sad." Corkin, a pieceworker in narrow binding on the third floor, with over twenty-five years, many as a single parent, understood the implications of the plant's closure for workers, their families, and downtown businesses.

Debra Lucas, who knew many workers with twenty, thirty, and forty years of experience, was worried. "These older ladies raised their families with what they made as an income and put them through college and stuff. Now they're elderly, working, and waiting on their pension. How were they going to live? Who would hire a sixty-year-old woman? The

Gossard was their whole life."

To be sure, a cloud of uncertainty permeated Ishpeming's plant. Who would be laid off first? Who would work until the last day? What would happen to workers' health insurance? What would happen to their pensions? How would a Gossard Girl continue to help with a daughter's or son's college expenses? What about utility bills, mortgages, groceries, or a car loan? These and other concerns weighed in the minds of women caught in an "economically-imposed limbo," said *MJ* reporter Brown.

While answers to these and other questions weighed heavily in the minds of workers—many of whom had already been laid off in November—a skeletal crew went to work. They completed remaining production orders and inventoried all equipment and notions. There was equipment to be sold, some to be transferred to Indiana plants, and a small number of machines (thirty) to remain "in Ishpeming as a possible aid in the development of a new sewing business," reported Manager Peterson. The Gossard Outlet Store, which sold "women's sleepwear, undergarments and socks," would remain and possibly move to Marquette to be closer to college students, reported the newspaper.

Knowing their plant would close, four Gossard Girls—Helmi Heinonen, Bertha Tamlin, Elaine Peterson, and Dorothy Windsand—hatched a plan to find another business for the Gossard building, one that would employ women. The foursome journeyed over one hundred miles west to Ironwood, Michigan, to tour Hansen Glove Factory, which had been manufacturing leather gloves since 1947. Regrettably, the manager was not interested in expanding the glove factory, and the four women did not pursue other ideas for the Gossard facility.

Closing the factory took longer than expected, reported the factory's manager in a December 30 *MJ* article. "We were supposed to be finished with shipping all this stuff to New York buyers by the end of this week, but we can't possibly make it. We've still got at least two more semi's left to send out." The skeletal crew of five, down from 170 workers, kept working into 1977.

Jennie Melka was one of the few remaining employees in January 1977. "Oh, there might have been a couple of men maybe someplace around there, but I never saw them. I know I closed the darn doors." Sad as she was to close the doors, Jennie said, "I really enjoyed my twenty-seven years. When you're working in a place, everyone's got problems. You know what I mean. There are some you don't like and all that, but again, you learn to get along, and I enjoyed it. To tell you the truth, it was a terrible thing when the Gossard left because they really put a lot of people to work."

After the factory closed in January 1977, good-paying jobs in Ishpeming and other rural towns were scarce. Debra Lucas found full-time work at Johnny's and part-time at Smitty's, but earnings from both restaurants fell short of her weekly Gossard pay of $200. Without the wages of a pieceworker, she and other former workers spent less. And "Main Street [which] used to be a great place to go," saw many of the "little family businesses close," she recalled.

Factory wages were important, but so were life's intangibles such as "relationship building," according to Debra, who learned this on her first day before she sat at her industrial sewing machine. Supervisor Elaine Peterson introduced Debra to every seaming operator—many twenty to forty-plus years her senior. Debra, who had moved to Ishpeming in her sophomore year, never forgot this simple gesture, a small act that showed "Gossard workers cared about each other." Moreover, workers forged deeper relationships in the factory's basement lunchroom during "all the life's celebrations," such as births, weddings, and birthdays.

When Ishpeming's factory officially closed its doors in January 1977, it ended the economic history of approximately 1500 workers for over a half century. Gossard Girls missed having their own money to spend. So did local business owners and city officials.

JOYCE AND DENNIS EVANS, GOSSARD COUPLE

Joyce and Dennis Evans, wife and husband and former Gossard workers, reflected on the legacy of the H. W. Gossard factory. It "was a good place for women to work, and the hours were good for mothers with children at home," Joyce explained. Furthermore, she observed, "mothers contributed to their families." The pleasure a young single man like Dennis found "working on machines" overshadowed occasional "nerve-wracking" incidents, and "the pay was sufficient for a young single man." These were meaningful legacies for these Ishpeming natives who also agreed that had it not been for the long tenure of the Gossard factory (1920–76), Joyce and Dennis would never have met. "The odds were *zero*," Dennis stated emphatically.

Joyce Kivisto, born 1940, and Dennis Evans, born 1944, did not grow up knowing each other or attend Ishpeming High School at the same time. The Kivisto and Evans families did not live in the same neighborhood; nor did their parents know each other. Joyce's father, Arthur, was a cutter at Ishpeming's plant prior to working in the mines, but neither of Dennis's parents worked in the undergarment factory. It would take more than thirty years and a matchmaker before the two

Gossard employees' paths crossed.

Between high school and their first encounter at the Gossard plant, Joyce and Dennis took different life paths. Joyce remained in Ishpeming, married, and raised a family of five. In 1969, she began working at the undergarment plant. Dennis, four years younger than Joyce, left the Upper Peninsula after high school to work in the field of electronics at Wright-Patterson Air Force Base near Dayton, Ohio. He soon tired of Ohio and returned to Ishpeming, where he worked at Bell Memorial Hospital and OK Auto Parts until 1970 when manager Roy Peterson hired the twenty-six-year-old.

Dennis was not concerned about being a minority, one of the 10–15 percent of men, in the woman-dominated plant. It "didn't really bother me at all," Dennis observed, because "I was hired to work on sewing machines, not socialize." Nor was he concerned about being a single male. In 1970, "most of the women were quite older than me," Dennis chuckled. The percentage of older workers persisted during his four years at the plant.

Like the women workers, Dennis began at 7:00 a.m. and punched in on the time clock. While the bulk of women workers headed up to their industrial sewing machines on the second and third floors, second-floor mechanics like Dennis headed "to a little work area" tucked into "the back of the second floor in the corner," a small space where "tools and parts were kept." He put on his tool pouch, surveyed the repair list posted on the wall, and picked "the first machine to work on it." From this point, Dennis's day was anything but slow. The mechanic never "worried about not having a job to do," not in a work environment that rewarded fast, efficient pieceworkers. Many pieceworkers "pushed their industrial machines to the limit. No doubt about that," he recalled. The rate at which some operators sewed would cause "a lot of those machines to break down," he added.

Dennis understood this environment, and for the most part, he "got along with pretty near everybody." However, there were a few operators, particularly those "earning good money," who occasionally gave him "a headache." Whenever "small things" got in the way of earning money (i.e., stitching not working or threads breaking), Dennis observed, "they wanted their machines fixed *right away*."

Within a short period of time, Dennis became a knowledgeable mechanic, thanks to his supervisor Bob Sihtala. "He was an excellent mechanic. If I ran into problems, I'd check with Bob and he'd help me. I believe after a couple of years, I was pretty good at it."

Joyce said, "He [Dennis] never worked on my machine before anyone else's or anything else like that." Dennis added, "I didn't get very many calls from Joyce because she would try to fix her own machine before she called the mechanic because she knew we had so many things on the board. It had to be something actually physically wrong with the machine before she'd call me." Sometimes, machine problems stemmed from incorrect tension settings. While a number of the pieceworkers "didn't like to change the tension," Joyce felt comfortable adjusting her machine's tension. This strategy enabled her to maximize her daily wages.

Fast and efficient workers like Joyce also knew how important it was to oil one's machine daily. Her husband explained the logic in circulating machine oil first thing each morning. "In the seventies the two-needle machines had oil pumps. There was a big tray underneath the machine where we put the oil. An oil pump would pump it up to the machine and pump it to the various spots on the machine to keep them oiled." Overnight when machines were not being used, "that oil would drain back." Therefore, prior to running one's machine, it was prudent "to put a few squirts of oil in the oil spots on the machine" to get oil recirculating because the industrial machines "would be going so fast they might burn something." In the case of hooks on the 1970s two-needle machines, if an operator failed to oil the machine's two hooks (hooks pick up thread and make stitches), they "could freeze up and stop," at which point, a worker would have had to wait for a mechanic, according to Dennis.

Over his four years, Dennis would learn it wasn't just the machine that needed fixing; it might also be the machine operator. "That's the psychological part," an older Dennis mused. "You had to kind of pamper the woman in a way, too, at the time when you go there. You tried to explain what's happening." For example, in one situation, Dennis was asked to fix a machine with a smoking needle. The mechanical mind of Dennis understood the situation. "Well there were times where the thread on these machines wasn't very thick, and they were sewing so fast the needle would get hot. It would smoke. Well, it wasn't the needle that was smoking; it was the thread. So then, when they stopped and started their machine again, it sizzled through the thread, and it would break the thread." Dennis tried to explain the causes: speed, thread, and fabric type, but the pieceworker was more interested in a solution. The more time it took to finish a bundle, the less money the pieceworker made. Furthermore, the longer it took to finish a bundle, the less profit for the Gossard. Time meant money for everyone. Thinking back on this situation, Dennis said proudly, "So we were spraying the thread with a silicone base spray. That helped somewhat."

A mechanics' repair list directed the sequence of work. "We had a list on the wall. They had to sign and put down their name. We were supposed to go accordingly, supposed to go one, two, three." However, floor ladies often disrupted the sequence, and with good reason, Joyce explained. Floor ladies knew which machines were important for production, "if something was getting backed up." This occasional disruption may not have pleased some pieceworkers, but Joyce knew it was necessary for production deadlines.

Ideas about dating wouldn't surface for Dennis and Joyce until after Joyce was widowed in 1972. And then it would take persistent nudging from a Gossard matchmaker to get them together. Dennis remembered this determined matchmaker and childhood friend of his future wife. "Margie is one of the reasons why Joyce and I got together. She was pushing me a lot." Marjorie (Margie) Ketola and Joyce had grown up in the same neighborhood, and the two Gossard Girls worked on the same floor close to each other. They shared a long history and the same mechanic: Dennis Evans. Matchmaker Margie somehow knew Dennis and Joyce would be good for each other. "You gotta go out with Joyce," Dennis remembered an insistent Margie saying. He did. They dated for three years. The two Gossard employees discovered what Margie had known. The couple was a good match.

Dennis and Joyce continued their courtship after the mechanic left the Gossard plant in 1974 "for better pay at CCI." An increase in pay and benefits was nice, and so was the opportunity to continue in a job he enjoyed. Four years (1970–74) working "on many, many, many different machines" (i.e., seaming, overlock, zigzag, bar tack, etc.) had helped prepare him for a thirty-two-year career in maintenance in the local mines.

In 1969, Joyce became a Gossard Girl not out of economic necessity. "It was something I wanted to do," she stated. Nonetheless, her income did help with family expenses. Joyce used her Gossard pay to supplement her first husband's income as milkman. Joyce said, "It wasn't that much, but it helped" with rent and household expenses. A pieceworker in the hooks and eyes department, she "made over minimum wage," due to her talent and speed.

Often Joyce would end up with spare coupons. Coupons were critical for two reasons. First, a pieceworker's weekly pay was based on the number of coupons she completed each day. "You have to take a coupon off the bundle. It was just a little piece of paper. It had the bundle number and whatever on there, and then you had to put it on your worksheet for the day. You got X amount of money per bundle, per little coupon," she said. At the end of each day, Joyce would turn in her worksheet, and office workers tabulated her earnings. The coupons were proof of work completed.

Second, while coupons were valuable receipts for payroll purposes, coupons might also be a tool to help management revalue the rate of pay for an undergarment. Joyce, a fast pieceworker, understood this unintended consequence of coupons. "If I went too fast, they would have cut the amount for the bundle. You would have made less for that bundle." In effect, Joyce would now have to sew even faster. So would her peers in the hooks and eyes department. However, an older Joyce reflected, some in the hooks and eyes department weren't as fast. "So I tried to go over the minimum wage but not enough to call their [management's] attention to it." In these situations, Joyce used her saved coupons for "a bad day" or she "shared coupons with some of the ladies if they had machine trouble." Joyce acknowledged her actions "probably weren't honest. That was okay." She did not regret her decision. Her peers were more than pieceworkers; they were part of "our little circle," said Joyce.

Nancy Finnila, Gossard Girl

"My immigrant parents believed in schooling. We all had to go to school," said Nancy Finnila, the youngest of eleven children, who dreamt of being a nurse. Nancy's father died in 1948 forcing her mother to work at "what she had always been doing: cleaning." Five years later, thanks to a scholarship from the veteran's association, high school graduate Nancy enrolled in South Chicago Community College. She quit school within two months when she discovered students were using outdated textbooks. "This was false advertising. I have the oldest books in the world," she told her mother. "A new textbook book would have been $50, an amount my mother earned cleaning in one month." No amount of persuasion from Nancy's college teacher or her mother would convince Nancy to continue her studies in 1954.

The day after a disappointed Nancy returned home, she was hired at Ishpeming's undergarment factory thanks to sage advice from an older sister. It wasn't Nancy's dream to work in an undergarment factory; nonetheless, her pieceworker wages would help her mother. "I had to give my mother money. I didn't feel like I should sponge off my mother. She worked hard cleaning stores for a little money, and my brothers were away in the service."

It may have been an economic imperative that kept bringing Nancy back to Ishpeming's factory three times, but she also "liked sewing. I was quick. I never went on unemployment," Nancy remarked of her long tenure.

Nancy learned if she wanted to make a lot of money, she'd need a coherent and consistent strategy to attach trim (scallops) to bras. "Do scallops on the top of bras. You had to push it through the right way. You put them all on one string. You keep sewing. You don't do one and cut it apart; that's a waste of time. You do the whole lot (three dozen), one side at a time, all on one string. Then you check them to see if you made mistakes. Cut them apart and tie them."

Nancy's system worked too well, much to the consternation of some pieceworkers on her shaft. "You can't go that fast. You caught up to us [in three weeks], and we've been here a long time," remarked one worker. Bewildered yet determined, Nancy replied, "Too bad. I am going to go as fast as I can and do it because I want the money."

After Nancy married Eino Finnila, she continued to help her mother, and in time the Finnila family moved into Nancy's childhood home to help her aging mother. Nancy's income would be even more critical in her immediate family when her husband Eino would be laid off several times from work in the mines.

Each time the pieceworker left the factory, whether it was for a few weeks or months, management said "they would always find a corner to put me on," high praise that kept her coming back to work wherever she was needed *and* to make money. Instead of applying scallops to bras, Nancy was moved to girdle assembly, a department where some of her peers lacked the patience, efficiency, and dexterity to sew elastic onto a special girdle. The needles required special attention. "The tips of these industrial needles had to be polished to remove the tiny end of the needle, so it could go through the elastic quicker. I could do only so many girdles, and then I would have to replace the needle," said Nancy. Because she was double jointed, Nancy would "hold the thread a certain way," in attaching the elastic to the girdle.

"It was strictly work, honey," said Nancy of her tenure at Ishpeming's factory where she worked "mostly with older women." It didn't matter where supervisors moved her, not even when they "stuck her on push-up bras, giving her every damn bag to finish." Taking care of her family was what mattered. Thirty-four years later, a circumspect Nancy declared, "the Gossard factory really helped us out."

....

Remigia Davey, Gossard Girl

"I stood there until they closed or threw me out," said a grinning Remigia Davey. This sharp-witted, independent-minded woman would use a different lens to encapsulate twenty-six years (1950–76) as a pieceworker in Ishpeming's factory. Making money was important in her early years, but there were other benefits from working a quarter of a century.

Two months after Remigia graduated from Negaunee High School, she "put her name in at the Gossard," joining a mother and older sister. Remigia's mother, Mary, "was a homemaker until her husband got real sick in the forties." At one point, mother and daughter sat across from each other on the seaming shaft for bras. They also ate together until company-sponsored meals were discontinued in the 1950s. Remigia's older sister Yolanda, who "couldn't sew worth a darn," worked in the cutting room. In 1949, mother and sister "never went on the picket line, but they supported the strikers by working in the kitchen," said Remigia.

For several years, she gave her mother "the whole check," which mystified Remigia's peers. "They thought I wasn't doing right." It didn't make sense for a young, single woman working five days a week to give her entire paycheck to her mother. However, the strong-willed teenager didn't agree with her peers. Looking back, Remigia said, "Lord only knows what they thought. My mother did everything she could to raise me even when my father had cancer." Remigia knew she could always ask her mother if she needed anything. In reality, she "didn't care what [her peers] thought." Helping her immediate family was the right thing to do.

"The girls": this is Remigia's fondest memory from working more than a quarter of a century. "Well, you sit there day after day and their families became your family. Your family became theirs. You talked about anything, anything and everything. And it was just like one happy family." Reflecting on an environment where women spoke freely, the former seamer chuckled, "We always gave advice. It was free. So, we gave it, and we took it."

The self-assured woman recalled a spirited exchange with a pieceworker sitting across from Remigia, when supervisor Carmella asked Remigia to model sample bras "for us." Wide-eyed, Remigia eyed Carmella cautiously, inquiring, "And who is the 'us'?" Her supervisor answered, "The manager, you know, the head one." To which Remigia replied, "Well, give me a few minutes to think about it." The exchange between Carmella and Remigia did not go unnoticed. The unnamed pieceworker said, "Rena, you're not going to model. What would Bob [Remigia's husband] think?" Remigia wasted little time responding, "I don't know what he would think, but I think that's entirely up to me." Unswayed, Remigia's coworker continued, "Well, I don't think Bob would like that at all." Carmella reappeared shortly and Remigia said, "Yes, I'll do it."

Bob would hear of his wife's decision from friends, not his wife. "When did you plan on telling me about your other job?" Bob asked his wife. Remigia responded quickly, "I don't even like the one I got. Besides, the modeling job isn't a big deal." Bob responded, "It's your body. You do what you want with it." And so, she did. Initially, Remigia modeled in front of women, "but then the big shots from Chicago came." In exchange for modeling, she would keep the sample bras.

Remigia liked spirited exchanges. "I could argue at the drop of a hat. Of course, I said once, 'I am never wrong. I thought I was once, but I was mistaken.'" Decades later, she held "nice memories of these times. No matter where you work, you'll find good and bad people. So you associate with the good people and try to ignore the bad people." The sagacious former Gossard Girl continued, "It *was* a wonderful thing they had the Gossard. There were times when I felt like quitting, and there were times they felt like throwing me out. But we still got along."

CHAPTER 8

Remembering the Gossard

IT'S NOT UNUSUAL TODAY FOR CHILDREN to shadow parents in their workplaces for a day. In fact, there is a designated day called Take Our Daughters and Sons to Work Day. At the very least, a child who sees a parent working might imagine what it would be like to work in an office, a factory, a science lab, a classroom, or other workplace.

During the 1940s and 1950s, some children of Gossard workers spent time in Ishpeming's factory, though not for the same purpose as today's national program. Children of Gossard employees used the factory as an informal after-school day care, and for some older children, the multiple-floor building was the ultimate place for an adventure.

When economics forced a mother to become the family's primary wage earner, some Gossard children had the opportunity to witness their fathers assume household duties. Additionally, sons and daughters watched their mothers cash their hard-earned checks, a message that continued to resonate with them throughout their lives. Collectively, these children experienced a cultural shift of experiencing women/mothers as wage earners, decision makers, and change makers.

The Gossard Quilt

The Gossard Quilt, a work of art by four women quilters from Marquette County, honors the contributions of more than 1,500 workers employed at two Gossard undergarment plants in Marquette County from 1920 to 1976. In years past, other quilts were made from Gossard remnants. Marilyn Andrew treasures a pale pink doll's quilt made by her Gossard mother. Kathleen Fredrickson completed a quilt begun on a treadle sewing machine by her great-aunt Lahti, whose sister Senia was a Gossard pieceworker. Robare sisters Virginia Johnson and Karen Bratonia still prize an apricot and yellow quilt made by one of their three Gossard aunts. Functional quilts, now valued artifacts from one's family history, held priceless memories.

The path from Gossard remnants to art quilt began at Northern Michigan University in March 2010 at a historical presentation celebrating the contributions of Gossard Girls. In attendance was antique collector Karen Johnson, who brought with her a cardboard box of pale peach-colored antique Gossard fabric, remnants that had been in the box she had purchased at an estate sale for the feed sack material that was also included.

In the two months after the presentation, the box of remnants traveled to a Gossard Girl's home, a local fiber expert, another Gossard presentation, and a local quilt business. Gossard Girl Elaine Peterson said the material was probably used to make combinations, otherwise known as one-piece foundations in the 1950s. Area dry cleaner Dan Dallas, with a background in chemistry and antique garment restoration, reported the 1950s reversible antique material, made from cotton and silk threads, was classified as damask.

The box then traveled to a local women's philanthropic organization. Few in the membership knew of the Gossard factories' rich history. The club's membership endorsed the idea of a memorial quilt with the remnants that would honor the women of long ago and bring together four Marquette County textile artists. The collaborative project would be another opportunity to expose new generations to the Upper Peninsula's nascent women's labor history.

The box's next contact at a local sewing business was fortuitous. Owner Chris Wiik was not only an experienced quilter, but she had worked briefly in Ishpeming's Gossard factory. Four quilt artists—Wiik, Esther Johnson, Judy Parlato, and Toyo Kaumeheiwa—met in July and set an ambitious goal to create a memorial quilt from the remnants within three months for the area's regional quilt show running in mid-October.

The quartet of quilting artists met their goal, and the Gossard Quilt became a featured exhibit, generating new conversations, connecting strangers, and educating visitors. Karen Johnson attended and was surprised to see the Gossard remnants had been repurposed so beautifully.

Four months later, the Gossard Quilt was displayed in Marquette's Peter White Public Library where library patrons, visitors, and tourists viewed the art quilt and learned about its relevance.

In her letter to the *Mining Journal*, Negaunee native Edith Danielson Wills thanked "two ladies from Northern Michigan University [and workers from] Peter White Public Library for their assistance in contacting me when the quilt was up for display." The Gossard remnants from her mother's 1998 estate sale were now an intimate piece in a memorial work of art.

....

GERALD HARJU, SON OF LYDIA HARJU

"Because it employed so many women, the Gossard started a wave of stay-at-home dads who had never stayed at home before," said Upper Peninsula writer Jerry Harju, whose father took on that role in the 1940s.

Jerry's mother, Lydia, became a Gossard Girl in 1941. "We were pretty poor. My father grew potatoes and a little hay on family property west of Ishpeming, but around 1940 there was no market for potatoes." Jerry's father traded potatoes "for groceries and other things." His father owned two draft horses and a wagon, which he used to haul "garbage for places like the A & P." When grocery stores "threw out all the old vegetables," Jerry's father took some home. Father and son also repurposed empty wood crates for firewood and other wood projects. That was "how we were getting by."

Lydia worked long hours at the Gossard factory, and Jerry's father assumed additional responsibilities around the home. "So now with her working at the Gossard, somebody had to be around to make sure I got breakfast, some lunch, got dressed, and got off to school. So that was the old man. That was his job," said Jerry.

Meals prepared by Jerry's stay-at-home father were often memorable. One cold morning Jerry's father said, "What do you want for breakfast?" Lydia usually made oatmeal, especially during the winter, but a young Jerry seized the opportunity to request his favorite breakfast. "I want *pancakes*," knowing his mother reserved pancakes for special occasions. His father, an expert in horses and farming, was a novice in cooking, even cooking something as simple as pancakes.

Nonetheless, Jerry's father agreed. "He took down the pancake mix and then he was kind of stirring it up, and it was kind of lumpy. And we had a *big, big* frying pan. He poured the whole thing in this frying pan, covering the whole bottom. We had a wood stove in the kitchen, and he put it on there. It bubbled and bubbled. My father realized this was going to be tricky to turn over. I don't know exactly how he did it, but he got it over." A pancake so large "it didn't even fit on the plate," laughed Jerry. Lunches were generally simple: "a lot of baloney, canned soup, and stuff like that."

House cleaning became another job for the stay-at-home dad and his son. "We took whatever was laying around and stuffed them in drawers."

House cleaning may have been fast, "until you opened up drawers and tried to find something or looked in cupboards," Jerry mused.

Lydia refused to delegate two housekeeping jobs: laundry and cooking dinner. Drying clothes was the biggest challenge. The Harju family lived next to railroad tracks used by the mines. Iron ore dust from the uncovered train cars coated clothes drying outside, so Lydia became familiar with the train's schedule.

Even though the Harju family "was getting by" between Lydia's Gossard pay and his father's work with the horses and wagon, World War II employment opportunities helped the family improve its economic situation. They moved to Milwaukee where Lydia found employment as a seamstress and Jerry's father worked for International Harvester.

An older Jerry observed, "Men didn't really want to consider they were staying at home cooking and all that. But when there wasn't any choice, there wasn't any choice." For a young boy in the 1940s, "having a stay-at-home dad was comical *and* comforting to have someone home all the time. I never, never felt neglected."

JUDY CHARBONNEAU, DAUGHTER OF ANITA LEHTINEN

Two ideas, "full-time housewife *and* full-time Gossard Girl," helped shape Judy Charbonneau's images of her role model and mother Anita Lehtinen. In 1960, Anita returned to Gwinn's factory, and Judy said, relatives "saw that my brother and I got off to school in the morning and had the proper breakfast . . . and they greeted us when we got off the school bus." After school and homework, Judy "put the roaster pan in the oven" and cooked potatoes her mother had prepared before leaving for the factory. These and other chores underscored a family belief: "family came first."

"It benefited me in the long run," Judy said of her mother's Gossard work. "If it wasn't for my mom working, I wouldn't have had a prom dress or my suit when I graduated from high school. And there were extras like new shoes, a graduation ring, graduation pictures, a school yearbook, trips to the Escanaba fair, and eating pasties on the trip home." More importantly, Judy said because her mother "got out there," she had the example she needed to know "I could do it too." When Judy raised her family, she worked two jobs: homemaker and manager at Ishpeming's Gossard Outlet Store. Like her mother, Judy "made a point of being there" for her family.

JOAN LUOMA, DAUGHTER OF CLIFFORD AND EDITH PERRY

Clutching a small bag of mementos, Joan Luoma walked purposefully into the former Gossard factory, now repurposed into small businesses. It was quite a contrast from days when Joan, as a child, spent "many, many, many, many hours" at her parents' workplace. Gone was "the particular odor from satin and heavy, very decorative material." Now Clifford and Edith Perry's daughter would muse about special sewing needles needed to penetrate "very hard material and very, very rough lace." Gone was the unmistakable sound of "women crowding each other" as they descended the factory's wide staircase and headed home. "My dad was in charge of all those women," Joan said. These and other childhood memories from the late 1930s and 1940s came flooding back as Joan made her way to the third floor, one of two assembly-line floors.

Over a span of five years, the Gossard factory served as a daycare for Clifford's two children. At the end of many school days, Joan and her brother would spend afternoons at the Gossard while her father and mother worked. With their father's permission, the siblings highjacked wooden crates used to transport material for imaginary play. "We used to push each other in these big wooden crates. We weren't misbehaving, but we had a lot of fun at the Gossard with the big wooden crates with little steel wheels." Unless the sister and brother were bothersome, their father left them to their own devices. Sometimes, Joan recalled, they would hear "the buzzing of machines" on the second floor, but "we were not allowed to disturb these machine operators." When the buzzing ceased and stairs began creaking, the sister and brother quickly moved out of the way of the oncoming herd. Clifford "loved having his children at the factory," and Joan loved racing wooden crates with her brother.

Superintendent Clifford supervised the women workers, including Joan's mother. Growing up, Joan learned about her father's responsibilities from conversations she overheard between her parents. "All I heard was the word production. Production had to be up. I understood there were lines of women, and each line had a supervisor. My father would keep track of the production at all times, by the hour perhaps, through these supervisors."

Joan spoke of her father's dedication. The biggest part of his work was talking to women who had problems. Women "would go into his office and share what bothered them about their job. He would try to solve it. He'd carry that home and talk to Edith." Through these overheard conversations, Joan learned that an environment that rewarded speed and accuracy *also* created "a lot of tension" among workers. "It was mostly personal problems the girls had like 'this girl bothers me' or 'it's too tense to keep up.' They were all timed. There was a lot of this tension about keeping up the time. If they didn't keep up the time, they were not good workers. A lot of them were under pressure, and my father tried to help them."

Years later when Joan socialized with Gossard workers during club meetings and other social settings, she heard many stories about her father. Comments such as "he was so understanding," "I could always talk to your father," or "he would always listen, never condemn" reinforced Joan's admiration of her father, "a very dedicated man" who *listened* without judging.

The Gossard strike proved challenging for Joan's father. "It was a very hard time, because my father had to work. . . . It became rather loud, name calling and things like that. They called him many names, and they hurt my feelings, of course." Joan's father worked "many hours over his regular day," including evenings to keep picketers from entering the factory. Passions ran high in the early weeks. "They were mostly in big groups. And the more you get in a big group, the braver you'd get," said Joan. When she witnessed a few picketers "spitting on her father," she stayed away from the factory. Joan's father did not have that choice.

Clifford continued to earn a salary, but he was "hurt emotionally by the strike, which also affected the family." Within a year or two the superintendent was transferred to Gwinn's factory where Gwinn's workers came to know "a quiet and intelligent man."

Joan said the Gossard factory empowered women. "They loved this independence and being able to spend money that was theirs. Not their husbands', or parents', but *their* money." Perhaps Joan's father, whose Gossard career spanned more than four decades, understood this more than most.

Barbara Gauthier, Daughter of Viola Medlyn

"Funds were limited in 1941" when Viola Medlyn became a Gossard Girl. "My father didn't make much as a barber, and we lived with my grandmother," said Viola's daughter, Barbara.

At six o'clock each weekday morning, Viola walked to Ishpeming's Gossard factory while her mother dressed, fed, and walked her five-year-old granddaughter Barbara to kindergarten. "When I was slightly older,

I was permitted to meet my mother halfway when she was returning from work," Barbara recalled. Later, she met Viola at the factory and waited quietly at "the top of the wide Gossard stairs" where she watched her mother and other pieceworkers at "their big machines and where they put their piecework in the big bins when they were finished. It was a noisy place with all those big machines going, the elevator going, and big carts being rolled around."

Payday Fridays were special in the 1940s. Viola and her daughter would head downtown after visiting her father's barbershop opposite the factory. From there, mother and daughter cashed Viola's paycheck and walked to Olson News in search of comic and music books for Barbara. Their Friday ritual frequently included stops "at the Five and Dime Store and Penney's where Viola hoped to purchase nylons, one of the many rationed items during the war." They also bought and mailed care packages to Barbara's soldier brother stationed overseas. Before heading home, Viola and Barbara treated themselves to ice cream cones. Payday Fridays were special excursions for the Gossard mother and her daughter.

The 1949 Gossard strike affected the Medlyn family financially as Viola was not a picketer. Barbara's father "was so against women striking. People in those days didn't talk about issues like they do today. They were more closed mouthed. So, I am sure there were a lot of conversations that went on that I wasn't privy to," said Barbara. Nonetheless, she did see picketers as she walked to school, and there were "a lot of political discussions in my father's barbershop."

Though Viola wasn't a striker, she held firm on other family matters such as education. "It wasn't unusual in those days that my parents did not finish school. My grandmother had a third grade education. There were the haves and have nots." Even so, when Barbara considered a future beyond high school, her mother was inflexible. "No daughter of mine will ever work at the Gossard. You're going to do something to get an education and do something besides what I am doing." Barbara became a high school history teacher and incorporated the history of the Gossard factory in her American history class. Students learned about "strong women, widows, and single women [who] provided for their families when they had no Medicaid, state subsidies, and food subsidies." And when Viola's husband wanted a car, she agreed as long as she got a driver's license.

Decades later, a photo of "a beautiful white eyelet, strapless prom dress, and little white jacket" made by Viola from Gossard surplus material for $1 signifies her "strong, sweet and resourceful" mother.

PETER JOHNSON, SON OF HAROLD AND GERTIE JOHNSON

Peter, son of Gossard workers Harold and Gertie Johnson, grew up five blocks from Ishpeming's factory. While he did not spend afternoons at the factory, Peter has fond Gossard memories of multiple times he accompanied his uncle, who transported Gossard material in the late 1940s and 1950s. "I had an uncle who drove a truck for Ameen Transfer Line, and quite often I would go with him in the truck, and we would pick up whatever material it was at the Ishpeming Gossard and bring it down to Gwinn." These were memorable trips because Peter's uncle always stopped at the Mussatto Grocery Store in Gwinn where Peter always received a treat.

MICHAEL MORISSETTE, SON OF HENRY AND ALICE MORISSETTE

"The Gossard factory wasn't just a job but their life," said Mike Morissette, the place where Mike's parents, Henry and Alice, forged lifelong friendships and made their son's childhood home feel as if it was an extension of the workplace. Henry worked "as a shipping clerk until the day he died," while Alice worked as a seamer, inspector, chief inspector, and shipping clerk. Their combined years of employment exceeded sixty years.

The birth of Mike in 1951 would lead to other Gossard connections. Lucy Collins in accounts payable became Mike's godmother. Office worker Cecilia Conte and "her lifelong boyfriend" cutter Bill Cox played cribbage with Mike's parents every Saturday evening "for as long as Mike could remember." When the foursome tired of the card game, they played Smear. Card games, food, and friendship were sacred traditions in the Morissette home.

Gossard truck driver Joe Tollman became a fixture during Mike's childhood. Joe lived in Chicago, and three times a week he drove an eighteen-wheeler loaded with Gossard raw materials north almost four hundred miles. After Joe's truck had been unloaded and reloaded with the finished undergarments, "Joe rode home with my dad in the car, he ate dinner with us, [and in the evenings] Joe stayed at the Mather Inn." Despite the distance, the friendship between the families endured long after Henry and Joe retired.

There was the "Hungry Ten" a group of ten Gossard Girls who regularly converged on Mike's childhood home on Jasper Street. "My mother had a club, people who worked at the Gossard. My father called them the Hungry Ten because he said it took a week's wages to feed them every time they came over." These and other social events at his parents' home made it seem as if Mike, an only child in the 1950s and 1960s (his sister was twenty years older), was raised in the Morissette Community Social Center.

"The Gossard Company was one of those companies that allowed nepotism to exist within the work force," according to Kristine Antcliff, Mike's first cousin. Mike's connections to the Gossard continued at his mother's family gatherings (picnics, birthdays, and holidays), since Alice's four siblings worked at the plant. Boxer Signe worked during the 1940s. Ida, who worked forty-five years, was plant production supervisor. Carl, the fourth sibling, worked as a cloth layer before joining the military during World War II. And Iner, the fifth sibling (and his wife) worked briefly at the factory.

Nepotism may have benefited the Swanson clan economically, but the undergarment factory was much, much more than that. The Swanson family "talked, ate, and lived the Gossard operation 100 percent. They did not differentiate between the Gossard or the Swanson families. It was one family," Kristine said emphatically.

"It was unique," said Mike of the many months he spent every afternoon at the factory. Most Gossard workers—machine operators and pieceworkers—had already left by 3:30 p.m. when fourth grader Mike walked from Central School to his father's shipping room office. Rarely did Mike stay in his father's first-floor office because there were any number of adults (janitor, cutter, head inspector, boxer, clicker machine operator, plant manager, or office worker) willing to show a boy the inner workings of the undergarment factory.

Consequently, there would be Mike Morissette sightings on any given day. One day the fourth grader might be seen sweeping the dirty wood floors with janitor Oscar Gjlome. At least once a week, Mike and Oscar entered a special trap door on the fourth floor. "We used to go up and check on the clock in the northwest corner of the building. We would actually go up inside the clock." Once inside, they inspected the clock's gears and adjusting mechanisms. Before leaving, they "wound up" the mechanical clock. Another day, a cutter might have escorted a wide-eyed Mike to the cutting room to observe men skilled in minimizing "the waste of the fabric." Cutters worked their magic laying metal patterns strategically, "almost like a jigsaw puzzle." The curious boy was awed by manual cutter Bill Cox who cut through twenty-five layers of raw material effortlessly.

Even more exciting were afternoons spent in the basement where Mike watched Bill operate "a behemoth hydraulic machine" capable of cutting through at least three times the layers of material as a manual cutter. Bill again worked his magic positioning metal blades "almost like a jigsaw puzzle." Loud sounds—"bang, bang, bang"—pierced the basement as "sharp metal patterns passed through layers instantaneously, like a punch." Afternoons with Bill and the hydraulic behemoth were fresh fifty years later.

There was no area in the undergarment plant the fourth grader did not visit. Often, he accompanied production manager Aunt Ida, the highest-ranking female employee. "I used to watch the ladies sew these garments together. They'd come down from start to finish. It was just like putting a car together really, but it was putting a garment together."

Plant manager Kenneth Strengberg brought Mike into his office to broaden the boy's understanding of the plant. "He would explain what was going on in the different areas" and "no one ever complained" about a young boy hanging out at the plant. Other times Mike hung out with his godmother Lucy Collins, who "took care of the payroll and accounts payable." Mike knew about boxing from Francis Kepler, who was around while Mike waited for his parents. He had seen all parts of the assembly process, or so it seemed. Not many young boys or girls could brag about having the run of a woman's undergarment plant, mused an older Mike. He pursued degrees in math and science, yet he never forgot his unique afternoons at the Gossard. "That was fun. There were no bad memories of the Gossard."

....

CHRIS WIIK, GOSSARD GIRL

"It went full circle. We found everyone it touched over the years," said Gossard Girl Chris Wiik, quilt artist and owner of the Viking Sewing Village. The fabric's circular path would take about forty years, touch four women, and spark remembrances of a time when the influence of the Gossard Company was felt across the world.

Chris's connection with the Gossard Quilt began in 1970 when her husband, a United Parcel Service (UPS) employee, was transferred to Marquette. An apartment shortage in Marquette forced the couple to move to Ishpeming. "It was very, very cold. We had to shovel our way into the house." The young Ohio native knew little about Ishpeming's number one industry—mining—except "at noon every day the blast would go off, and the dishes would shake." She also knew nothing about another large employer, the Gossard Company, until her husband's coworker urged the experienced sewer to apply.

Sewing had been part of Chris's DNA since she was five. "I began sewing for money for my friends in junior high school," and then "I sewed for my friends' moms in high school. Sitting at a sewing machine was natural for me." It wasn't easy for young workers from outside Michigan's Upper Peninsula to integrate the closely knit mining community. In the 1970s, veteran workers (twenty-five-plus years of employment) with roots in the U.P. outnumbered young energetic workers like Chris. Veteran "motherly" pieceworker Cecilia Kangas would invite the Wisconsin native over for coffee and conversation.

Chris, who worked in narrow binding, excelled in piecework, and within a short time, she met her "goal: to buy a new car." Even so, the experienced sewer learned that speed, a maintenance-free machine, and well-maintained snippers (specialty scissors that cut quickly through thread and fabric) were no match for an occasional lapse in judgment and focus. Chris smiled as she described the time she joined the list of workers injured on the job. "Someone sewed their finger. She was sitting down the row from me, and I glanced down that way. I blurted out loud, 'How can anyone do that?' Immediately, I sewed my finger." Her injury was more serious, one that required X-rays. Chris returned to her machine, albeit a bit humbler. Each machine operator, she learned, must be attentive at all times. Chris worked at the Gossard for almost two years until she moved to a neighboring town so her husband would be closer to his workplace.

Chris credited her brief tenure at the factory as one of the most significant "stepping stones" in her life. Working at the factory "gave me confidence to move to a new area and establish myself as a person." She became owner of Marquette's Viking Sewing Village. Over the years, Chris's sewing business connected her with former Gossard Girls. These encounters did more to educate her about the Gossard plant. "The women were *proud* of what they did. I did not think of them as a common laborer. They had a higher standing in the community."

In 2010, Chris was initially drawn to the antique pale peach damask remnants. "It was part of history, and I admire fiber that is of good quality. I was fascinated with [the material]." Over the next four months, the collaborative quilt project would enlarge her appreciation of and commitment to creating an art piece commemorating hundreds of Gossard workers.

Chris, who originally envisioned a corset-shaped quilt, credited Esther, Judy, and Toyo for the final quilt design. "My partners in crime" thought the memorial art piece should preserve the integrity of the original design since some remnants had been "hand-sewn into quilt squares." Esther, Judy, and Toyo sewed additional quilt squares and constructed the quilt.

Chris used her computer to create a quilting stitch design that reflected a corset of the period and the antique material.

Throughout this design and quilting process, Chris often found herself thinking about the diverse group of workers: single, divorced, married, and immigrant women. She also thought about the 1940s, a period of high employment, a world war, clandestine union-organizing activities, and a four-month strike. "I thought more about the different women who worked there, and I couldn't imagine what it must have been like to work there in the forties, but I've seen pictures. I thought more about the women, the families this involved. It's quite amazing. The quality just shines through."

Her computerized quilt machine—a Long Arm Quilt Machine—was set up in the storefront in full view of customers. "People [men and women] would come in and tell me stories about their past or their connection, or they knew someone who worked at the Gossard." Often stories focused on corsets. A male quilter talked about his aunt who wore a corset every day, while another customer described a female relative who requested to be buried in her favorite corset. A third story focused on differences in culture and generational attitudes. Chris learned her friend's mother wanted her college-bound daughter in the 1960s to purchase a corset. Failure to wear a corset, the mother maintained, meant her daughter's body wouldn't "be configured properly" for childbearing. The daughter said to her mother, "Native American Indians did not wear corsets, and they had children." Mother and daughter compromised. The daughter would wear a panty girdle, less constricting than corsets.

The Gossard Quilt project yielded another story with roots on the African continent about the power of branding. In the summer of 2010, Chris discussed her project with a close friend who had grown up in South Africa before settling in Canada. Chris's friend often heard her elders speak about their "Gossards." "My friend had no idea that the word had to do with a specific brand until she moved to Canada during the 1960s and saw billboards for the H. W. Gossard Company."

During her October interview with a local TV reporter, Chris said, "I could feel the spirit of those women while working on the quilt, and it was a great feeling."

"Satisfying and special." That's how Chris felt when she learned the Gossard Quilt would be housed permanently at the Marquette Regional History Center in Marquette, Michigan. The knowledge of having helped create a memorial quilt preserved in perpetuity was humbling. But more than that was the knowledge she had helped create art that "paid honor to our women who came before us."

CHAPTER 9

....

Reemergence

FOUR DECADES AFTER Ishpeming's Gossard factory closed, no large-scale factory has ever moved into the building. In 1981, Hematite Development bought the building, renovating the exterior and turning the first floor into a mall. In 1985, Ishpeming native Paul Arsenault purchased the building, which was then known as Pioneer Square. At the time, the young businessman had no interest in the building, but bank officials kept pressuring him "to just go look at it." Decades later, Arsenault, president and CEO of Concepts Consulting, reflected on his visit. "I took three steps into the store. . . . I fell in love with it. In less than three minutes, I knew I wanted to buy the building . . . and make a home for small businesses, while promoting the rich history of our community." The building's character, such as its maple wood flooring and tin-lined ceiling and walls, would "become a showcase for Ishpeming."

In 2015, the building, now named the Gossard Building, was granted entry on the National Park Service's National Registry of Historic Places. Since then, the interior of the building has been remodeled to accommodate a variety of businesses, service industries, nonprofits, and counseling services. Gossard Girl Debra Lucas located her business, Little Miss Sew & Sew, in the former factory she once sewed in. The presence of the Women's Center, an outreach of Marquette's Women's Center is noteworthy, as Geraldine Gordon Defant, the International Ladies Garment Workers Union (ILGWU) organizer who played such a critical role in helping the Gossard Girls unionize, played a big part in 1973 to help lay the foundations for what would become the Marquette Women's Center, a valuable resource for Upper Peninsula women. The Ishpeming Area Historical Society and Museum is housed on the third floor.

The legacy of the former Gossard Factory permeates many areas of the historical building, in its well-worn maple hardwood floors and stairs, its tin-lined ceiling and walls, and the elevator used to transport raw materials and finished garments. However, the most important tribute to hundreds of Gossard workers is a collection of artifacts artfully displayed on three floors. Workers' names, machine photos, and Gossard advertisements grace some first-floor walls. An exhibit of the basement cafeteria (table and chairs), as well as Gossard strike photos further document the history on the second floor. Artifacts on the third floor, among other things, depict the Gossard office—a wood desk, chair, and clock—as well as office machines: telephones, manual typewriter, and manual adding machines.

Whether one is a visitor, a relative of a Gossard worker, or a customer in one of the Gossard Building's small businesses, one cannot help but be inspired by the Gossard worker tribute, thanks to Paul and Sandy Arsenault, proud owners and stewards of the century-old historic building. "The girls kept the town going, and they always spent their money in Ishpeming," said Gossard Girl Elaine Keto, a veteran of twenty-seven years, reflecting on the economic power of the Gossard Girls.

RUTH CRAINE, GOSSARD GIRL AND UNION ORGANIZER

She was sixty-eight; he was sixteen. She lived on Deer Lake Avenue, and he lived 0.2 miles away on Poplar Street. It was 1966, the summer between his junior and senior year at Ishpeming High School and her first summer as a retired Gossard Girl. Their worlds merged when Thomas Solka inherited his older brother's newspaper route. Six days a week and well before sunrise, a distributer dropped off a bundle of papers at the Solka home. Tom loaded copies of the *Mining Journal* into monogrammed canvas bags and delivered newspapers by foot to customers in the Deer Lake area and "into an extended part of the route" known as the flats. If customers hadn't received their newspapers by 5:30 a.m. due to late delivery of the bundle, they called his home. "Where's our paper?" they asked the teenager. And once a week, Tom went door to door for subscription payments.

In the national election year of 1966, he spotted unusual landscaping on Deer Lake Avenue. Ruth's front yard was "a proliferation of political yard signs for the August primary." It was "a nerdy thing in the sixties" for high school students "to be interested in politics," Tom mused. Decades later, the Honorable Tom Solka, a longtime judge, couldn't remember if his sixty-eight-year-old customer had invited him into her house or if the sixteen-year-old had invited himself. This detail was of little importance to Tom. The more important part was that a teenage boy "came of age politically" in Ruth's kitchen, where she taught him "organization politics, not coffee table politics." For this, Tom considered Ruth a vital political mentor in his life.

Coincidentally, a brother and sister from Ishpeming's Deer Lake neighborhood also benefited from a relationship with Ruth. In the mid 1960s, Ruth hired teenagers Bob and Gerry Saxwold to do odd jobs. Bob did outdoor and indoor work—weeding the garden, mowing the lawn, cleaning the refrigerator, oven cleaning, and garbage removal—while Ruth hired his sister to "sew house dresses." The retired Gossard pieceworker provided her sewing machine, fabric, sewing notions such as thread and scissors, and an old house dress, which Gerry used for a pattern.

Decades later, Gerry observed, "Ruth had a great sense of humor who spoke with authority and always made sure you were paid what you were worth. She just felt that things should be good for the person who got up in the morning and went to work." Her brother, Bob, described "a tall husky" Ruth as a mellow person around her house, but serious when she spoke about politics. Gerry recalled numerous "little donkey knick-knacks—Democrat memorabilia—scattered about her house." Politics, the siblings agreed, was Ruth's passion.

When a young Bob got his driver's license, Ruth hired him to take her to Democratic fundraisers, where his lessons in politics continued. Gerry, on the other hand, would have received her lessons in politics at Ruth's home, when the teenager was sewing house dresses. "Ruth would put in a little word about politics and Democrats," Gerry said, and that's when she saw Ruth's eyes sparkle, as she "talked faster and louder." An animated Ruth was advocating for "a good work environment and good pay" for workers. The siblings viewed "Ruth as a mentor to many young people."

A circumspect Tom felt his mentor had cut her teeth in politics when she was a Gossard Girl. "It was clear to me that she came to her politics from her labor organizing days at the Gossard." Those early organizing days, the judge also observed, would help shape one of Ruth's political views. "Business was Republicans and Republicans were bad." Ruth was a proud and active Democrat, whose political career included vice chairman of the Marquette County Democratic Committee, district organizer of the international union, and manager of Ishpeming's Local 286. All things Democratic, all things union.

Five years before teenage Tom had noticed Gossard Girl Ruth's yard packed with political signs, she received a medal of honor from Michigan Governor G. Mennen Williams. Perhaps as a result of Ruth's political activities and her "fine relationship [with] Governor [John] Swainson," she also received official invitations to the Swainson and President John F. Kennedy inaugurations, high honors, according to ILGWU vice president Morris Bialis, who congratulated Ruth in a letter sent January 11, 1961. "The thrill one experiences from honors like these cannot be bought for any amount of money. I am sure that is exactly the way you feel." The path to these accolades may have started almost twenty years earlier in Ishpeming's Gossard factory where the pieceworker worked in the seaming department.

As a teenager, Tom spent evenings at his mentor's kitchen table listening to Ruth's involvement in the "nuts and bolts" of political campaigns. One of Ruth's stories was set at a Democratic campaign event at the Landmark (formerly known as Hotel Northland). In 1966, men outnumbered women at these political events Tom would learn. One of those in attendance was local author, celebrity, and attorney John Voelker, whose cigar smoking bothered Ruth. She insisted the Upper Peninsula celebrity stop smoking his cigar. Though her request may have been considered unusual in 1966, Ruth banned all smoking in her home. Voelker extinguished his cigar, whether out of respect for Ruth's work in unionizing the Gossard factory, her position and work in the ILGWU, or because Gossard Girls like Pauline Toivonen knew "[Ruth] was a force to be reckoned with."

Stories were but a small part of Tom's lessons in the rudiments of politics. A more important part of the lessons would be *the doing*. Working alongside Ruth, Tom folded and bundled campaign literature. He learned about Ruth's simple system for tracking Democratic voters. Shoeboxes stored names, addresses, and phone numbers on three-by-five-inch index cards. Ruth also taught Tom the inner workings of canvassing households and distributing campaign literature. This precomputer system may seem labor intensive by today's standards, but not for a young man eager to absorb everything he could about political campaigns. The kitchen table lessons would come in handy years later when Tom ran for office.

According to Tom, Ruth did not talk about her eight years as a Gossard organizer with the teenagers. Nor were they aware of her work as ILGWU manager of Local 286 or her job as a business agent for ILGWU. Nonetheless, fifty years later, Tom reflected on his mentor's legacy. Ruth "was a hard worker and an organizer. She was a worker and an action person, who achieved results for the good of working people in the community. She didn't waste time on politics and the policy of things. And she wanted to see results from the political and community-organizing standpoint. By and large between the Gossard and the Marquette County Democratic party, she was a success at what she set out to do."

GERALDINE GORDON DEFANT, ILGWU UNION ORGANIZER

At the end of her 1990 interview with Jennifer Grondin, Geraldine Defant, Chicago native, union organizer at the H. W. Gossard plant in Ishpeming, and former Marquette County commissioner, reflected on her life's commitment to social changes. "My basic value system has not changed from when I was seventeen. It still is pretty much the same." Two decades later, Karlyn Rapport, retired clinical speech pathologist and close friend of Geraldine, offered her thoughts. "Geri was just a champion," someone who worked on behalf of others. Though Karlyn had not witnessed Geraldine's activism at the Gossard plant between 1948 and 1949, she had heard others (usually men) talk disapprovingly of Geraldine. "If I mentioned Geraldine's name especially with men, there would be hackles, palpable hackles. The phrase, 'oh, she was the union organizer,' would be connected with her name. It was somewhat pejorative, which kind of set her apart." Karlyn viewed these and other comments as "a show of strength." From Karlyn's perspective, her forward-thinking, feminist friend and mentor was "a troubleshooter and community organizer."

Karlyn's friendship with the former union organizer had roots in the 1960s at Northern Michigan University (NMU) at a time when Geraldine had been retired from her work as business agent for the ILGWU. Geraldine and her second husband, Michael Defant ("known as the union lawyer in the community"), would settle in Marquette where they raised a family and Geraldine would earn a bachelor's degree in political science in 1964. Karlyn had moved to Marquette in 1958 when her husband became director of theater at NMU. When she researched preschool options for her young family, Karlyn discovered "there was only one preschool and the woman took in only five children." Limited options for the professional and mother.

Geraldine was sympathetic to Karlyn's concerns, and so the former ILGWU union organizer and social activist did what she had been doing most of her life: she brought together like-minded people to solve a social problem. In this case, the problem was the shortage of preschools in Marquette during the 1960s. Years later, Karlyn reflected on their initial meeting. "Geraldine invited Dr. Jane Bemis, who was a faculty member at Northern in home economics, to meet with us [other like-minded women] and talk about possibly getting together a preschool, at least so we'd know what was involved in setting up such an arrangement. That meeting was the first time I met Geraldine as an organizer."

Bringing people together was but one of Geraldine's strengths, said Karlyn, who observed her "facilitate a discussion so that *everybody* had their say. Inevitably we decided to build a cooperative nursery which is now Marquette Cooperative Nursery." Karlyn became chair of the Marquette Cooperative Nursery, launching four decades in a unique friendship between two like-minded women. "Geraldine was a dear friend and mentor."

Compassion, Karlyn recalled, was another quality of the former ILGWU organizer. Geraldine "could see what people were going through, particularly the unfairness, and she would feel justice was needed." It was this idea that would catapult the social activist and union organizer into action: to right a wrong. From their meeting in the 1960s, the like-minded women would work together on other social issues. For example, they were concerned their voices weren't valued during an academic freedom issue at the university. "Geraldine and I were soul sisters at this particular time. And so we had a conference on women's rights. Out of that grew the identification of a need for a spouse abuse shelter and the women's center." Karlyn would take leadership of the spouse abuse shelter, and Geraldine took leadership of the women's center.

Geraldine was a problem solver and community organizer, Karlyn observed. When demand for services exceeded the women's center's space at NMU, Geraldine brought together "different elements of Marquette's labor workforce (carpenters, electricians, etc.)" to help renovate a building on Front Street in the 1980s. When the demand for fundraising at the nonprofit center rose, Geraldine viewed bingo games as "an entrée into getting women to organize and help, which kind of horrified us," Karlyn recalled.

But it was an effective strategy, Karlyn said years later. "Geraldine would be able to encourage them to take leadership in these roles, and yet she was a driving force. As you watched her, you could see her giving everybody else a voice but then kind of shepherding the group toward a successful conclusion." Geraldine was masterful at empowering like-minded women who were "interested in making something happen." Today, Marquette Women's Center is a valuable resource for women, providing services in three additional areas: Munising, Gwinn, and now Ishpeming's Gossard Building. A fitting legacy to a woman who "demonstrated her philosophy by example," Karlyn mused.

Jack LaSalle, a retired trade union leader, got to know Geraldine Defant "from a distance" in the 1970s during his junior and senior years at Northern Michigan University, and actively involved with the Marquette Democratic party.

Reflecting on his early union years, Jack observed, it was "through the Marquette County Dems, we became much closer, and I very much respected Geri. And I think she looked at me as a sincere, young trade unionist who was worthy of being taken under her wing." Geraldine did just that, becoming "a mentor [to Jack] in a political context." The smart and experienced mentor would, over the years, give her mentee "advice on running campaigns, advice on organizing political efforts, advice on organizing trade unionists, as well." It wasn't just that Geraldine knew more about politics; it was also that Jack saw in his mentor "the kind of heart and commitment to working people." She was "unafraid to hide her intellect." Jack stated, "She helped make me who I am."

Decades later, interviews with former workers and community members suggest Geraldine was admired and respected by many for her advocacy of workers, particularly women workers. For example, Gossard Girl Antoinnette "Toni" Certo named her daughter after Geraldine. Not only did Toni like the name "Geraldine," but she was also grateful for the union organizer's help when Gossard management wanted to fire a pregnant Toni. "Women weren't used to fighting for their rights at that time," according to Toni's daughter, Gerry Nault. But Geraldine Gordon did fight. "Geraldine was bent on what she was going to do, and probably wasn't bothered by being under the microscope by management. She would have stayed within her legal bounds within the workplace," said Gerry.

For Gerry, Karlyn, Jack, and others, the ILGWU organizer wasn't a thorn but a forceful, intelligent, and kind woman who valued workers, a person who helped empower many women to own their own voice before the women's movement in the twentieth century, a woman who is remembered for doing what was right.

....

Dorothy Windsand, Gossard Girl

Outside temperatures struggled to reach forty-five degrees on June 22, 2009, as former Gossard Girl Dorothy Windsand, now eighty-eight and hugging a treasured photo album, eyed the interior of the H. W. Gossard. It had been more than three decades since she had worked in the factory. Absent was the daily hubbub of activity before 7:00 a.m. when hundreds of women filed through three entrances: some needing to speak with payroll, some heading to numbered coat racks, and some engaged in conversations with their Gossard family members. Today Dorothy, who worked at the Gossard factory from 1940 to 1976, walked deliberately, absorbing the first-floor changes.

Walls reconfigured an open space where once box lid printers, boxers, and shippers prepared undergarments for delivery to Gossard warehouses. Another wall obscured the Gossard office window, where in 1940 Dorothy applied, walking a few blocks from J.J. Newberry to the factory because she "just heard the Gossard was looking for workers. All I did was write my name on paper. That's about it." Today's tour, she said, made her think about her daily work in the main office "checking the slips the girls submitted each day," and Friday afternoons when workers picked up their weekly paychecks. Dorothy noted she still has her last "cancelled check from the Gossard," the only "good working place" for rural U.P. women from 1920 to 1976, a place where her wages helped three daughters earn their college degrees.

Another wall concealed wood stairs to the second, third, and fourth floors Dorothy had traversed daily, so today she'd use an elevator that had been installed twelve years after the Gossard factory closed, *not* the 1920s freight elevator used by men to transport raw material and finished undergarments.

Gripping her photo album tightly, Dorothy stepped cautiously onto the second floor, eyeing the now unfamiliar narrow hallway and more walls. Absent was an enormous space where women sat in rows at tables facing each other, and where overhead wiring powered their industrial sewing machines mounted on tables. Dorothy had worked on this floor as a machine operator on "regular sewing," until management assigned her to check girl. "I checked the orders from the office each day and made sure machine operators were working on the day's orders." Orders bearing a yellow tag required her immediate attention since yellow-tagged items had to be shipped by the end of the day. Special tags were also used on factory orders for women soldiers serving in World War II. "When we had those orders, we were told it was for the service, and we worked longer hours," said Dorothy. The white noise from hundreds of machines never disrupted her focus. "I never thought of the machines' noise."

The calls from a nation at war were felt in Dorothy's family; three brothers joined the military at the same time. Whether her brothers' commitment inspired her or whether Dorothy overheard her brothers talk about the country's urgent need for "women to join the service," Dorothy planned to enlist. "I'm joining, too," she vowed. Her father, Richard, who worked at the Athens Mine in Negaunee, said, "As soon as the boy down the street goes, I will let you go." The young boy her father referenced "was a conscientious objector." A disappointed Dorothy did not quit the Gossard. Years later, the mother of three, grandmother of three, and great-grandmother of two giggled about that young naïve girl. "What a dumb thing to do," said Dorothy.

Dorothy's duties at the undergarment factory increased during the 1940s. She opened her photo album, careful not to tear the fragile pages while she searched for images from over sixty years ago. She didn't remember the year or names of everyone in the black-and-white photo, but without hesitation, Dorothy pointed to her first image: a group photo in the kitchen of the Gossard basement lunchroom. Pointing to a young woman with dark hair in the photo, the former check girl said proudly, "That's me." With a workforce well over five hundred in the 1940s, check girls like Dorothy helped lunchroom workers. Eyeing the antique photo more intently, Dorothy pointed to a group of workers dressed in white. These workers were hired "just for work only in the kitchen." Then there was Gossard chef Paul Maloney, her neighbor, and Manager Harold Peterson, "the factory's boss." Dorothy knew the impact of daily free meals meant a lot, especially for women who were the sole providers in their families.

Dorothy paused again as she delicately turned the album's pages to a series of images at a large outdoor gathering. Dorothy treasured these 1947 photos from a day-long Gossard picnic held at Al Quaal Recreation Area in Ishpeming for seven hundred workers from the Ishpeming and Gwinn factories. Many of the details were sketchy, but Dorothy's photos gave witness to a day of food, competitive games, dancing, and a special Gossard Queen competition. "I was the queen, and we won the baseball tournament," she said gesturing at the collection of images. "That was nice," Dorothy said, pointing first to her crown and corsage in the photo. She pointed to two more photographs: one that showed the athletic Gossard Queen swinging a baseball bat, and an image of four smiling Gossard Girls posing with their prize, Brach's chocolate candy bars. Many Gossard Girls remembered the historic picnic, but Dorothy's memories were especially meaningful.

She studied another photo, though it was not from her album but a newspaper: a black-and-white image from the Gossard strike in 1949. "They went on strike." Not Dorothy, who was an hourly worker in 1949. "We worked, and when we were ready to get the inventory out, somebody told them. Anyhow they wouldn't let us back in." Passions ran high in the early weeks. One day two Gossard picketers followed Dorothy and her friend around downtown Ishpeming. "They called us scab, scab, scab all the way around town. We weren't scabs because we didn't belong to the union in the first place." Unable to continue her work at the factory, Dorothy drove sixty-five miles south in her Ford, to Iron Mountain where she had spent summers with her aunt's family. When she returned in August 1949, "most of them were glad to see you."

Like many women of the period, Dorothy left the factory to raise her children. When she did return, it was at the behest of her friend Gossard Girl Elaine Peterson, who felt the undergarment factory needed workers like Dorothy. "I enjoyed the work. It was good experience. It was good to get out of the house." When she did return, the Gossard brand was undergoing declining sales. Factories were closing, including the factory in Gwinn. Dorothy who had "helped out in Gwinn's factory when it first opened in 1947," now helped "clean out Gwinn's factory." The loss of wages would be a tough pill for Gwinn's rural families to swallow. Fast forward to 1976, office worker Dorothy helped close Ishpeming's factory, whose economic impact would be felt even more.

Dorothy did not dwell on these losses. The factory "was a good place for a lot of people to work. It wasn't that much money, but at that time it was good." She studied the first of two final photos, a stylish white wedding gown made from surplus Gossard material: silks and laces. "I'll be darn. They had good stuff." Dorothy looked intently at another photo: a sewing machine needle embedded decades later in the century-old wood floor. "They had a long life," she joked and continued, "we all tried that," referencing accidents, times when sewing needles were removed from machine operators' fingers.

Gesturing to her high-tech running shoes, a treasured hand-me down from her daughter, a marathon runner, Dorothy wanted to see areas obscured by walls. Now perched at the top of wood stairs worn down by hundreds and hundreds of women's shoes, she paused again, quietly absorbing the ornate tin-tiled walls and ceiling, faded strips of yellow paint on the stairs, and worn wooden handrail. "The Gossard was important to so many people, so many women, so many families," she said, heading down the stairs. "It was important to me."

Acknowledgments

The support from a host of individuals, family, friends, and colleagues from the Upper Peninsula of Michigan and those with roots in the Upper Peninsula, inspired this book. Regrettably time and space do not allow me to list everyone. You should know that your stories fill the spaces between every line of this book with the Yooper spirit found nowhere else in my life experiences.

There are no words to adequately convey the depth of my appreciation to Cindy Paavola, friend, former colleague, and mentor. When I first uttered the idea of this book almost ten years ago, she supported the idea wholeheartedly, offering help at every turn and on every page. Nor have I forgotten her gentle directive: "just write, Phyllis." Month after month, year after year, your helpful comments, patience, and wisdom yielded a manuscript that pays tribute to hundreds of unheralded rural women workers.

I am grateful to readers Robert Archibald, PhD, Gwinn, MI; Eve Bowen; Jill Compton; Russell M. Magnaghi, emeritus professor of history, Northern Michigan University; Mike Marsden, emeritus professor of English, American studies, and media studies and emeritus dean of the college and academic vice president, St. Norbert College; Alison Sanders; Fram Virgee; Rick Wills of the Forsyth Township Historical Society in Gwinn, Michigan; and Isaac Wong. Your thoughtful and constructive comments made this book far better than I could have imagined.

I am indebted to Paul and Sandy Arsenault, owners and stewards of the historic Gossard Building in Ishpeming. The building and numerous artifacts on public display tell visitors an important story of Michigan's Upper Peninsula. Thank you, Jack Deo of Superior View, for improving photos that weren't top quality and were low resolution. My deep appreciation to the staff and faculty of Northern Michigan University and San Francisco State University who helped me on a number of occasions. You are friends forever. Thank you.

I am thankful to the Michigan State University Press staff and editorial board who put their faith in me. I am especially indebted to editor Julie Loehr who first saw potential in the manuscript. Reworking a topic-based manuscript into a chronological manuscript was daunting yet necessary. I am deeply appreciative to Catherine Cocks, assistant director and editor-in-chief, for your patience, support, and guidance; you are editor extraordinaire. I am immensely grateful to Anastasia Wraight, project editor, for your advice, your wisdom, and for listening. Many thanks to Elise Jajuga, publicity manager, and Kristine Blakeslee, managing editor, for their expertise and assistance to a first-time author.

This book took shape during informal and formal conversations with family, friends, colleagues, writers, historians, librarians, archivists, and even occasional strangers. You know who you are. I am grateful to each of you for listening to mini stories of these inspiring women who have left an indelible mark on me.

To my soul mate and husband, Les, who championed this project in countless ways from the beginning to the end. You shined a light on this project among your colleagues and in many professional settings as a university president. You encouraged me to get away for extended weeks at a time so I could better concentrate on the writing. You listened when the weight of writing seemed impossible, as well as in those moments of pure joy. I am also deeply appreciative to my sons and their wives, good people and exceptional parents. Your excitement, pride, and cheerleading warms my heart. I must acknowledge eight delightfully curious and supportive grandchildren. I love your questions, your enthusiasm, and your book art ideas. Maybe this book will encourage you or others to discover unheralded stories from your neighborhoods or communities.

Any errors, inaccuracies, oversights, or other unintended mistakes in my retelling of the history of the U.P. Gossard factories are, of course, mine and mine alone.

Appendix: People Interviewed for the Book

CGP—Child of Gossard Parent(s)
CM—Community Member
GG—Gossard Girl
GM—Gossard Man
RGW—Relative (i.e., aunt/grandmother/uncle/cousin) of Gossard Worker
Note: When known, birth last names of women are provided in parentheses.

Denise (Dussart) Anderson, GG, war bride from Esneux, Belgium, worked twenty-eight years (1948–76) in Ishpeming's factory. The immigrant pieceworker started in zigzag and worked as a floor lady and instructor.

Marilyn Andrew, CGP of Ishpeming, is the daughter of a Gossard pieceworker who made a doll quilt from Gossard remnants.

Frank Andriacchi, CM of Ishpeming, was owner of the Venice Supper Club in Ishpeming.

Marjorie (Tripp) Annelin, CGP from Ishpeming, is the daughter of Claude and Grace Tripp. Manager Claude Tripp worked from 1921–43, and Personnel Director Grace worked 1944–54

Kristine Antcliff, CGP originally from Ishpeming, is daughter of Alice Swanson, one of five siblings who worked in Ishpeming's factory.

Robert Archibald, CM, of Ishpeming, is a writer and author of Upper Peninsula history.

Paul and Sandy Arsenault, CM, are owners of the historic Gossard Building.

Virginia (Forchini) Ayotte, GG, New Swanzy native of Italian immigrant parents, was an office worker at Gwinn's factory from 1948 to 1962.

Dorothy Baldini, GG, of Negaunee, worked on the assembly line in Ishpeming's factory in the 1940s.

Audrey (Boase) Bergman, GG, whose ancestors hailed from Cornwall, England, is a native of Ishpeming. As a teenager, she worked in the office from 1947 until 1949.

Donna (Pascoe) Bergman, GG, of Ishpeming, began as a teenager in zigzag in Ishpeming's factory in 1945, working until she married in 1947.

Bertha Boase, GG, originally from Wisconsin, worked on and off for twenty-five years as a pieceworker in Ishpeming's factory.

Alvera (Pezzotti) Brisson, GG, Negaunee native of Italian descent, worked in Ishpeming's factory during the 1940s as a zigzag pieceworker.

Judy (Lehtinen) Charbonneau, CGP, who was raised in Palmer, worked at the Gossard Outlet Store at Ishpeming's factory. She is the daughter of a pieceworker who worked in Gwinn's factory almost ten years.

Willard "Bill" Cohodas, CM, of Cohodas Brothers Produce, supplied fruits and vegetables for company-sponsored lunches during the 1940s and early 1950s in the Ishpeming and Gwinn factories.

Rose (Nardi) Collick, GG, Ishpeming native of Italian descent, worked in Ishpeming's factory for twenty years over two periods. She began as an underage teenager in 1937, working in medium and wide binding and zigzag ends until she married in 1942. She returned in 1961 and worked in stripping, boning, boxing, as well as department head until the factory closed in 1976.

Evelyn (Larson) Corkin, GG, of Ishpeming, started as a teenager in Ishpeming's factory on narrow binding and worked two stints during 1947–76.

Elizabeth (Gauthier) Coron, GG, an Ishpeming native of French Canadian descent, worked on the assembly line five years, 1940–45.

Rita (Roberts) Corradina, GG, of Ishpeming, was an office worker in Ishpeming's factory from 1958 to 1961.

Dan Dallas, CM, owner of Dallas Cleaners in Marquette, inspected and cleaned Gossard remnant material for the 2010 memorial Gossard Quilt.

Remigia (Zopetti) Davey, GG of Italian descent, was a pieceworker in Ishpeming's factory on seaming for twenty-six years beginning in 1950 until the factory closed in 1976.

Madeleine (Barbiere) DelBello, GG, Canadian immigrant of Italian descent, was a seamer in Gwinn's factory from 1947 to 1964.

Dennis and Joyce (Kivisto) Evans, GM & GG, both of Ishpeming, worked in Ishpeming's factory. Dennis, a mechanic, worked from 1970 to 1974. Joyce was a pieceworker in hooks and eyes between 1969 and 1976.

Ruth (Webb) Fagerberg, GG from Gwinn, worked in Gwinn's factory for three years (1947–50). She began in boxing and moved to seaming when she was eighteen.

Arleen (Pearce) Felt, GG, whose parents came from Cornwall, England, was raised in Negaunee. The wife and mother worked two years in Ishpeming's factory during the 1960s.

Pearl (Filippi) Filizetti, GG, Palmer native of Finnish descent, was a pieceworker in Gwinn's factory twice: 1947–49, 1951–53.

Nancy (Vizena) Finnila, GG, of Ishpeming, was a pieceworker in Ishpeming's factory several times between 1954 and 1968. She worked in a variety of assembly jobs, which included applying scallop trim to bras and elastic to girdles.

Betty Fosco, GG, Negaunee native of Italian descent, worked nineteen years in Ishpeming's factory. She began as a teenager in 1947 and worked in seaming, end finishing, circular stitching, and girdles until 1966 when she left to care for her mother.

Kathleen Fredrickson, CGP, preserved a Gossard quilt made by her grandmother, a pieceworker in Ishpeming's factory during the 1930s or 1940s.

Barbara (Medlyn) Gauthier, CGP, of Ishpeming, is the daughter of a pieceworker who worked in Ishpeming's factory between 1941 and 1962.

Trudy Gray, CM, and her mother used material purchased from the Gossard Outlet Store to upholster the interior of an old car for Trudy's brother in the 1960s.

Judy (Raihala) Green, GG, of Finnish descent from Midway, worked in Gwinn's factory twice. She worked as a narrow binder from 1956–57 and for two years in the 1960s.

Alice (LaBeau) Haapala, GG, of French descent, grew up in Republic, Michigan, and worked sixteen years (1949–65) in Ishpeming's factory on narrow, medium, and wide binding.

Gerald Harju, CGP, an Ishpeming native of Finnish descent, is the son of a pieceworker who worked four years in the 1940s.

Verna (Stansbury) Holmgren, GG, Ishpeming native of English descent, worked twenty-five years in Ishpeming's factory over two stints. She was a pieceworker from 1940 to 1941 but returned in 1952 and worked as an instructor training new workers until the factory closed in 1976.

Maxine Honkala, CGP, is the daughter of pieceworker Olga (Koskela) Honkala who worked thirty years (1930–42, 1958–76) in Ishpeming's factory.

Mary (Valela) Jacobson, GG, Ishpeming native of Italian descent, worked briefly after high school as a pieceworker until she married in the 1940s.

Cecilia (Paris) Jafolla, GG, Ishpeming native of Italian descent, worked in Ishpeming's factory. In 1943, the teenage pieceworker worked four years until she married and moved from the area in 1947.

Catherine (Barbiere) Johnson, GG, Ishpeming native of Italian descent, worked eight years (1939–47) in Ishpeming's factory. She started as a teenager in seaming and became an instructor training new workers until she married.

Esther Johnson, CM, was one of four quilters who created the 2010 memorial Gossard Quilt.

Peter Johnson, CGP, son of Gossard parents who worked in Ishpeming's factory, accompanied his uncle who drove a truck delivering raw materials from Ishpeming to Gwinn's factory in the 1950s.

Virginia Johnson and Karen Bratonia, RGW, sisters from Gladstone, preserved a Gossard quilt made by their aunt, who was a pieceworker in Gwinn's factory starting in 1947.

Clara (Valela) Joseph, GG, of Ishpeming, started at Ishpeming's factory in 1945 and worked in wide binding less than a year until she married.

Cecilia (Marra) Rovedo Kangas, GG, Ishpeming native of Italian descent, worked in Ishpeming's factory for more than forty years. In 1925, the underage teenager began in seaming, and over the years, she worked in other areas, including sewing sample bras.

G. Mae (Kompsi) Kari, GG, of Finnish descent, was a pieceworker in Ishpeming's factory fourteen years: 1962–76. She worked in seaming, double-needle seam binding, and underwire bra assembly.

Toyo Kaumeheiwa, CM, was one of four quilters who created the 2010 memorial Gossard Quilt.

Madeline (Paris) Kaupilla, GG, a Negaunee native of Italian descent, was a medium binder in Ishpeming's factory for sixteen years (1941–57).

Marlene Kautz, GG, of Negaunee, worked three to four years over two stints in two-needle narrow and wide binding at Ishpeming's factory during the 1950s.

Elaine (Arseneau) Keto, GG, grew up in Ishpeming and worked in zippers, hooks and eyes, and brassiere straps for twenty-seven years in Ishpeming's factory (1945–48, 1952–76).

Marjorie (Kucher) Ketola, GG, a Menominee native of German descent, finished high school in Ishpeming. She worked on zigzag ends in Ishpeming's factory in two stints for almost thirty years between 1941 and 1976.

Gloria (Koski) LaFave, GG, Gwinn native of Finnish descent, was an office worker for four years (1948–52) in Gwinn's factory.

Jack LaSalle, CM, of Marquette, met Geraldine Defant through the Marquette County Democrat functions beginning in the 1970s.

Bill Lehmann, GM, of Ishpeming, worked as a timer for Ishpeming's factory during the mid-1960s.

Anita (Kestila) Lehtinen, GG, born in Finland, grew up in Rock, Michigan. In 1947, the teenager worked in seaming and two-needle binding until 1950. She returned in 1960 and worked until the factory closed in 1964.

Dona (Johnson) Lenten, GG, Negaunee native, began as a teenage two-needle binder in 1948, working until 1952 when the wife and mother left Ishpeming's factory.

Debra Ann (Beck) Lucas, GG, of Ishpeming, worked four years from 1972 until the factory closed. The teenager operated one-, two-, and three-needle machines. She also worked in the shipping department.

Joan (Perry) Luoma, CGP, of Ishpeming, is daughter of Clifford and Edith Perry. Her father worked in management in both plants over forty years. Edith was a pieceworker in Ishpeming.

Russ Magnaghi, CM, of Marquette, is an author and former director of the Northern Michigan University Center for Upper Peninsula Studies.

Carlo Maki, CM, who attended Ishpeming High School in 1940, worked for Cleveland-Cliffs Iron Company for forty-five years.

Elaine Maki, GG, a Republic native, was a teenage worker in binding, boxing, inspection, and office work for two years (1950s) in Ishpeming's factory.

Karen Marietti, CGP, of Ishpeming, is the daughter of pieceworker Martha (Korpi) Brown who, as the eldest sibling in her family, left high school early to support her family in the 1930's. Karen's mother worked over thirty years in Ishpeming's factory.

Jennie (Luca) Melka, GG, of Negaunee, worked multiple times totaling twenty-seven years as a pieceworker and instructor in Ishpeming's factory.

Donald Merrill, GM, who was raised in Sheboygan, Wisconsin, began working at Ishpeming's factory in 1959. He worked seventeen years in different positions: mechanic, hand cloth cutter, machine operator, and truck driver.

Phyllis (Jensen) Miller, GG, of Sands, Michigan, worked for two years (1949–50) until she married and moved to Marquette with her husband, James Miller.

Michael Morissette, CGP, Ishpeming native of French Canadian and Swedish descent, is the son of Henry and Alice Morissette whose combined work years in Ishpeming's factory exceeded sixty years. Henry worked in the shipping department. Alice, who began in seaming, was an inspector, then a chief inspector, and a shipping room clerk.

Dora (Fountain) Mussatto, GG, Gwinn native of Italian descent, worked as a teenage pieceworker in binding for three years in Gwinn's factory: 1947–50.

Paulette (Denofre) Nardi, GG, Ishpeming native of Italian descent, was a pieceworker in Ishpeming's factory from 1965 to 1976.

Gerry (Saxwold) Nault, CPG, originally from Ishpeming and the daughter of pieceworker Antoinnette, was hired by Ruth Craine in the 1960s to sew dresses for Ruth.

Pam Nault, GG, originally of Sault Sainte Marie, was a pieceworker in Ishpeming's factory from 1975 to 1976.

Joan (Holmgren) Nelson, GG, of Ishpeming, was a pieceworker in Ishpeming's factory four years during the 1960s.

Barbara (Husby) Nuorala, GG, Ishpeming native of Norwegian and Swedish descent, worked in Ishpeming's factory beginning in 1947. The teenage worker started in seaming and also worked on end seaming for many years in two periods.

Judy Parlato, CM, was one of four quilters who created the 2010 memorial Gossard Quilt.

Barry Patron, CGP, of Ishpeming, is the son of pieceworker Marie Patron who worked in Ishpeming's factory for many years.

Elaine (Millimaki) Peterson, GG, National Mine native, worked in Ishpeming's factory for twenty-two years over two periods. She began in piecework in 1944, working until 1950 when she married. She returned in 1960, working in ten different jobs until the factory closed in 1976.

Laila (Heitala) Poutanen, GG, of Palmer, was a pieceworker in the Ishpeming (1940s) and Gwinn (1960s) factories.

Karlyn Rapport, CM, of Marquette, worked with Geraldine Defant beginning in 1970 to help start a women's center in Marquette.

Hilda (Hemmila) Rivers, GG, of Negaunee, was a pieceworker in Ishpeming's factory for a number of years.

Edna (Pelkie) Roberts, GG, Gwinn native of Finnish descent, worked as a teenage pieceworker in Gwinn's factory for two years from 1947 to 1949.

Bob Saxwold, CPG, son of Gossard Girl Antoinnette, grew up in Ishpeming. During the 1960s, the teenage neighbor of Ruth Craine worked odd jobs, including driving Ruth to local Democratic events.

Bob Sihtala, GM, Ishpeming native of French Canadian and Finnish descent, worked thirteen years as a mechanic in Ishpeming's factory.

Margaret (Paris) Sippola, GG, a Negaunee native of Italian descent, was a pieceworker in Ishpeming's factory multiple times totaling twenty-five years between 1944 and 1976.

Gwen (Emmanuelson) Skewis, GG, of Ishpeming, was a pieceworker in narrow and medium binding and in boxing for eighteen years (1944–62) in Ishpeming's factory.

Thomas Solka, CM, was a neighbor (and newspaper carrier) of Ruth Craine during the 1960s.

Ann Marie (Barbiere) Stieve, GG, of Ishpeming, worked four years in Ishpeming's factory. The teenager worked as a finishing binder from 1951 to 1955 until she and her husband moved from the area.

Helmi (Lakso) Talbacka, GG and Champion native of Finnish descent, was a pieceworker in Ishpeming's factory on hooks and eyes and on corsets for fifteen years from 1947 to 1962.

Shirley (Talus) Terzaghi, GG and Negaunee native of Finnish descent, was a check worker and pieceworker in seaming who worked two stints in Ishpeming's factory from 1948 to 1954.

Pauline (Salson) Toivonen, GG, Ishpeming native of Scottish descent, was a pieceworker in Ishpeming's factory from 1946 to 1950.

Lucy (Grasso) Tousignant, GG, Ishpeming native of Italian descent, was a pieceworker in Ishpeming's factory, who worked multiple stints from 1940 to 1976.

Genevieve Valenti, GG, Ishpeming native of Italian descent, was a pieceworker in zigzag and featherstitch for six years (1959–65) in Ishpeming's factory.

Nancy Valenzio, GG, who grew up in Republic, was a pieceworker in Ishpeming's factory multiple times between 1947 and 76 for a total of twenty-five years.

Alice (Gill) Vallier, GG, of Gwinn, Michigan, worked part time in the seaming, zipper, and boning departments in Gwinn's factory during the 1960s. The wife and mother stayed until the factory closed in 1964.

Dorothy (Hemmila) Waters, GG, Ishpeming native of Finnish descent, began in piecework in Ishpeming's factory in 1944. She was also an assistant instructor and repair worker during her eight years.

Chris Wiik, GG, of Marquette, was a pieceworker for two years in the 1970s and one of four quilters who created the 2010 memorial Gossard Quilt.

Edith (Danielson) Wills, CM, of Negaunee, donated antique Gossard remnants for the 2010 memorial Gossard Quilt project.

Rick Wills, CM, native of Gwinn and president of Forsyth Township Historical Society, lived next to Gossard Girl Nathalie (Boogren) Hutchens who worked in Gwinn's factory for a number of years.

Dorothy (Carlyon) Windsand, GG, of Ishpeming, worked more than two decades in Ishpeming's factory over two stints. She started as a teenage pieceworker in 1940 in seaming, then moved to check worker, and eventually to office work until the factory closed in 1976.

Glossary

Bar tack machine: A machine that applies a series of back-and-forth stitches in the same spot to attach bows or reinforce stress areas on undergarments (bras, corsets, girdles).

Bias tape: A narrow strip of fabric cut on the bias, or at a forty-five degree angle, to make the fabric stretchier when sewing.

Bias tape machine: A machine that makes bias strips for covering seams and raw edges.

Bones or stays: A narrow strip of rigid material to reinforce and shape corsets.

Box lid printer: A machine used for printing information (model, size, color, and number of garments) onto cardboard box lids, which were used for boxing finished undergarments.

Bra cup iron: A revolving electric ironing machine for removing wrinkles in bra cups.

Bundle: A bundle is a durable cloth bag used for unassembled (and finished) undergarments, which were held together in bunches of twelve, twenty-four, or thirty-six. A bundle contained only one undergarment model.

Check girl: A worker who collected bundles of finished garments, removed the inventory tags (aka "the corners"), and delivered the inventory tags to the female production manager.

Clamps: Metal fasteners used by men to secure multiple layers of raw material and metal undergarment pattern pieces.

Cleaning fluid: A special fluid used by repair women to remove stains on finished undergarments.

Cloth layer: A male worker who laid out twenty-four to forty-eight layers of raw material on a large wood table.

Coupon: A piece of paper that displayed the units (i.e., a seamer $.10, or narrow binder $.80) earned in each step of bra, girdle, or corset assembly. Coupons that were detached as each worker finished her assembly step were glued onto a "sticky."

Cutting table: A special wooden table used by men for cutting out undergarment pattern pieces.

Department head (also called supervisor): Women who supervised pieceworkers within their department (i.e., seaming, binding, boxing, and zigzag). Some of her duties involved distributing bundles, dispensing sewing needles, bringing workers' scissors to mechanics for sharpening, and helping oversee quality control in one's department.

Findings: Components like bias tape, bobbins, elastic, threads, lace, snaps, and needles that are used in sewing undergarments and stored on metal racks on assembly line floors.

Gauge: A metal measuring tool used by female inspectors to check the accuracy of seam widths, stitches per inch, or stitches per area on a garment.

Hand elevator: The manual hand elevator—bucket on a rope—was used to transport small items such as a bra or small bundles between the first, second, and third floors.

Head floor lady: A worker responsible for monitoring first-, second-, and third-floor assembly lines so they ran smoothly, and at times she assisted check girls by bringing bundles to the next worker in the assembly process. Other duties included meetings with department heads regarding worker issues (missing work, quality of work, tardiness, etc.), meetings regarding new undergarment models, and selection of skilled pieceworkers for sample bra or corset model assembly.

Industrial machine operators: Workers on the second and third floors who operated a variety of industrial sewing machines. Each operator was assigned a unique three-digit number that corresponded to her assembly job (i.e., 200–400 seamers; 700 zigzag ends; 500–600, 800 binders). A partial list of pieceworkers included seamer; narrow, medium, and wide binder; overcaster; zigzag ends; zigzagger; boxer; lace edge operator; zipper operator; bone stitch operator; shaper; applique operator; featherstitch machine operator or faggot machine operator; bar-tack machine operator; ironer (regular iron and bra cup machine iron); ladder stitch machine operator (a loose stitch used to sew two bra pieces together); hook and eye operator; circular stitch operator; Reece machine operator (a machine that popped out a piece of elastic with the eye on it); boner operator (a worker who inserted steel or plastic stays into corsets).

Inspectors: Female workers on the production floors who checked as each operation was completed in a section (i.e., seaming, binding, overcasting). Inspectors examined assembly work for flaws (i.e., loose threads, uneven stitching, or sloppy bias tape binding).

Janitors: Male workers who cleaned the multistory plant. A partial list of daily duties involved removing sewing debris (threads, broken needles, fabric lint) from production floors, sweeping two separate staircases, cleaning the men's washroom, and servicing the Gossard clock.

Machine operator work box: A rectangular wooden box with an attached wooden handle used by operators for holding supplies such as scissors, extra thread, bobbins, and lace.

Needles: Specialized industrial sewing machine needles for assembling fine, lightweight, medium, and heavy weight fabrics.

Oiling can: A small metal container used by sewing machine operators for oiling their machines.

One-piece foundation: An undergarment that combined a bra and girdle.

Production manager: A female worker who helped supervise the flow of undergarment production.

Repair operators: Skilled female workers (one person from each department) who repaired garments damaged during the assembly process.

Repair table: A wooden table used by repair operators to remove and replace flawed pieces of material.

Scissors: A cutting tool used by pieceworkers for clipping threads, lace, and bias tape. Machine operators were required to own scissors, which could be purchased from the company or from local stores.

Sticky: A piece of paper on which a pieceworker kept track of her work hours and daily wages.

Stockroom worker: Male workers unloaded raw materials from the loading dock, transported the heavy materials to the factory's top floor, inventoried them, and distributed findings to the factory production floors. During the sixties and seventies, a female stockroom worker distributed findings to the three production floors.

Tag: A piece of tan cardboard-like paper embedded with a tracking number and attached to a bundle (a cloth canvas bag). The left side of the tag listed piece rate units for each assembly step. The right side of the tag listed the operations.

Tag printer machine: A machine used by a female worker to create price tags (model, size, price) for finished undergarments.

Thread: A special type of yarn (i.e., silk, cotton, or nylon) constructed to pass through sewing machines rapidly.

Timers: Two individuals—a representative from the company and a union representative—who conducted time studies for each step in the assembly of undergarments.

Truck: A large wooden box on three metal rollers/wheels used by department heads to transport unassembled and finished undergarments from one section/department to the next.

Twelve-needle machine: An industrial machine that puts reinforcements on the bottom of bras.

Women's washroom cleaner: A female worker who cleaned women's washrooms on three floors, made coffee for the workers' breaks, and worked in the basement lunchroom.

Sources

Books

Corset and Underwear Review, The, vol. 10. New York: Haire Publishing Company, 1917.

Corset and Underwear Review, The, vol. 15. New York: Haire Publishing Company, 1920.

Farrell-Beck, Jane, and Colleen Gau. *Uplift: The Bra in America.* Philadelphia: University of Pennsylvania Press, 2007.

Fields, Jill. *An Intimate Affair: Women, Lingerie, and Sexuality.* Berkeley: University of California Press, 2007.

Leonard, John William. *The Book of Chicagoans: A Biographical Dictionary of Leading Living Men of the City of Chicago.* Chicago: A.N. Marquis & Company, 1905.

Emails

Archibald, Robert: March 26, 2016; November 2, 2017; January 16, 2020.

Arsenault, Paul: October 28, 2020; November 21, 2020; December 29, 2020.

Arsenault, Sandy: September 23, 2015; November 9, 16, 2017; March 19, 2018 (numerous email, telephone, and in-person contacts).

Magnaghi, Russell M.: April 19, 2019; May 6, 2019; January 15, 2020 (numerous email, telephone, and in-person contacts).

Nault, Gerry: October 11, 2017; October 17, 2017.

Wills, Rick. March 4, 2019; April 16, 2019; February 9, 2020; December 18, 2020 (numerous email and telephone contacts).

Interviews

Anderson, Denise, in-person, March 1, 2010.

Andriacchi, Frank, in-person, August 14, 2008.

Annelin, Marjorie, telephone, July 2009; February 2015.

Antcliff, Kristine, telephone, November 2008.

Archibald, Robert, telephone, April 2, 2016.

Arsenault, Paul, in-person, March 29, 2007.

Ayotte, Virginia, in-person, April 28, 2010.

Baldini, Dorothy, telephone, August 11, 2008.

Bergman, Audrey, in-person, May 26, 2009.

Bergman, Donna, telephone, October 19, 2010.

Boase, Bertha, telephone, January 7, 2011.

Botero, Gina, telephone, January 2, 2014.

Bratonia, Karen, in-person, May 27, 2010.

Brisson, Alvera, in-person, July 22, 2008.

Charbonneau, Judy, in-person, March 24, 2009.

Cohodas, Willard, in-person, September 2009.

Collick, Rose, in-person, May 6, 2008; November 2, 2011.

Corkin, Evelyn, in-person, February 22, 2007; April 1, 2008.

Coron, Elizabeth, in-person, May 6, 2008.

Corradina, Rita, in-person, January 31, 2011.

Davey, Remigia, in-person, October 23, 2008.

DelBello, Madeleine, in-person, May 5, 2008.

Evans, Dennis, in-person, September 13, 2010.

Evans, Joyce, in-person, September 13, 2010.

Fagerberg, Ruth, in-person, August 10, 2010.

Felt, Arlene, in-person, February 17, 2012.

Filizetti, Pearl, in-person, May 13, 2010.

Finnila, Nancy, in-person, September 27, 2010.

Fosco, Betty, in-person, April 5, 2010; March 2019.

Fredrickson, Kathleen, in-person, September 30, 2010.

Gauthier, Barbara, in-person, January 18, 2010.

Gray, Trudy, telephone, October 21, 2010.

Green, Judy, in-person, April 28, 2010.

Haapala, Alice, in-person, April 25, 2008.

Harju, Gerald, in-person, November 10, 2008.

Holmgren, Verna, in-person, February 22, 2008; March 2018.

Honkala, Maxine, telephone, 2015.

Jacobson, Mary, telephone, March 12, 2008.

Jafolla, Cecilia, telephone, April 20, 2009.

Johnson, Catherine, in-person, October 31, 2007.

Johnson, Karen, telephone, March 29, 2011.

Johnson, Peter, telephone, October 2017.

Johnson, Virginia, in-person, May 27, 2010.

Joseph, Clara, in-person, November 7, 2008.

Kangas, Cecilia, in-person, April 21, 2009; May 7, 2009; January 18, 2010.

Kari, G. Mae, in-person, April 6, 2009.

Kaupilla, Madeline, in-person, July 22, 2008.

Kautz, Marlene, in-person, April 25, 2008.

Keto, Elaine, telephone, March 19, 2008.

Ketola, Marjorie, in-person, March 18, 2008.

LaFave, Gloria, in-person, August 10, 2010.

LaSalle, Jack, in-person, February 15, 2010.

Lehmann, Bill, telephone, September 18, 2009.

Lehtinen, Anita, in-person, March 24, 2009.

Lenten, Dona, in-person, November 5, 2008.

Lucas, Debra Ann, in-person, February 17, 2016.

Luoma, Joan, in-person, May 15, 2008.

Marietti, Karen, telephone, April 5, 2016.

Maki, Elaine, in-person, April 25, 2008.

Melka, Jennie, in-person, March 20, 2007.

Merrill, Donald, in-person, May 5, 2008.

Miller, Phyllis, telephone, November 11, 2008.

Morissette, Michael, in-person, April 20, 2009.

Mussatto, Dora, in-person, May 11, 2010.

Nardi, Paulette, in-person, October 23, 2008.

Nault, Geraldine, telephone, October 19, 2017.

Nault, Pam, in-person, April 17, 2007.

Nelson, Joan, in-person, March 2018.

Nuorala, Barbara, in-person, October 20, 2008.

Patron, Barry, in-person, July 5, 2010.

Peterson, Elaine, in-person, April 1, 2008; June 10, 2009; March 17, 2011
    (numerous in-person and telephone contacts).

Poutanen, Laila, in-person, March 18, 2009.

Rapport, Karlyn, in-person, March 12, 2010.

Rivers, Hilda, telephone, April 30, 2008.

Roberts, Edna, in-person, April 28, 2010.

Saxwold, Bob, telephone, October 19, 2017.

Sihtala, Bob, in-person, May 8, 2009; telephone, September 25, 2017;
    October 9, 2017.

Sippola, Margaret, in-person, October 20, 2008.

Skewis, Gwen, in-person, February 27, 2007.

Solka, Thomas, in-person, March 26, 2009.

Stieve, Ann Marie, telephone, February 26, 2008.

Talbacka, Helmi, in-person, March 12, 2010.

Terzaghi, Shirley, in-person, September 27, 2010.
Toivonen, Pauline, in-person, July 5, 2010.
Tousignant, Lucy, in-person, September 22, 2008.
Valenti, Genevieve, in-person, April 5, 2010.
Valenzio, Nancy, in-person, May 26, 2009.
Vallier, Alice Gill, telephone, March 13, 2009.
Waters, Dorothy, in-person, May 8, 2008.
Wiik, Chris, in-person, August 29, 2010.
Wills, Edith, telephone, 2010.
Wills, Rick, telephone, December 5, 2020.
Windsand, Dorothy, in-person, June 22, 2009.

Letters

Annelin, Marjorie, letter to author, July 2009.
Antcliff, Kristine, letter to author, November 23, 2008.
Johnson, Karen, undated note to author.

Magazines

Elliott, Erin. "Back in the Day of Lingerie." *Marquette Monthly*. March
   2005.
The Gossardian 1, no. 4. January 1921.
The Gossardian 3, no. 12. September 1923.

Newspapers
Belvidere Daily Republican

"Claude Tripp Departs to Canada." October 13, 1915.

Ironwood Daily Globe

[Missing title]. April 7, 1954.

The Bessemer Herald

"Ishpeming Garment Factory Busy One." December 29, 1933.

The Daily Banner, Greencastle Indiana

"Strike at Corset Plant." December 2, 1941.

The Daily Mining Journal or Mining Journal:

Advertisement. August 5, 1949: 11.

"Average Pay Raise of Six Cents for Gossard Workers." August 9, 1949.

"Banner Year for Gossard; Payroll Up." December 24, 1940.

Bauer, John. "Despondency Is the Feeling of Gossard Workers." November 2, 1976.

Bauer, John. "Uncertainty Facing Former Gossard Employes [*sic*]." December 30, 1976.

"'Big Ben' Atop Gossard Factory Chimes No More." October 3, 1959.

Brown, Peter. "Plant Shutdown Tough Situation for 'Gossard Girls.'" January 3, 1977.

"Capacity Crowd Attends ILGWU Protest Meeting." April 25, 1949.

"City Stunned by Death of C. H. Tripp, Civic Leader." September 30, 1943.

"Closing of Gossard Area Plant Confirmed." November 1, 1976.

"Club Urges Strike Law Enforcement." June 1, 1949.

"'Committee to Preserve Rights of Labor' at County Mass Meeting." June 13, 1949.

"Conference on Gossard Strike Called." July 14, 1949.

"Employment at Gossard May Reach 600 this Month." September 6, 1946.

"Felonious Assault Charge Brought in Gwinn Accident Case." April 23, 1949.

"15 Strikers Face Conspiracy Charge." June 10, 1949.

"Gossard and Union Chiefs Meet Monday." July 30, 1949.

"Gossard Branch Plant in Gwinn Gives Area $250,000 Payroll." September 13, 1947.

"Gossard Employees Awarded Citation by U.S. Treasury." September 15, 1961.

"Gossard Officials Meet Ishpeming Men at Dinner." March 27, 1920.

"Gossard Plant Became Stabilizing Factor in Economy of Ishpeming." July 13, 1954.

"Gossard Plant Finishing Big Remodeling Project: Sun Clothing Produced at Two Plants." March 25, 1950.

"Gossard Plant Finishing Big Remodeling Project: Ishpeming's Factory Gets Face-Lifting." March 25, 1950.

"Gossard Plant Has Record of 19 Years' Continuous." June 20, 1939.

"Gossard President Urges Employes [*sic*] to Go to Work, Negotiate 'While Earning.'" June 29, 1949.

"Gossard Productive Capacity Increased." July 3, 1953.

"Gossard's Chiefs Return to Chicago." June 18, 1949.

"Gossard's Workers Go Back to Jobs." August 5, 1949.

"Governor Sends Fox to Ishpeming to Call Meeting." June 29, 1949.

Heisel, Bruce. "ON STRIKE! The 1949 Gossard Labor Action." March 5, 1989.

"Ishpeming in Line for Plant of Gossard Company." March 9, 1920.

"Local Girls to Work at Ishpeming." March 26, 1920.

"Mediation Fails To Settle Strike At Gossard Company." May 4, 1949.

"'Model Town' Quiet after Near-Tragedy." April 21, 1949.

Trethewey, James. "Operations at Peak Capacity at Gossard Factory; 389 on Payroll." October 2, 1962.

"Over 500 Employes [*sic*] Idle after Union Calls Strike at Gossard Company Plant." April 12, 1949.

"Picket Lines Set Up around Gwinn Factory." April 19, 1949.

"Picnic Today for Employes [*sic*] of Gossard." July 3, 1947.

"Remodeling of Gossard's Ishpeming Plant to Begin Next Week; No Shutdowns." March 26, 1948.

"Strike Ends at Gossard, Union Reports." August 3, 1949.

"Style Award Presented to Gossard Firm." April 12, 1950.

"Sun Clothing Produced at Two Plants." March 25, 1950.

Treloar, W. H. "Gossard Gives Noon Meals in New Cafeteria to 550 Workers." March 25, 1944.

"25 Gossard Strikers Plead Not Guilty to Mass Picketing Charge." June 8, 1949.

Wills, Edith Danielson, Letter to editor. May 6, 2011.

The Evening News from Sault Sainte Marie

[Missing title], June 11, 1954: 9.

Iron Ore

"Direct from Division Street." May 7, 1949.

"Direct from Division Street." May 14, 1949.

"Direct from Division Street." May 21, 1949.

"Direct from Division Street." June 4, 1949.

"Direct from Division Street." June 11, 1949.

"Gossard Company Changes Name." September 1, 1928.

"Gossard Factory Deal Is Closed at Meeting Monday." March 27, 1920.

"Gossard Plant a Busy Place." May 1, 1920.

"Gossard Plant Makes Headway." October 23, 1920.

"Gossard Plant Busy." May 21, 1932.

"Gossard Plant Has Large Force." June 9, 1928.
"Gossard-Union Meet Ends in Failure." May 7, 1949.
"Helping Ourselves Good Business." March 6, 1920.
"Ishpeming May Land Factory." March 13, 1920.
"Ishpeming's Bright Spot." December 19, 1931.
"Ishpeming's Second Largest Industry." June 16, 1928.
"Lunch Room at Gossard Plant." July 31, 1920.
"Our New Industries." October 1, 1921.
"Our Women Laborers All Taken." May 8, 1920.
"Pickets Injured at Gwinn Plant." April 23, 1949.

Milwaukee Journal

Romney, George. Photo. September 23, 1962.

The Wakefield News

"In the Left Hand Corner." August 1, 1931.

Newscasts

"Quilt Honors Ishpeming 'Gossard Girls.'" TV 10 ABC News 5:55 pm.
Thursday, October 14, 2010.

Special Collections

Grondin, Jennifer, "Interview with Geraldine Defant," March 22, 1990.
Central Upper Peninsula and Northern Michigan University Archives,
Northern Michigan University Olson Library: Geraldine Defant
Papers, Collection-Box 26-04-01, Identifier MSS-027.
"ILGWU Organizational History." International Ladies Garment Workers
Union Organizational History. Chicago Joint Board. ILGWU Local
105 Records. Collection Number: 5780/053. Kheel Center for Labor
Management Documentation and Archives, Martin P. Catherwood
Library, Cornell University Library, https://rmc.library.cornell.edu
/EAD/htmldocs/KCL05780-053.html#d0e185.
International Ladies Garment Workers Union Organizational History.
Chicago Joint Board. Records, 1914–1975 [bulk 1922–1975]. 5780/044
Kheel Center for Labor-Management Documentation and Archives,
Martin P. Catherwood Library, Cornell University Library.

- Letter from Winnifred Boynton to Abe Plotkin, October 1941.
- Letter from Winnifred Boynton to Abe Plotkin, December 1941.
- Letters from Ruth Craine to Abe Plotkin, undated; February 9, 1944; March 7, 1944; November 2, 1944; March 16, 1945; May 29, 1945; August 10, 1945; August 17, 1945; September 12, 1945; September 17, 1945; September 20, 1945; October 3, 1945; October 19, 1945; February 23, 1948.
- Letter from Ruth Craine and Narcissus Suardini to Abe Plotkin, December 22, 1944.
- Letter from Morris Bialis to Ruth Craine, January 11, 1961.
- Letters from William Davis to Abe Plotkin, December 11, 1941; December 12, 1941.
- Letters from Ruby Dingman to Abe Plotkin, April 1, 1944; November 2, 1944; March 27, 1945; May 26, 1945; August 16, 1945; August 30, 1945; November 9, 1945; November 16, 1945.
- Letter from Ruby Dingman to Gossard Workers, June 26, 1945.
- Letter from Ruby Dingman and Ruth Craine to Abe Plotkin, October 2, 1944.
- Letters from Marie Gernet to Abe Plotkin, January 1941; January 30, 1944; February 21, 1944; February 22, 1944; March 1944.
- Letter from Abe Plotkin to Morris Bialis, March 4, 1948.
- Letters from Abe Plotkin to Ruth Craine, March 10, 1944; August 2, 1945; January 11, 1961.
- Letter from Abe Plotkin to Ruby Dingman, August 22, 1945.
- Letters from Abe Plotkin to Marie Gernet, February 12, 1944; February 23, 1944.
- Letter from Joseph Zukerman to Abe Plotkin, October 24, 1941.
- Postal Telegraph from Abe Plotkin to William Davis, December 22, 1941.
- Postal Telegraph from Abe Plotkin to Ruth Craine, October 19, 1945.
- Report on Michigan and Indiana from Abe Plotkin, undated.

Other

Autumn Comforts 2010 Quilt Show. Pamphlet. Sponsored by Marquette County Quilters' Association.

"The Building: F. Braastad and Co. General Store." A collection of Braastad documents from Paul Arsenault, owner of Gossard Building. Unknown authorship and date.

Magnaghi, Russell M. *Gender and Work in the Upper Peninsula through 1976*. Marquette, MI: 906 Heritage Press, 2021.

Websites

Braastad-Gossard Building. National Register of Historic Places Registration Form. https://www.nps.gov/nr/feature/places/pdfs/15000946.pdf.
"Our Heritage." Gossard Website. http://www.gossard.com/About-Gossard/Heritage.
"Our Finnish Heritage." Finlandia University. http://www.finlandia.edu/about/our-finnish-heritage/.

Index

145; noise, 17, 21; timings, 24,
105–6, 109, 119, 169. *See also*
Ishpeming plant; meals; production; unionization
workplace injuries, 28, 49, 82,
120, 145
World War II: Battle of the Bulge,
90; female service members
in, 154; male service members
in, 27, 34, 62, 102, 121, 143;
postwar effects of, 60, 111; U.S.

production and employment
during, 33–34, 60, 138; war
bonds for, 34, 38

Z

Ziegler, C. G., 32
zigzag work, 47, 101, 111, 115–16.
See also production
Zukerman, Joseph, 52